Tearmoon Empire

Volume 6

Author
Nozomu Mochitsuki

Illustrator
Gilse

Kingdom of Sunkland

Keithwood
Prince Sion's attendant. A cynic. But a competent one.

Sion
Crown Prince. All-round genius. In the previous timeline he was Mia's archnemesis, aided Tiona and eventually became known as the "Penal King." In the present he accepts that Mia is the Great Sage of the Empire.

ASSISTANCE

[**Wind Crows**] Sunkland's intelligence service.

[**White Crows**] A team within the Wind Crows formed for a certain project.

Holy Principality of Belluga

SUPPORT

Rafina
The Duke's daughter. Saint-Noel Academy's de facto decision maker. In the previous timeline, she supported Sion and Tiona from behind the scenes. Her smile can be lethal.

[**Saint-Noel Academy**]
A super elite school attended by all the highborn children of neighboring nations.

Kingdom of Remno

Abel
Second Prince. In the previous timeline, he was known to be an extraordinary playboy. Now, as a result of meeting Mia, he works to diligently improve his swordsmanship instead.

[**Forkroad & Co.**]
Chloe
The only heir of Marco Forkroad, whose company spans multiple kingdoms. She is Mia's classmate and book buddy.

SUPPORT

Chaos Serpents
A group of chaosmongers trying to wreak havoc upon the world. They are deeply hostile toward the Holy Principality of Belluga and the Central Orthodox Church. Traces of their clandestine misdeeds can be found throughout history, but the details are shrouded in mystery.

Story

Mia, the reviled selfish princess of the fallen Tearmoon Empire, is executed, only to wake up a twelve-year-old again after somehow leaping backward through time. With this second chance at life she resolves to fix the ills that plague the Empire... so she doesn't end up at the guillotine again. With the help of her previous life's memories and a healthy dose of overly-generous interpretation of her actions by those around her, she successfully averts a revolution, only to be told by her time-leaping granddaughter, Bel, that in the future Mia and her entire lineage end in ruin. Furthermore, she finds out from the "The Chronicles of Saint Princess Mia" — a book from the future — that she's going to be assassinated on the night of the Holy Eve Festival.

Characters

Tearmoon Empire

Mia

Protagonist. The sole Princess of the Empire. Ex-selfish brat. Actually a coward. A revolution leads to her execution, but she somehow leaps back through time and wakes up a twelve-year-old again. She successfully avoids a repeat encounter with the guillotine, but then Bel shows up...

ARCHENEMESIS

GRANDDAUGHTER AND GRANDMOTHER

Miabel

Mia's future granddaughter who leapt backward through time. Goes by "Bel."

REVOLUTIONARY
ARCHENEMESIS

Outcount Rudolvon's Family

Tiona

The eldest daughter of Outcount Rudolvon. Looks up to Mia. In the previous timeline, she led the revolutionary army.

Cyril

Tiona's younger brother. Super smart.

Ludwig

Young, motivated government official. Sharp tongue. Ardently believes in Mia and is trying to make her Empress.

ARCHENEMESIS

Anne

Mia's maid. Born into a poor family of merchants. Mia's loyal subject.

Dion

The strongest knight in the Empire. In the previous timeline, he was Mia's executioner.

The Four Dukes' Families

Ruby

The daughter of the Duke of Redmoon. A gallant lady with a wardrobe to match.

Citrina

The only daughter of the House of Yellowmoon. Bel's first friend.

Esmeralda

The eldest daughter of the House of Greenmoon. Self-proclaimed best friend of Mia.

Sapphias

The eldest son of the House of Bluemoon. Got into the student council thanks to Mia.

※ —— Future Timeline Relationship   ※ ·········· Previous Timeline Relationship

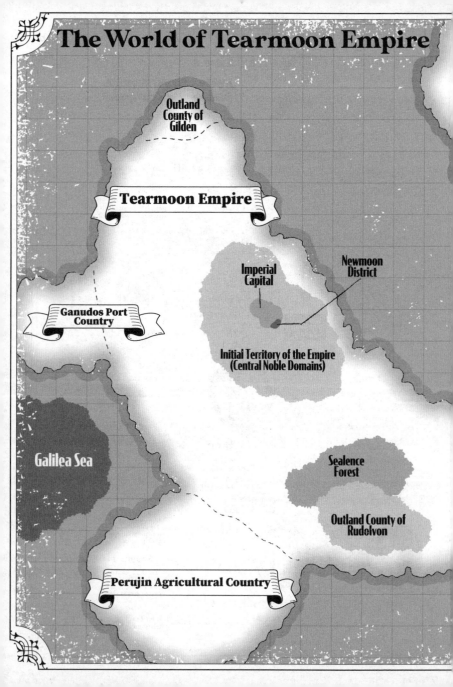

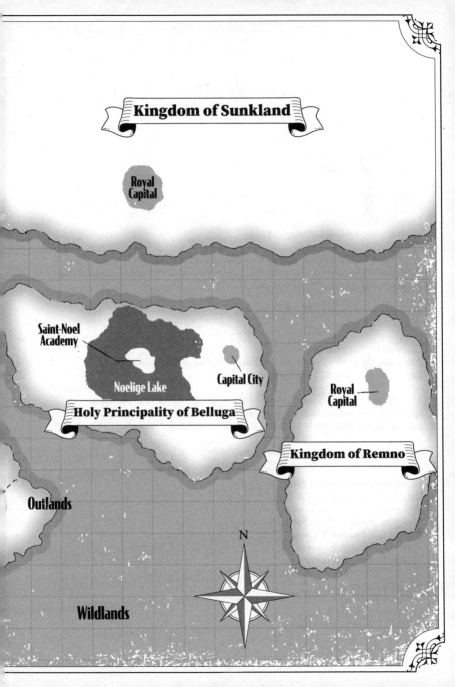

Tearmoon Empire: Volume 6
by Nozomu Mochitsuki

Translated by David Teng
Edited by Hannah N. Carter
Layout by Cheree Smith
English Cover & Image Lettering by Meiru

Copyright © 2021 Nozomu Mochitsuki
Illustrations by Gilse

First published in Japan in 2021
Publication rights for this English edition arranged through TO Books, Japan.
English translation © 2021 J-Novel Club LLC

Find more books like this one at www.j-novel.club!

Managing Director: Samuel Pinansky
Light Novel Line Manager: Chi Tran
Managing Editor: Jan Mitsuko Cash
Managing Translator: Kristi Fernandez
QA Manager: Hannah N. Carter
Marketing Manager: Stephanie Hii
Project Manager: Kristine Johnson

ISBN: 978-1-7183-7445-4
Printed in Korea
First Printing: July 2022
10 9 8 7 6 5 4 3 2 1

Part 3: A New Oath between the Moon and Stars II

Part 3
A New Oath between the Moon and Stars II

Part 5
A New Oath
between the
Blood and Stars II

Prologue: Bad News! The Nefarious Plot Is at Last in Motion!

With the horsemanship tournament concluded, autumn was now in full swing, bringing to mind that poetic seasonal adage, *a time of high skies and portly princesses.* Wait, *ponies.* It was definitely *ponies.* The point is, it was the season when there were lots of tasty things to eat. Normally, this would be Mia's favorite time of the year.

"Oh, woe is me…"

Instead, she was currently letting out a forlorn sigh. You might assume the reason to be another episode of F.A.T. that was preventing her from devouring platefuls of sweets, and if you did, then you would be…wrong! The source of her misery was none other than *The Chronicles of Saint Princess Mia.* While her brain had the usually convenient tendency to suffer bouts of amnesia when it came to recalling unpleasant facts, it wasn't going to forget that winter's approach would bring with it her foretold doom. Meanwhile, the Princess Chronicles stubbornly refused to regain its original girth despite presenting an updated passage about her winning the horsemanship tournament. It even included a description of her victory lap, during which she purportedly "flew about the spectator stands like a fairy." That bit of embellishment had earned the book a scowl.

What kind of nonsense was Anne feeding to Elise?

"Hmm…" Mia murmured, her brows furrowing. "I think I'm going to need to ask everyone for help…"

Her experience in the horsemanship tournament had taught her the importance of seeking help from others.

"I can't just tell them about the Princess Chronicles, of course, but… Maybe I can say I caught wind of a plot to assassinate me?"

She could ask some of the boys for help. Abel's face flashed through her mind, followed by Sion's and Keithwood's. They were all capable fighters. If she had them take turns guarding her around the clock, wouldn't she be able to fend off any attempts on her life?

Though the plan seemed sound, it would soon prove futile. The next morning, she resolved to discuss her plan with them, but before heading off, she checked the Princess Chronicles only to discover that it had updated itself to reflect both the discussion she was about to have and how she'd die afterward. According to the book, although Abel would closely shadow her as a bodyguard, she eluded his watch and snuck out of Saint-Noel.

"Gah! Wh-What in the moons was this future me thinking?"

She held her head and shrieked in frustration. At the same time, she couldn't help but feel a sense of unease.

"The way things keep playing out in the book…it's almost as if I'm being manipulated by someone and keep heading off toward my own death."

She tried to imagine herself sauntering thoughtlessly out of the academy, lured by the Serpents. She succeeded. Far too easily. The vacant, clueless look on her envisioned face made her shudder.

"Also, now that I think about it, even if I survive the night of the Holy Eve Festival, it'll be pointless if they just carry out the plot against me soon after… Which raises another question. Am I really going to be assassinated?"

It was theoretically possible for her to surround herself with guards to ward off assassins, but that was neither feasible in the long term nor did it solve the fundamental problem. So long as the assassins' identities remained a mystery, she could treat only the symptom and not the disease. Particularly frustrating was the fact that she didn't even know what exactly would happen. The sole witness—herself—had been killed, so details were extremely sparse. Scouring the Princess Chronicles had told her nothing more than the simple fact that she'd somehow end up dead.

"Well, I guess I did learn one thing. I know now that I sneak past my own guards just so I can get myself killed. In that case, hm… Maybe for that one day, I should tie myself to a pillar somewhere… Or lock myself in a dungeon. But that still feels like it's just delaying the inevitable. Hmm…" she muttered as she passed the library.

"Ah, Princess Mia!" said Chloe, who happened to be at its entrance.

"My, Chloe. Hunting for more books, I presume?"

"Yes. They do say fall is the best season for reading."

Smiling, she showed Mia the books she was holding.

"Mmm, it's certainly a comfortable time. Not too cold, not too hot. Great for losing yourself in a book, isn't it?" Mia agreed, though a dreary thought prevented her enthusiasm from matching Chloe's.

If I end up dying in the winter, I won't get to finish reading Elise's novel. I do wonder what'll happen to the prince and the dragon…

That tale was yet to be finished. Having first heard it in the underground dungeon, she'd hoped to read the rest of the story.

Granted, considering I'd heard it at a point in time that's technically three years from now, and it still won't be finished then…I guess I'm out of luck.

For booklovers, there were few things worse than not being able to read a good story to its end. She continued to be occupied by this upsetting thought until...

"Oh?"

...Chloe held a book out to her. It was titled *Exotic Gastronomy 2*.

Oho ho, I see what's going on now. So that's the kind of reading you've been doing. I see you're a fellow comrade of cravings!

Autumn was a time of harvest. Inevitably, it was also a time of invigorated appetites.

"Now isn't that a rather delicious-looking book," said Mia.

"It really is. Exotic Gastronomy had descriptions of delicious foods from all over the world, and now volume two is out. This one focuses on seasonal dishes and... Look! It says here that mushroom stew is particularly tasty right now."

"You don't say..." Mia's eyes glittered. "Mushroom stew... How terribly tempting. All right, I shall give this book a thorough read!"

Keithwood's kitchen nightmares were about to begin once again.

Chapter 1: Rafina's Concern

"Lady Rafina, here are the documents describing the security protocols. Would you mind going over them with the student council?"

"Not at all. As always, thank you, Santeri."

Santeri Bandler respectfully lowered his head. A man nearing old age, he was a veteran guard-priest who oversaw Saint-Noel Island's security. Since beginning his employment there at the age of twenty-five, he'd worked for thirty-five consecutive years, never stepping off the island even once. He exuded the air of a true artisan who took pride in his work, and for good reason, for it was the robust system of policing and security protocols he'd developed that had established the island's reputation for being the safest region in the continent. The Duke of Belluga had on multiple occasions rewarded him with medals for his work.

Rafina quickly read through the documents he provided...and frowned ever so slightly.

It's almost the exact same procedures as last year...

"May I ask if any part of the protocols seem inadequate?" Santeri politely inquired, having seen her reaction. "It is my belief that these protocols are optimal for ensuring your safety and preventing any incidents from marring the esteemed reputation of Belluga."

He was right. The security measures laid out in the documents were impeccable. The island had always conducted strict inspections of those wishing to enter. It was almost impossible for anyone nefarious to gain access. Trying to bring in dangerous materials such as poisons or weapons was equally futile. One could of course try to swim across, but that would likely entail a taste of the aquatic snares encircling the island. Someone with skills and wits on par with Tearmoon's strongest knight, the renowned Empire's Finest, could perhaps sneak in, but that was far too tall an order for the average assassin. Saint-Noel was, for all intents and purposes, an insular haven. In Rafina's eyes, the island was a paradise isolated from the outside world.

The food to be enjoyed by students during the Holy Eve Festival was tightly controlled as well. Ingredients were stored deep within the academy where access was restricted, and they would be prepared for the table under the strict supervision of the chef-priest. Food tasters would also be present, ready to test each dish before it was served.

With the island's ordinarily strict security tightened even further on the day of the Holy Eve Festival, there was no way any incidents could occur. So believed Rafina. Or rather, so had she believed back when she'd been overwhelmed by the responsibilities of the student council president. But now, Mia was president. Free of the position's duties, Rafina had time to think. And because she thought, something occurred to her.

Even if our security protocols are perfect...isn't it risky to never change them?

Suppose the island's security was indeed flawless and its implementation foiled the attempts of all infiltrators. Would all those infiltrators be forever deterred? No, many would try again. And if they did, would they not plan around the island's existing defenses? Elaborate patrol routes... Carefully positioned guards... These were doubtlessly effective against *uninformed* foes.

But what if the transgressors they caught had others with them? Their capture might give their associates information about those carefully positioned guards and their elaborate patrol routes, which they could then take into account when planning their next foray.

Our security might be breached through a blind spot. It's...not impossible.

It was a tenuous concern revolving around a very nebulous threat. But for all its vagueness, it filled her with a sense of urgency. Somehow, she knew. Something *bad* was going to happen. Driven by this premonition, she questioned the guard-priest.

"Santeri, are you *certain* that these security measures will be sufficient?"

Nothing was more dangerous than ossified thinking. Habitual faith in a system hindered critical thinking, blinding people to reasonable doubt of the system's efficacy. When it came to safety, overconfidence came before the fall. She was just about to suggest a more careful look at the protocols when Santeri replied.

"I'm not sure what you mean." His tone bore the stiffness of dented pride. "As you are fully aware, Lady Rafina, we have always used these protocols, and they have never failed us before."

"That's true...but are you sure there are absolutely no oversights? No blind spots we can fix?"

"There are none. We priests tasked with this island's security stake our honor and lives on our work," he declared. Then, he indignantly added, "Should your ladyship find my protocols to be inadequate, you are free to dismiss me from my post."

Hmm... Now this is a bit of a pickle.

The situation was quickly proving to be a headache. Redesigning the security protocols without Santeri would be exceedingly difficult.

Decades of experience in safeguarding the island had given him an indispensable wealth of knowledge. It was, of course, also contributing to his mental inflexibility, but the utility of that expertise was indisputable and she couldn't afford to lose it.

The problem is that there are none. Nothing concrete, at least. His security protocols are very good. Even if I dismiss him and redesign them myself, there's no guarantee they'll be any better. They could in fact be a lot worse...

Fixing something only to break it more would be an exercise in futility. However, she couldn't leave things the way they were. She wasn't sure why, but she *was* sure.

If I order him to make me a new security plan, he probably will, but...

There was a problem with that too, and it was one of initiative. The difference in quality between work done willingly with passion and work done reluctantly under orders was incomparable.

If anything, that would just create an opportunity for the Serpents. They're experts at exploiting those kinds of psychological vulnerabilities.

The Chaos Serpents could slither into people's hearts in the most cunning ways. The slightest rift between Santeri and her would be an invitation for them to strike. Therefore, what she needed was for him to share her concern. Only by having him see the same danger she did could she ensure his experience was put to full use.

Oh, this is so hard. I can't even pin down what exactly it is I'm worried about, never mind explain it to him...

Had there been an obvious flaw in his security protocols, she could just point it out and have him fix it. Unfortunately, the nature of her concern wasn't quite so concrete. It was more about a mental readiness to look for flaws rather than any specific flaw itself.

In his current frame of mind, Santeri was probably incapable of identifying any flaws in the system he'd developed. Even if he did, she doubted he'd admit it. Chances were, she'd have no choice but to reuse the same protocols this year.

But there's no way the Serpents won't take advantage of an opportunity like that.

After Santeri left the room, Rafina's expression remained troubled as she kept mulling over the problem. With a frustrated sigh, she rubbed at the bridge of her nose. When she opened her eyes again, she noticed out of the corner of her eye a red strip of cloth. It was the symbol worn by Mia supporters during the student council election.

"Oh, I'm no good, am I?" she whispered before chuckling softly to herself. "I'm doing it again."

Just then, Monica walked into the room.

"Hm? Doing what again, Miss Rafina?"

Rafina grimaced.

"Trying to shoulder all the responsibilities myself. This is an issue that should be discussed by the student council. I need to get better at asking for advice."

She stood up and tilted her neck from side to side, then headed off to the student council office.

Chapter 2: Princess Mia...Opens Her Eyes to a Cosmic Truth!

"Huh? Mushroom...stew?"

Unable to believe what he'd just heard, Keithwood's mind went blank for a second. A few minutes ago, everything had been perfectly fine. Now, it was a full-blown emergency. The sheer abruptness defied comprehension.

Wai— What? But...how? We were discussing security during the Holy Eve Festival?

It was rare for Rafina to voice frustrations, so when she did so during the meeting, it had gotten the attention of everyone present. Her concerns were well-founded too, and everyone had agreed with the need for additional precautions.

So why? Why *are we talking about mushroom stew now?*

Crisis had struck, and it had done so without warning.

It had all begun with the student council convening to discuss the issue of security during the Holy Eve Festival.

"There will be lots of traffic in and out of the island that day, and much of it will be guests and foreign visitors. I'd of course like to assure everyone that we'll have impeccable security measures in place, but..."

Her hesitant tone spoke for itself, but she nevertheless proceeded to explain the challenges she was facing.

Well then. I see no country has it easy.

Standing a few steps behind Sion, Keithwood let out a quiet whistle of a sigh. It was the same everywhere. The old dogs were the most reliable...

until they had to learn new tricks. Lifelong expertise was nearly always accompanied by mental calcification; the more veteran, the more inflexible their thinking, and the likelier they were to commit a grave error. Experience, he lamented, could be such a mixed blessing.

The challenge was that these old fossils still had value, but said value had to be extracted with care. Their skills, however rigid, could be put to good use. The ability to optimally allocate and utilize all human resources was a trait required of those in positions of leadership.

I sure don't envy her position right now. I wonder if there even exists a decent solution to this problem... he thought with the kind of casual interest afforded only to those who weren't personally in the hot seat. The casualness of said interest was, however, short-lived.

"Hmm... In that case, why don't we go mushroom hunting?"

The student council president proceeded to light a fire directly under his rear. Heck, her suggestion didn't even make any sense! What did she mean by "in that case"? In what case? There was no logical connection to be found whatsoever.

Keithwood swallowed, forcing his complaints back down for the sake of propriety, and urged his mind to work harder. This was Mia talking. She was the Great Sage of the Empire. His own master, Sion, admired her greatly, and he'd been personally impressed by her on multiple occasions himself. Surely there was some deep wisdom to her suggestion. There had to be. Sweet suns high above, he hoped there was...

He prayed silently for the swift elucidation of this imperceptible wisdom, because he couldn't shake the worrying feeling that it might not exist.

When it comes to mushrooms, Princess Mia has a tendency to... lose her head.

For some reason, she had an intense obsession with mushrooms, and it baffled him to no end.

Is this some kind of "the way to a man's heart is through his stomach" thing? No, that's too ridiculous...

With worried brows, he silently studied her, waiting to see how this would play out.

"I'm sorry, Miss Mia, but could you perhaps explain your idea a little further? I'm not sure I understand," asked a similarly puzzled Rafina.

Rather than explaining, Mia simply nodded and said with supreme confidence, "Please, just leave this to me. I guarantee that the key to victory lies in a bowl of exquisite mushroom stew!"

If you want someone to listen to you, you have to grab them by the gut!

Mia recalled a few lines she'd recently read in a book borrowed from Chloe. It had said, *"Appetite is the most primal of desires for all humans. By taking control of the appetite, one can thereby gain dominance over the person."* The passage had deeply resonated with her.

"This book contains a fundamental truth of human existence!"

Moved by the book's profundity, she'd devoured it. As a result, her brain had evolved from romance mode to gourmet mode, allowing her to engage in mental fermentation. The final distillation of those efforts was the ultimate idea she just presented as a solution—exquisite mushroom stew!

That fellow in charge of security—Santeri, was it? He won't stand a chance against mushroom stew!

And that wasn't all. The Great Gastronome of the Empire would hardly settle for an idea with only one goal. This one was two-fold.

And feeding him will serve as a dry run for the night of the Holy Eve Festival…when we can get the student council together for a private stew party!

According to the Princess Chronicles, Mia would ask the princes to guard her during the festival, only to evade them and sneak off the island. She'd contemplated what would cause her to do such a thing and managed to produce a hypothesis of sorts.

"Something's going to happen…and whatever it is, it's going to make me want to leave the island."

It wasn't much. Frankly, she wasn't sure if she believed it herself. Her knowledge of her own tendencies made her doubt the likelihood of her going for a midnight stroll on horseback. Being someone who could see herself objectively, she knew she was a cautious, prudent person. Now, the validity of both those clauses was perhaps debatable, but…

"Even if a caravan bearing the most exotic pastries stopped near the lake… Knowing what I know, I'm pretty sure I still wouldn't go…" she'd muttered, figuring she couldn't possibly be lured by mere sweets.

Then she'd read Chloe's book, and her eyes had opened to a cosmic truth.

"Even someone with lots of self-control like me might find that their willpower falters before the primal desire of appetite."

For example, if she got a taste of a scrumptious delicacy the day before the festival, and someone then asked her to go get another bite the next day, could she resist? What if it was *really* tasty? More so than even that hare stew she'd once had? She rubbed her tummy. At the moment, she was full. She could resist. But what if the time came, and she happened to be extraordinarily hungry? Might she slip out, foolishly figuring that now that she could ride Kuolan properly, she had the ability to escape from the odd bandit or wolf?

"I'm definitely not a glutton...but still, I'm not sure if I could control myself. This is, after all, a primal desire I'm up against. Raw human nature. I bet lots of people would end up listening to their gut in a situation like that. And that...sounds exactly like the kind of thing those devious Serpents will try to exploit! Hmph, you can never let your guard down around them!"

What could she do to solve this dilemma, then? After much consideration, a thought occurred to her.

"Assuming this problem occurs because I voluntarily choose to leave Saint-Noel...don't I just have to make sure whatever's happening inside is more appealing than the outside? I could, say, get them to prepare lots of really tasty food in the academy so I'd be more tempted to stay put..."

Her conclusion then...

"My only way out of this is to throw a mushroom stew party with the student council!"

Thus, Project Mushroom Stew Party, courtesy of Mia, was quietly put into motion.

Chapter 3: Princess Mia...
Presents What Seem to be Reasonable Arguments

"I guarantee that the key to victory lies in a bowl of exquisite mushroom stew!"

The sheer confidence of her tone proved compelling, and the council members found themselves persuaded in spite of themselves. All except Keithwood who, horrified by what seemed to be a simultaneous relinquishing of good sense by everyone present, immediately spoke up.

"H-Hold on a minute."

As attendant to Sion, it was his job to stop his master from acting on lapses in judgment even if he'd incur Sion's temporary displeasure. He had a duty, and the time to do it was now! Driven by his concern for Sion and the instinctive knowledge that this was a very bad idea, he boldly stepped in front of the speeding wagon of momentum that was Mia.

"There are many types of mushrooms—some poisonous, some not—and telling them apart is, to my knowledge, exceedingly difficult. Attempting to do so ourselves seems rather inadvisable."

"Aha, I knew you'd say that, Keithwood. You've always been careful around mushrooms. And wisely so. But have no fear, for what you speak of is already a solved problem."

"Huh? A solved problem? H-How, exactly…if you don't mind my asking?"

Mia grinned slyly at his question.

"Consider, please, the nature of the island you currently stand upon. Is it not an island blessed by God? If so, then nothing poisonous could grow here, nor could it be brought in, correct?"

"Ah..."

Keithwood found himself at a loss for words.

The safest place in the continent... Paradise on Earth... These were descriptors often applied to Saint-Noel Island, for it was a land blessed by God. The pristine holiness of Noelige Lake's water ensured that nothing possessed of toxins, whether flora or fauna, could thrive on the island. It was a belief so prevalent as to be common sense.

"But, that's..."

He mounted a rebuttal, but faltered before her quiet smile.

"I know what you want to say, and I completely understand. In the unlikely event that a poisonous mushroom somehow slipped past the island's divine protection and ended up on our plates, we'd be in terrible trouble. That's your concern, yes?"

She spoke in a slow, pedagogical manner, as if she were speaking to a small child. It was, frankly, a little irritating.

"To that end, we can simply ask for an expert to accompany us, and as a matter of fact, I recently happened to come across such a person."

"An expert in mushrooms? Who might that be?"

"It's none other than the daughter of one of the Empire's Four Dukes, Citrina Yellowmoon. She appears to be very knowledgeable about them."

"...The young Yellowmoon?" Keithwood pensively furrowed his brows at this unexpected name. "But...isn't the House of Yellowmoon under suspicion for collaborating with the Chaos Serpents? Can we trust them?"

The question failed to shake Mia's composure.

"The House is under suspicion, yes, but I believe Citrina is unrelated. Suppose, however, that my trust is misplaced and she is indeed a Serpent. In that case, do you think she would do something so obviously suspect?"

"That's…"

It was actually a reasonable argument. Duke Yellowmoon was undoubtedly aware of the suspicions surrounding him. Surely, he'd know that his daughter Citrina was under scrutiny as well.

He could potentially sacrifice Citrina for an attempt to wipe out the student council in one go…but we already suspect him, so it's very unlikely that we'd all have a taste of the stew at the same time, and he must be aware of that…

If the first person to try the stew fell ill, the others obviously wouldn't eat it anymore. It was possible to employ some form of slow-acting poison, but the chances of finding mushrooms with such a convenient type of toxin on the island were, again, slim. In Keithwood's eyes, it wouldn't function as a plan; too much of it was left to luck.

"Also," continued Mia, "I believe that we as members of the student council need to foster more than just a working relationship with each other. We need to foster friendship, and the lack of opportunities to do so thus far is a personal failing of mine. I would therefore like to make up for it by taking advantage of a large-scale event like the Holy Eve Festival to organize a private celebration for the council to enjoy and deepen our friendship."

"That's…certainly very kind of you…"

Her arguments were sound, but for some reason, they grated on Keithwood's nerves. The problem with them, perhaps, was that they were too sound, resembling the kind of logic Sion tended to arm himself with when preparing to charge into danger.

"Besides, Bel is very good friends with Citrina, and they said they both wanted to come along if we were going mushroom hunting," Mia added before shifting her gaze. "Miss Rafina, I do believe there's a forest on the island that's perfect for this kind of thing?"

Rafina put a finger to her chin and frowned.

"It's...true that there's a small forest on the east side of the island. I'm not sure if any mushrooms grow there though..."

Mia brushed away this concern with a casual wave of her hand.

"Oh, it'll be fine. Citrina will be with us. Besides, I've also done a bit of reading into the matter myself. Right, Chloe?"

"Uh, yes. That's right. Lately, in preparation for the mushroom stew party, Princess Mia has been consulting books to figure out how to make it a success."

Ah, so this is premeditated. A plan rather than a whim.

Keithwood's interpretation was perhaps a tad generous. Regardless, he kept listening as Mia blithely continued her spiel.

"You'll be on the serene island of Saint-Noel, a blessed place where divine protection ensures nothing poisonous can grow, and you'll be led by Citrina and me, a pair of veteran mushroom guides. What can possibly go wrong?"

Keithwood regarded the confident posture of the self-proclaimed "veteran mushroom guide." For some reason, he could not recall a time when he felt less reassured.

"Okay, Rina, I brought a map."

After successfully inveigling a map from Rafina, Mia promptly paid Citrina a visit in her room. This was, of course, so they could draft plans for their big mushroom hunting trip.

"Oh my, Your Highness. Greetings."

Citrina's attendant opened the door. She was an older woman, maybe fifty to sixty years old, whose face was devoid of expression save for a striking sharpness to her gaze. Her image was that of a longtime servant who was competent but also stubborn about the way things should be done.

"Yes, greetings, um…Ms. Barbara, was it?" asked Mia with a frown.

The old attendant curtsied respectfully.

"I am most honored to know that Your Highness remembers my name."

"That's, uh…good. It's really not that big of a deal though…"

In truth, Mia was not particularly comfortable around stern-looking people like Barbara.

I'm getting a whiff of Ludwig from this lady! She seems like the type to give people two earfuls when she catches them slacking off!

Having perceived the danger of the old lady's presence, Mia hastily walked past her and entered the room. Inside, Citrina was helping Miabel with her studies. Lynsha sat nearby.

"Hello, Rina. Thank you for being so good to Bel."

"Oh, Your Highness is too kind. It's hardly worthy of thanks. Bel is a dear friend to Rina, after all," Citrina replied with a sweet smile.

Bel scratched her head with a bashful giggle and said, "That's so nice of you to say, Rina. Thank you."

The scene really drew out Mia's inner grandmother. She watched the pair of younger girls with a placid smile, pleased to know that her granddaughter was getting along well with her friend. A quick glance toward Lynsha elicited a small nod.

Hm, it looks like everything's fine here… It's good to know that Lynsha is keeping an eye on them.

She let out a sigh of relief before changing the topic.

"Okay, so, about the student council mushroom hunting trip we were talking about. I brought us a map."

This was the main purpose of her visit. Well versed in edible wild plants and herbs, Citrina's knowledge of flora extended even to mushrooms, and Mia had figured she'd be the perfect person to consult for drafting up some mushroom hunting plans.

"Ah, thank you very much. In that case, let's start figuring out the route," Citrina said, taking the map.

On a tangential note, the layout of Citrina's room was identical to Mia's. The only furniture present was a writing desk and a bed, both mundane in design. Even Mia with her penny-pinching tendencies had afforded her room a less austere atmosphere.

"I must say, Citrina, you, uh…didn't bring much from home, did you?"

"That's true… As I'm sure you're aware, though I was born to one of the Four Dukes, our house is known to be the weakest, notable only for its age. Our ability to afford luxuries is limited, unfortunately. I do apologize for the drabness of my room," said Citrina with an apologetic grimace.

Mia shifted uncomfortably in place, feeling like she'd just said something insensitive.

"Oh, um, don't worry about it. My room doesn't look all that different, to be honest. Are you…having any difficulties? I'm not exactly bursting with spending money either, but I can buy your school books or some—"

"The thought is enough, Your Highness. I'm doing fine. The library is always available to Rina when there's something I want to know."

After assuaging Mia's concerns, Citrina pursed her lips in thought.

"We can't possibly spread the map on the floor, so… It seems a tad crass, but…" She stuck out a playful tongue and spread the map on her bed. "How about here?"

"My, that looks fun!"

Mia's eyes glittered at the suggestion. There was a sense of mischief to discussing plans while huddled on a bed that she found appealing. It felt like secret girl talk, and she loved that kind of thing! Her enthusiasm, however, was tempered by concern.

Won't that Barbara lady tell us off?

She glanced toward the door to find Barbara watching them silently. The old lady made no attempt to approach.

Huh, that's surprising. I figured she'd have at least a stern word or two…

She spared the thought a quick lift of her eyebrow before turning around and hopping eagerly onto the bed.

The forest they were going to hunt in was located on the east side of Saint-Noel Island.

"So there's a forest over there, huh? I've never been," said Mia.

"It's not a very big forest, but lots of mushrooms grow there, so it should be fun. We'll start finding them as soon as we enter, so everyone should be able to have a good time without going too far in."

"That sounds wonderful!"

The fact that the mushrooms were easily accessible delighted her. As you all know, Mia was fundamentally a slacker, so the less legwork she had to do, the better.

"Also, we'd have to go deeper in, but I know there's a place in the forest where a lot of Belluga mushrooms grow," said Citrina.

"My, Belluga mushrooms! They grow here too? I read about them in Chloe's books. They're supposed to be perfect for stews."

"I'm impressed. Your Highness is certainly well-read. They're white mushrooms with a very rich flavor, but…"

Citrina frowned as she trailed off.

"Is there a problem with them?"

"There's actually another species called False Belluga Mushrooms that look very similar, but those are poisonous."

"My, poisonous, you say…"

"The poison isn't too strong though. At worst, it might give you the runs for three days along with an unpleasant stomachache, but it's said that even master mushroom pickers have trouble telling them apart…"

"Hm... Masters..." mumbled Mia, arms crossed in thought.

"That's why it's probably best for us to avoid picking any Belluga mushrooms," said Citrina as she pointed to the map, drawing out a course that entered the forest from the south and stayed near the edge. "I recommend a route like this where we don't go too far in. There shouldn't be much danger this way."

"I see..."

Mia studied the map for a while before straightening with a contemplative *hmm*.

Their discussion concluded shortly before dinner.

"We sure talked for a while, didn't we? Thank you for your time. You were most helpful. I'll be sure to repay you later," said Mia.

Citrina smiled her sweet smile in response.

"Please, don't worry about it, Your Highness. I'm just glad I get to go mushroom hunting with the student council. It really is an honor for Rina."

Saint-Noel Academy's student council was no mere school club. It had significant influence and real power, bolstered further by the roster of heavyweights that comprised its members. Just becoming acquainted with the Prince of Sunkland or the Holy Lady of Belluga would be worthy of celebration for the average noble. Therefore, though Citrina offered her help, she did not ask Mia for anything in return, because that was how people were supposed to behave. It was the *natural* thing to do...

"Well, by that logic, Bel should be in the same position, and you don't see *her* being so modest! Besides, you're accompanying us as our official mushroom safety expert, and you deserve to be rewarded for your efforts," Mia declared.

A princess with a heart of gold, huh? The rumors are true then...

Citrina presented another blossoming smile.

"Thank you very much, Your Highness."

Just then, Bel chimed in.

"You didn't bring anything as a thank-you gift, Miss Mia? That was rather careless of you," she said with a giggle before smugly tilting her head back. "Good thing I brought one then."

Citrina did not expect this. She floundered a little for a response. Bel studied her for a second before proudly holding out her hands.

"Here you go, Rina. This is for you."

In them was a small fluffy item. Closer inspection revealed it to be a stuffed…animal. A horse, maybe, but it was hard to say for sure.

"Um, Bel? What…is this?"

Bel grinned.

"It's a stuffed horse! I got Malong to teach me in secret, and I made it myself. It uses horse hair, and it's considered to be a good-luck charm in the Equestrian Kingdom."

A troya… She's right. This is a traditional Equestrian Kingdom charm.

Citrina knew about them. An Equestri had shown her one before. Made by carefully weaving strands of hair into the desired shape, they were no easy feat to make. As a result, Bel's attempt, owing to her inexperience, did not much resemble a horse. It could just as easily have been a dog, and that was being generous. Frankly, it looked a little creepy, like some sort of misshapen creature from an unpleasant dream. It was decidedly not a gift one would be happy to receive.

But it was still a gift, and the unexpected nature of its presentation caused something to stir ever so faintly in Citrina.

"Thank you, Bel. This is a wonderful gift, and I really appreciate it," she said with her usual head tilt and lip curl. It was a sweet smile—a perfect one—neither too emotive nor blatantly perfunctory.

With all the loveliness of a blossoming flower, it melted the hearts of all who beheld it.

"Hehe, I'm glad you like it, Rina. Thanks for helping me study today."

Bel beamed, all innocence and warmth. Citrina beamed back, tensing each muscle in her face just the right amount to match her friend's exuberance.

After seeing them off, Citrina shifted her attention to the charm in her hand. She regarded it for some time before tossing it into the corner of the room with a dismissive flick of her wrist. Barbara wordlessly walked over and picked it up from the ground.

"So? What do you think, Barbara? Was that enough of a nudge?" asked Citrina.

The old attendant nodded in response, her humorless expression unchanged.

"Yes, milady. I do believe you've convinced them to avoid exploring the forest's depths."

"Good. This way, they shouldn't see anything they're not supposed to."

Citrina laughed softly. It brought to mind the image of a charming little flower waving in the breeze. Then, her tone changed, gaining a touch of concern.

"Tell me, Barbara. Will father praise Rina now? Will he tell Rina that I'm a good girl?"

"Yes, I'm sure he will. Milord thinks very highly of milady. So long as the plan is brought to fruition, he will doubtlessly have many words of praise for you."

"He will, won't he? Yes... I'll see this plan through. It's going to work. And once it does, father will tell Rina how proud of Rina he is. Oh, I can hardly wait."

Citrina giggled as she twirled in circles around her room. Barbara watched the impromptu dance in silence until a thought occurred to her.

"By the way, milady…" She held out the troya Bel had brought. "What would you have me do with this? Shall I dispose of it?"

"You mean throw it away? Hmm…" Citrina gave her head a cute little tilt. "That seems like a waste."

"A waste, milady?"

She kept smiling at her puzzled attendant.

"I don't believe in good-luck charms, but this will be a useful tool for getting to know Her Highness through Bel. Keep it here for now."

"…As you wish."

Barbara regarded Citrina for a long second before walking over to the desk and depositing the charm in a drawer.

Chapter 4: The Meaning of "Oldest and Weakest"

While Mia was busy chattering away, Ludwig and Dion were already in the process of investigating the Yellowmoons. The two men would eventually become close friends and support Empress Mia as her most trusted retainers, but here and now they had never worked alone together before.

Dion stepped into Ludwig's office and immediately asked, "So, Ludwig, how exactly do you plan to go about this? Round up the suspects and beat the truth out of them one by one? I'd be up for that... It's a lot of work though. If you'd prefer something faster, we could also just..." He made a sound with his tongue while drawing his thumb across his throat. "Deal with them and not tell the princess. Not exactly fond of this idea, but I'll do whatever is necessary."

His roguish grin was clearly meant to provoke a response. Ludwig didn't bite. Instead, he calmly shook his head.

"That would run counter to the spirit of Her Highness's efforts. Such an option should only be employed as a last resort," Ludwig answered with a shrug, intentionally refraining from rejecting the idea outright. "I'd like to believe that we are yet capable of formulating more...civilized alternatives."

He then continued in a more thoughtful tone.

"As I said before, ever since we returned from Ganudos, I've ordered my men to monitor the Yellowmoons. We have eyes on the Duke's family, along with his butlers, maids, servants, the whole lot.

I'm also keeping a close watch on the main nobles in the Yellowmoon faction. But…for the time being, we have very little to show for it. There's been nothing. Not even an attempt to deter our agents. The Yellowmoons have made no moves whatsoever. Of course, no surveillance network is perfect, and I wouldn't be completely surprised if they were taking steps but managing to hide them from us…" He paused for a second. "It's also possible…that they were warned by Ganudos and are intentionally staying put."

"Probably. Still, they can lie low, but there must be *some* communication going in and out. They're probably sending secret messages."

Ludwig nodded at the suggestion.

"Indeed. There are regular letters going out to the Duke's daughter, who currently attends Saint-Noel."

"The princess's school, huh. Well, at least they've got their fangs pointed in the right direction. But you're telling me that there was nothing suspicious in those letters?" Dion said with a sharp gaze at Ludwig.

"I'll remind you that those are personal letters from a father to his daughter, Sir Dion. Do you accuse me of spying on such intimate correspondence?"

"I sure as hell do. Otherwise, I'd accuse you of incompetence," he said with a grin.

Ludwig grinned back and spread his hands.

"Fair enough. I admit that I may have partaken in some less-than-gentlemanly conduct. And unsurprisingly, the content of the letters was exactly what you'd expect from a father writing to his daughter attending school. He inquires about her present condition and encourages her to make the best of her time and abilities."

"Damn, I gotta say, anyone who says *I'm* a monster should get a good look at you. Intercepting a father's loving note to his daughter? That's downright vile," said a playfully abrasive Dion. "You sure you don't want to go with incompetence instead?"

"Quite sure," answered Ludwig primly. "Especially when it concerns Her Highness's safety. I'll go to hell and back if that's what it takes to keep her safe." He paused and took in a deep breath before continuing.

"But despite my best efforts, I've come away empty-handed. To be perfectly honest, I'm getting a bit desperate for some useful information about the Yellowmoons…"

Ludwig crossed his arms and let out a guttural sigh. Dion was amusedly appreciating the deepness of the creases on the spectacled minister's brow when a thought occurred to him.

"Huh. Question. Is it even possible for only a few people in the family to be involved in the conspiracy?" Dion asked abruptly. "I feel like these kinds of grand schemes require active cooperation from the whole house."

"Fair point…though I believe it's quite plausible for the Duke himself to be the only one involved," answered Ludwig with a classic finger-to-glasses-bridge gesture.

"Oh yeah? What's your angle?"

"The thing about secrets…is that the more people privy to one, the easier it will leak. It's an incontrovertible truth."

"Aha, and meanwhile, there's nothing circulating about the Yellowmoons. Not even a small rumor. The fact that they've managed to keep such a tight lip on things suggests there aren't a whole lot of lips involved to begin with. Maybe even just the Duke's own, and the rest of his family are clueless innocents. That what you're thinking?"

"Pretty much. Unless, of course, we're dealing with a particularly unique family… Hm…"

Ludwig fell silent, prompting Dion to ask, "What's the deal?"

"A thought just occurred to me… What role exactly do you think the House of Yellowmoon was supposed to fulfill?"

Dion cocked a brow.

"What do you mean by 'role'?"

"For example," said Ludwig in a calm, explanatory tone, "the House of Redmoon has a great deal of influence over the Ebony Moon Ministry, but there's a reciprocal aspect to the arrangement. That influence also comes with the expectation of relevant expertise that can be relied upon during emergencies."

"Yeah, that tracks," agreed Dion, nodding with arms crossed.

"The same logic can be applied to the House of Greenmoon, which has deep ties with foreign nations. By being the first to realize the value of goods and knowledge from abroad, they acquired significant influence over such matters. Excessive concentration of influence over education and scholarship from one source is, in my opinion, undesirable, but even so, the Greenmoons do need to be given credit for the role they've played."

"Gotcha. Which makes Duke Bluemoon the empire's official cat-herder," Dion quipped. A level look from Ludwig made him add, "He's the guy who rallies the powerful central nobility so they're easier to manage."

"Yes, more or less. The point is, throughout our history, each of the Four Dukes have had their own specific role to play. So…what was Yellowmoon's, then?"

There was a moment of silence before Dion answered in a contemplative tone.

"Hm… The oldest and weakest of the Four… Taken at face value, that means they're the longest-standing lineage. They were there when the empire was founded, sharing both the emperor's blood and the toil of his project's conception. Maybe that's it. Past glory and all that."

"These days, that might seem plausible, but I doubt the first emperor operated on such clement principles. At the very least, he didn't sound like the kind of person to hand out noble ranks based on friendship. This is purely conjecture, but…"

The man had sought to build an empire from the ground up for the sake of a personal goal. And he'd succeeded.

"I can't imagine someone of his caliber would tolerate waste. He wouldn't squander resources on the Yellowmoons out of gratitude. There had to have been a role they played. Or…a role they continue to play to this day. That, perhaps, is where we should look for answers."

"So if it's not about being the oldest, then is it the other part? Some sort of meaning to being the weakest?" said Dion before shrugging. "Can't see how being weak is useful."

"Well, maybe it can be useful… Being the weakest means that at the very least, they can avoid attracting a lot of attention. Were they as strong as you, Sir Dion, they would be known to friend and foe alike. Having so many eyes on them would, then, make it harder to get certain things done."

"I see… That's a good point."

"And with that… I believe I've finally figured out what we need to do. We need to *know*. About Duke Yellowmoon, but not just him and not just now. We have to look further back and find out what role the Yellowmoons played throughout the empire's history. That should give us some clues as to who we're up against… Maybe then, we'll be able to supply Her Highness with the information she desired regarding who in their house is actually connected to the Serpents."

Their course of action for the time being was thus decided. Ludwig and Dion would venture into the empire's dark past in search of answers. Mia, meanwhile, was about to venture somewhere too. In her case though, it was into Saint-Noel's forest in search of easily harvestable clusters of mushrooms.

44

Chapter 5: Grandmother Mia...
Engages in Embellishment!

After her planning session with Citrina concluded, Mia took a bath and returned to her room. Lounging there in soft sleep attire, she enjoyed a period of peaceful idleness. A glance at Bel revealed her to be sitting on her bed, grinning in pure pleasure as she rubbed her face against the sleeve cuffs of her fluffy pajamas. The young girl was especially fond of this particular nightwear. Every time she changed into it, she'd bury her face in its fabric and breathe in its scent. As Mia watched, her mind drifted into nostalgia.

That reminds me... I used to get worked up like that too.

A fluffy blanket and a pair of pajamas made with the soft, fuzzy wool of fullmoon sheep had been enough to keep her grinning for hours relishing their wonderful texture.

So easily moved... Such innocent exuberance... Ah, youth is such a gift...

The sight of her granddaughter brought a tender smile to Grandmother Mia's lips.

"Wait, hold on! I'm no grandma! I'm still young myself!"

Mia twacked the rearing head of her inner grandmother and stomped her back down, verbally reassuring herself of her youthfulness in the process. The outburst elicited a puzzled glance from Bel.

"Huh? Miss Mia? What did you just say?"

"Nothing. Don't worry about it. Also, I'd been wondering what you were spending so much time on by yourself lately. It was that thing you gave Rina, wasn't it?"

"Oh, yes it was. I made friends with Malong, and he taught me how to make it. Heh heh. Rina is the first friend I ever made, so I'm glad I got to give her a gift," Bel said with a bright smile.

"Mmm. That's nice to hear."

Pleased to see that her granddaughter was developing healthy friendships, a tender smile spread across Mia's lips. It had a distinctly senior aura to it. Her inner grandmother proved particularly hardy today, having clawed her way back up and reared her boot-printed head again.

"I must admit, I didn't know you were—" Remembering how the troya had looked, Mia snuck a glance at Bel's hands to find her index fingers wrapped in bandages. Victims of the girl's attempt at sewing, presumably. She decided to pretend she hadn't seen anything. "Uh, so good with your hands. Maybe you're an artisan in the making."

Alas, her inner grandmother had taken the upper hand. Faced with Bel's earnest delight at having handmade a present for her friend, Mia could hardly speak the awkward truth of its dubious quality. Instead, she went with a small white lie.

"Heh heh, right? I know I don't look it, but I'm actually pretty talented." Bel proudly puffed up her chest. Then, her eyes narrowed a little with nostalgia. "It's all thanks to Mother Elise. She was a really good teacher. Oh, but it was tough because at first, she didn't want to teach me housekeeping. She said I shouldn't be doing stuff like that because I'm a princess. So I told her that the girls in town all know those things, and it would look weird if I didn't, and that convinced her."

"Bel…"

The anecdote was brief but poignant, evoking the cruel reality of Bel's earlier life—one in which she was used to thinking on her feet and crafting persuasive arguments to achieve even a simple goal.

"Heh heh, Mr. Ludwig told me to say that to Mother Elise, and it worked."

"...Bel."

Mia's expression grew appreciative as she listened to Bel's method of persuasion and she thought about how the young girl's difficult early life must have forced her to always be ready for anything.

Mia's expression promptly grew less appreciative as she smelled a whiff of her own tendencies in Bel's behavior. Suddenly, the story felt less poignant.

"Once I convinced her," continued Bel, "she taught me all sorts of things. After the situation in the empire got really bad, she started focusing a lot on cooking and sewing. She told me it was so I could survive on my own..."

"I see..."

Poignancy restored. Mia imagined the harsh environment Bel had to endure. She was manually dexterous (...was she?) because she'd needed to be. If she was good at sewing (a big if), then that would also be a consequence of her circumstances requiring it. Between Mia's year spent in a dungeon and Bel's life in hiding and on the run, it was hard to tell who'd had it worse. What she could say for sure, however, was that Bel had suffered a good deal of hardship.

Just as the beginnings of tears were welling up in Mia's eyes, Bel placed her hands on her hips and declared, "I can do housework too. *All* of it. In fact, in terms of marriageability, I think I've got you beat, Miss Mia. I mean, you've never cooked, have you?"

"M-Marri— What?"

Mia winced. For some reason, Bel's statement felt like a hammer to the gut. Deeper, even. It hurt her *soul*. The word "marriageability" did not ring a bell for her. Being a princess, she had never concerned herself with the competencies the term entailed.

She didn't *need* to know how to cook or sew. That's what servants were for. She could be clueless about all forms of housework, and it would be perfectly fine. There was no shame in it. No shame at all, but...

Hnnngh... Marriageability...

Her aching soul begged to differ. Being told she was of inferior marriageability came uncomfortably close to a repudiation of her very identity as a young, healthy member of the female population. It made her feel like she was past her prime, as if her inner grandmother wasn't actually all that inner.

Th-This is a problem! What if Abel loses interest in me? Augh, I've been too focused on figuring out how to survive this winter lately. When was the last time I reminded him what a charming young lady I am?

Driven by desperation, Mia resolved to demonstrate that she did, in fact, possess a great deal of marriageability. More than Bel, at least. This was a contest she couldn't afford to lose.

"W-Well, actually, I can be pretty marriable when I want to be. I made some sandwiches a while back, you know?" she said in a desperate attempt to mount a counterargument.

"You did? Really?" Bel asked in genuine surprise.

"I certainly did! It was a piece of cake!" Mia declared with confidence. But she didn't stop there. She proceeded to embellish the story, adding frosting to her figurative cake. "And it wasn't just any old sandwich. It was horse-shaped!"

"H-Horse-shaped?!"

Pleased by the response to the first dollop, she proceeded to add more.

"Let me tell you, that sandwich was *art*. Innovation at its finest. It looked so majestic, you'd think it was about to gallop off at any moment."

Then, emboldened by Bel's widening eyes, Mia was overcome by a sentiment known colloquially as *Ah, what the hell* and proceeded to dump the whole bowl of frosting on.

"The taste too. It was just...*mwah!* On par with the best of imperial cuisine. The fragrant juiciness of roasted meat...the crunchy texture of vegetables...and the soft bread enveloping them all... That was the kind of food that *changes lives*."

"Wow! Wow! That's so amazing, Miss Mia!" Bel bounced with earnest, unsuspecting wonder. "I wish I could have tried one. It sounds so good..."

"Oho ho, they sure were."

Mia savored the admiration in Bel's eyes for a moment before a thought came to her.

"Huh... In that case, I should get Abel to... Mmm, I think I just had a very good idea!"

She smiled with glowing enthusiasm, entirely heedless of the fact that her "very good idea" was going to be an unqualified nightmare for a certain workhorse of a man who'd kept his yeasty brethren from turning a picnic into a massacre.

Chapter 6: A Heartfelt Friendship Forms!

The attendant to the esteemed Sunkland prince, Sion Sol Sunkland, was an outstanding young man by the name of Keithwood. As a swordsman, he could hold his own against the genius that was Sion. As a lady's man, his refined etiquette and reserved smile won him the secret affections of many young women. He was quick on his feet, both in action and in thought, and he proved an invaluable moderator to Sion, whose passion to do what's right had a tendency to veer into recklessness. With composure, good sense, and a trusty blade, he'd kept his master safe through thick and thin. Even in the worst of times, he'd rarely failed to meet his challenges with a calm smile. Never failed, in fact. Until he came to Saint-Noel, that is…

…How? How is it that these problems just keep coming one after another?

His head spun as he stared at the walking disaster that was the princess before him. The disaster smiled, brimming with enthusiasm, and said, "I'm thinking of making some sandwiches like we did that other time. Could I ask you to help us again?"

"I— But… Huh?" he stammered, too distraught for coherence. All he knew was that trouble was brewing, and he was sitting in the cauldron with it.

To put things in context, this conversation occurred a few days after the mushroom hunting trip was finalized. At Mia's request, Keithwood had come to the student council office, only to be immediately told that she was making sandwiches, and she wanted him to help. First he thought he'd heard wrong. Then he *wished* he'd heard wrong.

"M-My apologies, but I'm not sure I follow," he said as he stared wordless *don't do this to me*s at her.

She didn't get the message.

"Well, we're going mushroom hunting soon, right? So I thought it'd be nice if we made sandwiches to bring for lunch. I was hoping you'd come help us make them."

Keithwood battled his throbbing temples with his fingers. *Something* about this situation wasn't right. It just had to be. But a good half of his wits had been shocked into oblivion, forcing him to struggle through a haze of confusion with the few that remained.

"I'm…terribly sorry, but could you perhaps explain this idea in more detail? I'm having trouble figuring out which part of it is unreasonable."

"How rude! There's nothing unreasonable about it. We decided a few days ago that we're going mushroom hunting, correct?"

"Yes, to my deep dismay."

He wished they hadn't, but what was done was done. The mushroom trip was happening.

"I'd prefer to have enough time to wander and just enjoy the scenery in the forest, so I think we should go in the morning and come back in the afternoon. That way, we won't have to rush."

"That does sound like a reasonable proposition."

The route they'd carefully drawn using Rafina's map was admittedly a good one. It would afford a sufficiently comfortable pace for even the less athletic members like Mia and Chloe to enjoy themselves.

"We'll be in the forest for most of the day. According to this map, it looks like there's a clearing in the forest that's perfect for a picnic. I think we should have lunch here." She indicated a spot on the map.

"This place, huh? The goal of the trip is for everyone to get to know each other better... To that end, lunch in a forest clearing *does* seem like a good social activity."

It was a good plan. There was nothing unreasonable about it. He nodded in approval.

"So, I figured I'll make some sandwiches and bring them—"

"Bingo!" exclaimed Keithwood, his usual courtesy faltering before a sense of triumph. "That's it, right there!"

"Huh? What's where?"

"The problem! I fu— finally found it. Okay, so I understand why you want to bring sandwiches. But the question, you see, is *why must you make them yourself?*"

"Well, I'm not making them on my own. Anne and Chloe will be helping. I'll get Tiona and Liora to help too."

Mia Rangers Assemble! The Floundering Five was back for round two with all cast members reprising their roles. They weren't exactly incompetent, but they were definitely less than the sum of their parts. Recalling his past experience leading the motley crew of young ladies gave his headache a headache.

"It was only our first attempt last time, and we all did such a great job," Mia continued, ostensibly unaware of the monumental effort required of Keithwood to bridge the first clause to the second. "Now that we have experience, we'll do even better. We could just ask the kitchen cooks to do it, but I bet they'll be tastier if we make them ourselves."

Keithwood barely managed to choke back an acerbic comment. The sheer *oblivious* confidence in her smug expression was almost too much.

"And it gets even better, because guess what? This time, Miss Rafina will be joining us!" she declared with all the pomp of divine decree.

He wheezed in amazement. Well, what Mia assumed was amazement, anyway. In truth, it was more of a fight-or-flight response to the Floundering Five's abrupt upgrade to the Stress-Inducing Six.

"Lady…Rafina?" he stammered, trying to work through the implications of this new addition.

"Yes. I asked her to join us, and she agreed. I'm so glad we'll have someone so reliable with us."

…Reliable? Is that actually true? The Holy Lady of Belluga is admittedly endowed with wisdom. Her displays on the dance floor suggest she's also fairly coordinated. I suppose it's not too much of a stretch to imagine she dabbles in cooking.

He couldn't dismiss the possibility. Still…

That's like throwing a dart and hoping it lands on a specific grain of sand on a beach! I can't be counting on something like that to pan out!

The rationalist in him bristled at the thought. It was far too risky a bet.

"Th-That's…certainly promising. But let's not forget that everyone is busy these days. Maybe it would be best to speak to the kitchen and, you know, let the *professional cooks* do the cooking. I'm quite busy myself too, so I might not be available to supervise…" he said, figuring his absence would be a terminal blow to her plan.

He woefully overestimated his own worth. Or perhaps underestimated her folly.

"My, I'm sorry to hear that. Well, if you're too busy, then don't worry about it. We girls will handle it ourselves this time."

"…Never mind. I'll be there. Please don't try anything without me watching."

He quickly back-pedaled. The implications of an unsupervised Mia given free rein over food preparation were too much to bear, never mind her with five other clueless girls.

Scorching suns… Here I was worrying about losing Sion to poisonous mushrooms. Turns out, he might not even make it that far.

Just as Keithwood was feeling like all was lost, a new voice threw him a lifeline.

"Have no fear, Keithwood. I heard the story and I'm here to help."

A figure appeared at the door.

"Lord Sapphias?"

Son of a duke, heir to the House of Bluemoon, and the student council's official assistant to the secretary, Sapphias Etoile Bluemoon strolled into the room with an easy smile. Keithwood eyed him with perplexed surprise. Sapphias walked over and laid a reassuring hand on his shoulder before turning to Mia.

"Oh? Sapphias, what are you doing here? I don't believe your help is required. Or do you mean to suggest there is something wrong with my plan?"

"It pains me to say this, Your Highness, but as a matter of fact…" His tone grave, Sapphias shook his head. "There's something missing from your plan."

"My! Missing? From my perfect plan? And just what exactly might that be?"

Mia piped up, half surprised and half indignant. Beside her, Keithwood gritted his teeth as his vision began to swim.

Ugh, just… For the love of the sun, please don't give her any more crazy ideas…

To Keithwood's profound dismay, Sapphias proceeded to explain his idea.

"Simple. It's the element of surprise, Your Highness."

"...Surprise?"

Mia blinked a few times. Seeing that his suggestion had caught her off guard, Sapphias continued with a pleased smile.

"Absolutely. Surprise. You need to keep people on their toes. Consider the nature of the event you're planning. It's a mushroom hunting trip. What a marvelously unique idea! One sure to be filled with new experiences and fresh delights. And yet, for this extraordinary occasion, you propose to preface it with the making of sandwiches which, to my knowledge, is an activity you've already partaken in. Don't you see? Next to the thrill of the fresh and new, the sandwich making will feel trite. There won't be any novelty to it."

"Novelty..."

"Your Highness's idea, if I may be so bold, is lackluster, as bland as tea brewed with used leaves."

"U-Used leaves?" Mia winced. That one hurt. "I...suppose that's true. The sandwiches had so much impact during the swordsmanship tournament because I wasn't expected to make them, but I did so anyway. This time, that element of surprise won't be available to me..."

After some thought, she clapped her hands once.

"All right, I see your point. So basically, sandwiches aren't enough, right? I need to make something more elaborate!"

"No, you misunderstand me," Sapphias hastily corrected. "What I mean is that since the girls team made the sandwiches last time, I propose that you let us boys handle it this time."

"You? Make sandwiches?"

Mia frowned at the idea, but Sapphias continued.

"Absolutely. I plan to solicit the assistance of the princes as well. Oh, Keithwood, fetch us a couple of prince-quality aprons, would you?"

"A-Aprons?!"

At the mention of aprons, Mia's frown disappeared.

"…Much obliged, Lord Sapphias. Your help couldn't have been more timely," said Keithwood with a weary sigh after Mia left the room.

It took some convincing, but they managed to talk her out of getting personally involved in any form of food preparation. Sapphias gave a wry shrug.

"Eh, it's fine. No skin off my nose. Besides, judging by how white your knuckles were, I assume Her Highness's prowess in the kitchen is…better left unwitnessed?"

Sweet sun high above… I think I'm going to cry…

Keithwood was pretty sure he now knew what it felt like to be on the cusp of losing a battle and suddenly see an allied army charging down the hill. It felt *good*. Doubly so, because the person coming to his rescue was someone he'd previously written off. His emotions were having a moment right now.

Mia Luna Tearmoon was endowed with overwhelming charisma. Those who beheld it quickly found themselves enthralled and bereft of reason. Almost no one could escape its influence. Not even the Holy Lady Rafina. Both his own master, Sion, and the Remno prince, Abel, had experienced lapses in judgment owing to their admiration for her.

Humans were not monoliths. They had facets, and not every facet was of equal quality. No one could do everything perfectly. Yet, for some reason, people seemed willing to think so of her. To assume things would work out fine so long as the idea came from her. It had somehow become the norm to place this kind of faith in her capabilities.

But it was an irresponsible faith. The norm was wrong. Because, at least when it came to cooking, Princess Mia was *not* to be trusted. And after all this time, at long last, Keithwood had found a *comrade* in the student council. A fellow skeptic who could still perceive the shadow of reasonable doubt before her blinding radiance.

"It's actually because, uh," said Sapphias, scratching his head sheepishly, "I've sort of gone through something similar. There was a time when my fiancée was really into cooking. I mean, she's the daughter of a high-ranking noble, so I obviously told her to knock it off and leave it to the servants. But wouldn't you know it, she just got more adamant and insisted that she make a meal herself, so… Ha ha, this was a long time ago, but, well… It's a pretty funny story now, but at the time, I think I had nightmares for weeks."

He laughed. It was an earnest laugh, free of lingering trauma. Then, he continued.

"In general, I'm of the opinion that if someone you love makes you food, then you do not leave any on the plate. But." He paused for emphasis before his voice grew more impassioned. "Let me just state very clearly that this stance of mine applies exclusively to *food*. And I do not consider charcoal or raw meat to be food. If I bite into a thing and end up looking like I'd licked a chimney or attempted live cannibalism, then—"

Keithwood coughed.

"…I believe you've made your point, Lord Sapphias," he said, pointedly glancing around before nodding a silent reminder at Sapphias that this particular grievance of his was best left unheard by others.

"R-Right. Anyway. The point is, what I just did was the same method I used back then to convince her to stop. It is, you see, a fundamental desire of women to try to cook by themselves, but they are also possessed of an equally strong desire to watch men cook."

"I see… Wise words. They have been duly noted."

Keithwood was, as a general rule, pretty popular with the ladies, but he'd never engaged with any particular girl for long nor developed a deep relationship with one. Being Sion's attendant kept him far too busy for such ventures. As a result, he felt a hint of admiration for Sapphias, who'd committed himself to his fiancée for long enough to have seen all her bad sides and yet was still willing to openly declare his love for her. Furthermore…

"So," Sapphias continued, "what followed was, put simply, a trial by fire for me and her younger brother. We cooked. A lot. It was pretty intense. We were literally fighting for our lives, because if we made something bad, she might just decide that she should cook after all. In the end, we got pretty good at it."

This was just about the last skill Keithwood would have expected Sapphias to have, but nevertheless, it meant that the student council boys team was now balanced. Though Sion and Abel knew nothing about cooking, they'd have a pair of experienced kitcheneers in Keithwood and Sapphias. If Sapphias's attendant could cook, then they'd have access to even more help. Overall, the situation was looking far more optimistic. Feeling like a heavy burden had been lifted from his shoulders, Keithwood let out a long breath.

"All right. If that's the case, then I could hardly ask for a better plan. I'll convince milord."

"And I'll talk to the others. We'll get through this predicament together."

Sapphias held out his hand and Keithwood clasped it with a firm grip. Thus began a curious new friendship.

This international camaraderie would persist even after Sapphias graduated from the academy and returned to the empire, serving as the basis of a rare episode among the tales of the Great Sage of the Empire, in which the titular character, Mia Luna Tearmoon, played the role of the villain.

Chapter 7: Sapphias Screams...

Talks went smoothly. After some choice words from Keithwood, Sion readily gave his consent. Abel too threw his name in, and with no small amount of enthusiasm. With the two princes on board, it was officially decided that the picnic sandwiches would be made by the boys of the student council.

Hnnngh... This was the perfect chance to show off my marriageability too. How did I let myself get talked into giving it up? Ugh, I wish I could give my past self a good smack to the noggin.

Now regretting her misstep, Mia made her way to the kitchen in the morning. They'd reserved it, turning it into a private cookhouse for the student council's male members to make their sandwiches.

"Gosh, Mia. You're certainly here early," greeted an already-uniformed Rafina as she entered.

Citrina had explained to them that while their mushroom hunting trip would take them into the forest, they would be staying in the sparser periphery. It would, according to her, be no different from a mild hike, so their school uniforms would suffice as protective attire. Consequently, the group decided that they'd all wear their uniforms today.

"Hello, Miss Rafina. You're no late riser yourself, it seems. Keithwood and the others haven't even shown up yet."

"Mmm, I suppose I did come a little too early. I just couldn't wait to see what everyone is making though. After all, I didn't get to participate last time. I felt a little left out, you know?"

"Oh my. Were you looking forward to making sandwiches then?"

"Well, of course. I thought I'd finally have the chance to enjoy cooking with you and the girls…"

To Mia's horror, Rafina's shoulders sagged slightly in disappointment.

"O-Oh no. I'm so terribly sorry," she said, hands waving in panicked apology. "This is all because I let Sapphias talk me into changing the plan…"

Rafina looked at her and giggled.

"Oh, I'm just joking, Mia. I was a little disappointed that I didn't get to join you, but I'm not mad about it."

Reassured, Mia put a hand to her chest and was just about to let out a breath of relief when…

"But hm… Sapphias, you say… I see."

…Rafina quietly murmured those words in a voice that seemed to lack its prior humor. Mia couldn't help but feel that she'd just inadvertently dragged Sapphias into…something. Before she could figure out what, several figures stepped into the kitchen, so she stopped thinking about it and turned her attention toward them.

"My!" she cried, marveling at the sight of the boys before her.

Standing at the front was Sapphias, whom her eyes promptly skipped over to appreciate the other three behind him. Next was Keithwood. Draped over his usual black butler outfit was a white apron. The lady-killer aura he always radiated was…not muted but somehow transformed by the presence of the apron, imbuing him with a curious new appeal. If she had to pick a word for it, it would probably be…hubbiness.

Third in line was Sion, who'd also donned an apron over his uniform. Normally, blazers did not go with aprons, but such rules of fashion were powerless before the Sunkland prince, whose sheer charisma refused to be bound by such concepts as "aesthetics" and "coordination." He somehow pulled off the apron-on-blazer look and looked damned fine doing it, proving to an awestruck Mia that Sion was simply incapable of looking undignified no matter what he wore.

Ugh, he looks so good in everything that it's actually upsetting. If Bel saw him right now, she'd be screaming in delight. It's a good thing the girl's such a sleepyhead, thought Mia, belittling her granddaughter's tendency to sleep in like a true hypocrite.

Finally, her eyes shifted toward the final member.

"Hey, Mia. Are you here to spectate too?"

Abel waved at her with an easy smile. Like Sion, he was also sporting the aproned uniform getup. One look at him, however, and Mia froze on the spot. This in turn unsettled Abel, who frowned at her and asked, "Uh, what's the matter? Do I look weird? I've never worn something like this before, so if there's something that looks off, I'd appreciate it if you told me."

He scratched his cheek, which had gained a mild rosy hue. Mia, faced with the endearingly bashful gesture of her charming sweetheart, managed only a "Can't...handle..." followed by a tiny, delighted squeal before her vocal cords tapped out.

"M-Mia?"

Abel's bewilderment deepened into concern. She hastily shook her head and forced her voice to work again.

"I-I'm fine. You, uh... You look really good in that. Oh, but..."

A dangling strand poking out from behind Abel caught her attention. One of the strings of his apron had come undone. Figuring she'd fix it for him, she walked over. As she was about to go behind him, however, she paused. Then, she stepped in front of him instead and reached around him in an impromptu hug to tie the strings behind him.

"There you go. All fixed. Now you look perfect," she said, smiling affectionately as she glanced up at him.

Such shameless flirting! The Great Seductress of the Empire clearly lives up to her name!

Mia easily succumbed to surprise displays of affection when she was on the receiving end. When she was the one dishing them out though, she did so with the composure of adulthood, relishing the experience of toying with the delicate sensibilities of the young boy before her. Paragon of dignified womanhood, she was not!

"Th-Thanks, Mia. I'll…try my best to make something good for you," said Abel.

Seeing his embarrassed smile, she realized that, as a matter of fact, she quite liked the current arrangement.

Oooooh, he's so cute! I can't get enough of this! Mmm, good going, past me!

So, having decided that her past self had indeed made the right choice, she proceeded to savor the morning's activities.

…Sapphias, meanwhile, was also wearing an apron over his uniform. Though Mia had paid him no attention, someone else had.

"Gosh, Sapphias." Rafina put her hand to her mouth and let out a short, humorless giggle. "You look lovely in an apron too. By the way, I heard from Mia that you were the one who came up with the idea of having the boys do the cooking today. Not that it matters, of course. It's not like I was looking forward to cooking or anything. I simply found it…intriguing."

"E-Eeeeeeek!"

Sapphias might have let out a terrified scream in the kitchen that day. Not that it matters, of course.

Chapter 8: Mushroommeister Mia...
Hears the Call of the Forest!

"Wow! Look, look, Miss Mia! The Libra King is wearing an apron!"

As soon as Miabel stepped into the kitchen, she immediately squealed in delight. Her wide, sparkling eyes became glued to Sion. Maniabel was clearly still alive and well.

I swear, sometimes I'm almost ashamed to have Bel as my granddaughter. That girl can be so embarrassing...

This, of course, was coming from the one who, in the previous timeline, had taken her first look at Sion and promptly exclaimed, "My! It's him! Prince Sion! And he's wearing a uniform! Moons, is there anything more beautiful in this world? No, there isn't!" Maniabel Luna Tearmoon, meet your grandmother, Mania Luna Tearmoon. Given the dubious nature of her recollective faculties, however, this particular event had long drifted past the irretrievable horizon of her memory.

A number of other girls soon filed into the kitchen. Chloe, Tiona, Liora, and even Lynsha had all shown up with the kind of enthusiasm typically seen in the moments before a live idol show began.

"Now then, let us begin preparing the sandwiches we will eat for lunch today," announced Keithwood.

Amidst the excited chatter of their fangirls, the team set about their work.

"As usual, I'll be helping milord Sion. Lord Sapphias, could you please assist Prince Abel?"

"I certainly can. What about the actual menu though? What kind of sandwiches should we make?" asked Sapphias as he crossed his arms and regarded the ingredients Keithwood had laid out.

"Well... To play it safe, how about we do the same thing as last time? Grilled meat with white sauce. Oh, and since we have some here, why don't we add fried eggs?" suggested Keithwood.

"Sounds good. We do have a lot of girls with us today though, and they might appreciate some with extra veggies instead."

"Ah, I see. It's true that meat alone can make for a rather dense meal. In that case, let's make a few different kinds. One with vegetables and fried eggs, and another with grilled meat. Then, we'll add a third option with thin slices of smoked meat on a bed of greens."

Mia regarded the pair's exchange with pursed lips.

Hmm, not bad... I didn't think Sapphias could hold his own in a conversation with Keithwood about cooking. He's got some serious marriageability! Well then, I'd better up my game!

She huffed out a pugnacious breath as if accepting a challenge and said, "Are you sure you have enough hands there? I've got nothing to do anyway, so I might as well help—"

Her dangerous proposition was shot down with extreme prejudice. Normally, Keithwood would have to deal with such hazards himself, but this time, he had help from Sapphias. After twitching simultaneously at the mention of her encroachment, the two boys shared no more than a brief moment's eye contact before mounting a swift and coordinated retaliation. Sapphias made the first strike.

"No, no, Your Highness. We couldn't possibly trouble you so. Please, feel free to stay right where you are and continue observing us."

Not missing a beat, Keithwood added the cross to Sapphias's opening jab.

"This is a chance for milord and Prince Abel to impress you with their creations. Surely, you wouldn't wish to rob them of their time in the spotlight?"

"I-Is that so? Well, I suppose in that case…"

With her advance masterfully repelled by the pair, Mia awkwardly scratched her head and returned to enjoying the royal cooking show as a spectator.

"All right then, Prince Abel, let us chop these vegetables. Ah, hold on. Make sure you curl your fingers on the hand you hold them with. Yes, yes, just like that. That way, you won't cut yourself."

Mia couldn't help but gape as Sapphias carefully guided Abel through the basics of knife handling.

"Huh…"

After a period of staring at the two boys, she broke into a grin.

Oho ho, this is great. Abel's so adorable. I love how he's a little clumsy with the knife but still trying so hard to use it properly. Ah, it's just too good!

It was charming to see him struggle so earnestly, and she enjoyed watching him learn. Until, that is, she noticed the motions of his hands growing steadily faster and more practiced.

W-Wait… Is it just me, or does it look like he's better with the knife than me now?

She wished she hadn't noticed. Now that it was on her mind, she couldn't keep from comparing herself to the others. Sion, being his flawless self, was kneading dough like a pro while drawing the gazes of the other girls. That was expected though. What she didn't see coming was the skill that Sapphias displayed. He was clearly a better cook than her as well. In other words, when it came to prowess in the kitchen, Mia… No, not just her, but every last one of the young, eminent ladies present…

We're losing to the student council's guys?!

This terrible revelation left her aghast. The whole point of this sandwich making exercise had been for her to show off her marriageability. To that end, a very big wrench had been thrown into her plans.

"O-Oh, I just had an idea. Why don't we make the shape more elaborate? Food should also be appealing to look at, after all. Last time, we made them horse-shaped, so this time, why don't we try mushroom-shaped—"

The dynamic duo reacted swiftly again, cutting her off before she could even finish her proposal.

"Don't worry about it, Princess Mia," said Keithwood with whirlwind speed.

"But—"

"There's no need. Everything is fine," added Sapphias with iron resolution.

Furthermore...

"Yeah, relax, Mia. I appreciate your concern, of course, but could you just let us handle this one ourselves?"

Even her beloved Abel spoke against her, leaving her with no choice but to back down. In the end, she was forced to sit there watching the princes demonstrate their superiority in the kitchen. The experience left her feeling utterly defeated.

Ugh, I hate to admit it, but they're obviously better than me...

Sion was superhuman, so he didn't count. Abel, however, was no genius, and yet he was still better at this than she was. Realizing that she was no match for them on the cooking front, Mia desperately racked her brains trying to figure out a way to make herself seem competent. She thought and thought...and finally arrived at a simple truth—she'd been going about this all wrong!

67

That's right. What was I thinking? I'm not the Great Gastronome of the Empire—I'm the Great Sage. I got too caught up in all this talk about marriageability. What I should be impressing people with is my wisdom. Specifically, my knowledge as a veteran mushroom guide!

The fact that her mushroom know-how skewed so heavily toward consumption made the distinction a tad suspect, but some truths were, perhaps, better left unrecognized.

"All right! For the sake of my delicious mushroom stew, I'm going to knock this one out of the park! Mushroom hunting, here I come!"

Galvanized by the superior marriageability of the boys, Mia felt something flare to life within her. Whether it was motivation or desperation, she could not tell, but the fiery emotion drove her to return to her room, whereupon she declared to her trusty maid, "Anne, get me a change of clothes. No self-respecting mushroommeister would walk into a forest wearing a school uniform!"

"Right away, milady!"

As if pulled by some invisible force, both Mia's heart and body gravitated toward the forest's depths.

Chapter 9: Oddity Alert!
Mushroom Princess Incoming!

With the sandwich making having drawn smoothly to a close, the group was now ready to hunt some mushrooms. Each of the student council members went off to finish their last-minute preparations before gathering at the academy's front entrance. Currently everyone except Mia was present, and the group was wondering where their president had got to when they saw *it*. In the distance was the slowly approaching silhouette of…a mushroom!

It was actually Mia, of course, but plopped on her round little head was a white hat in the shape of a mushroom cap. She wore a thick, long-sleeved top and equally thick trousers, which were tucked into a pair of hunting boots sturdy enough for mountain climbing.

Someone let slip an astonished "Huh?" No one knew who, but the equally stupefied look on their faces made all of them likely culprits. Her outfit was *that* weird.

"Well, hello, everyone. Isn't it a wonderful day for mushroom hunting?" asked a beaming Mia.

Citrina was the first to speak. She promptly voiced the burning question on everyone's mind.

"Um… Your Highness? Wh-What exactly…is that outfit?"

"Ah, Rina."

Mia looked at Citrina and, seeing that she was in her regular uniform, cracked a triumphant smile.

"This summer, you see, has provided me with the rare opportunity to experience what it's like to be stranded on a deserted island."

"Huh? You were stranded on a deserted island?"

"Yes, during the cruise with Esmeralda. It was...a learning experience, to say the least. And a rather stressful one. But it did teach me a few things, one of which is that when you're out and about in the mountains or forests, bare skin is a big no-no," Mia said with the patient smile of a teacher explaining the dangers of reckless behavior to an impulsive child. "When you leave your skin exposed in the woods, it might get bitten by bugs or scratched by branches, right? That's why the wise thing to do when going into a forest is to always wear long sleeves and long trousers."

"B-But, we'll be staying near the entrance to the forest today..."

"The entrance to the forest is still the forest. You can never be too careful. Underestimating the difficulties of an activity leads to sloppy planning, and sloppy planning is how you get tripped up by surprise problems. Prudence and preparation are key in staying safe outdoors."

The legitimacy of her admittedly sensible spiel about safety was unfortunately undercut by her outfit, which just screamed "Look at me, I'm a veteran mushroom guide!" Many in the group correctly deduced that she had every intention of going deeper into the forest. Citrina was one of them. Her expression went blank for a split second before reverting to her usual smile.

"I see. Your Highness is so smart. Prudence and preparation, yes?"

"Absolutely. There is a method to these things. An unspoken accord between man and mushroom. You'd be doing the mushrooms a disservice if you went in unprepared," she declared with a stately air as if she were some sort of oracle of fungi here to speak to humans on their behalf.

Citrina looked up at the mock mushroom deity and found herself of two minds.

It's pretty clear that she wants to go deeper into the forest...but why? Is it because she wants to see the Belluga mushrooms I told her about? Or because...she found out about the other thing?

She maintained her sweet smile as she pondered this possibility.

No... It can't be that. She's probably just curious about the Belluga mushrooms, in which case that was clearly a bad move on my part. I shouldn't have mentioned them.

Asking someone to be careful around or stay away from something also draws attention to it. Sometimes, the best way to hide something is to have it go unmentioned. Nonetheless...

Oh well. I'll be with her the whole time. If she tries to wander deeper into the forest, I'll just subtly point her in a different direction. Besides, those are at the bottom of a cliff. Unless she knows exactly where to look, she almost certainly won't find them...

Her thoughts were interrupted by Bel, who bounced over to her, giggling.

"Are you excited, Rina? I'm so excited."

Like Citrina, she was wearing her uniform.

"I've never gone mushroom hunting before. Have you?" asked the brightly smiling Bel.

"Hmm... Never with such a big group. This is a first for Rina too," Citrina answered before noticing something on Bel's bag. "Ah... That's..."

A small charm, identical to the troya she'd received from the girl the other day, dangled from its side.

"Oh. Heh heh, I was hoping we could have matching charms, so I made another one."

"I guess I should have brought mine too. Sorry about that. I didn't want something so precious to get dirty, so I left it in my drawer."

71

Bel gave her a funny look and giggled.

"Oh, you're so silly, Rina. Precious or not, everything gets dirty eventually. Just put it on and have fun. Don't even worry. If it breaks or gets lost, I'll just make another one for you."

She regarded that pure, trusting smile on Bel's face. Something stirred in her.

Whatever. None of it matters.

With a shake of her head, she dismissed the budding sentiment.

"Thank you, Bel. I'll start using it when we go back."

As usual, she made her face blossom into a disarming smile.

Chapter 10: Mushrooms First!

A brief hike after leaving the academy led the group to their wooded destination, whereupon they all let out a breath of wonder. A sea of golden foliage greeted them. Sunlight percolated through the leaves and trickled down onto the amber-colored path. The whole of the forest was dyed a brilliant yellow, brightly illuminated and dazzlingly vibrant.

"What a strange forest..." murmured Mia.

Behind her, Rafina chuckled.

"Gosh, Mia. Is this your first time seeing autumn foliage?"

"'Autumn Foliage'? Is that what these trees are called?"

Previous-timeline Mia'd had zero interest in forests. Having paid no attention to the life cycle of trees, she now gawked in wonder at the enchantingly strange hues on display.

"No, no," said Rafina, giggling. "Autumn foliage refers to the phenomenon of leaves changing color in the fall. Some tree species end up with red leaves, but it looks like the ones growing here all turn yellow."

"My... What a mysterious phenomenon..."

Mia proceeded to indulge in a bit of fantasizing.

Hm... This forest is pretty close to the academy... Maybe I can get Abel to come again later... It'll be just the two of us, and we can walk around in this forest...and maybe even hold hands... Mmm, what an excellent idea!

Just then, she heard a soft murmur.

"A forest of yellow…"

Turning toward the voice, she found Citrina gazing at the forest. Her usual flawless smile had vanished, replaced by…nothing at all. There was no discernible expression on her face at all.

"Rina? Is something wrong?" Mia asked with a curious frown.

"Hm? Oh, no, there's nothing wrong. I just felt, um…a connection with these trees, I guess you could say. I mean, I'm a Yellowmoon, and these leaves are all yellow, you see?" she explained with the hasty tone of an off-the-cuff excuse. Then her lips regained their usual curve.

"Mmm, I get what you mean. If I were a member of the House of Yellowmoon, I'd probably feel a connection with an all-yellow forest too."

"I'm glad you agree, Your Highness. Now then, let's keep going. Follow Rina, please," said Citrina as she took the lead.

Golden tones permeated the forest. The glow of the yellow canopy overhead reflected off the amber carpet of leaves underfoot, bathing the eyes in gilded hues.

"Wow! Amazing! This place is amazing!"

Miabel bubbled with excitement as she dashed through the trees with bounding steps.

"Ah! Be careful, Bel. These leaves on the ground are slippery."

Citrina hastily ran after her like a protective older sister, which then prompted Lynsha to give a helpless shrug before jogging off as well.

"So this is what autumn foliage looks like. It's my first time seeing it too," said Chloe, staring inquisitively at a yellow leaf she'd picked up.

"Yes, yellow leaves are a pretty rare sight, aren't they?" Tiona said in agreement as she fetched one from the ground as well. "I should press a few and send them to Cyril as a souvenir."

"Aaah… It's so nice here… I've been missing forests… I never knew there was a place like this in Saint-Noel…" said Liora, humming happily as she trailed Tiona.

The boys were gazing curiously about as well. Anne, standing beside Mia, regarded the group with a placid smile.

"This is such a beautiful place, isn't it, milady?" she said, closing her eyes to take in the scents and sounds of nature. "I do hope we have lots of fun today."

Everyone basked in the peaceful, pleasant atmosphere. Everyone except Mia, whose response to Anne's comment was a simple "Yes, fun…" Her reply's terseness was due to the fact that she'd barely even heard Anne speak. Unlike the others, Mia was not here to luxuriate in the aureate glory of autumn. No, she was a girl with a goal. She was a *hunter*, and whereas her companion's eyes were gliding about the swaying branches and fallen leaves, hers were locked onto the bases of trees, sweeping from one to the next in search of her fungal prey.

As of this moment, Mia's guiding principle had become Mushrooms First! She was now a fungal extremist espousing the ideals of fungus supremacy! With the sharp gaze of a predator, she scanned the surroundings. Then, pupils dilating, she pounced.

There! Found some! Mushrooms!

Mushroom Hunter Mia charged across the leafy ground, claws brandished and fangs bared, to descend upon her prize. In that moment, woman and mission had become one. She was mushroom, and mushroom was her. Nothing else mattered. The world faded from view, leaving only her and the fungi she so craved.

The problem, of course, was that the world was still there; failing to see something did not make it stop existing. For example, that pile of slippery-looking leaves in her path remained quite slippery, and when she stepped in it the leaves gave way in a decidedly inconvenient fashion, causing her foot to shoot outward against her will.

"Eh?"

Her impromptu kick sent up a geyser of yellow leaves, and the momentum spun her body backward. By the time her brain could begin to process what had happened, she was already at the mercy of gravity.

"...Eh?"

Her view tilted on its axis until all she could see was the tree canopy. She pressed her eyes shut, bracing for the inevitable impact.

"Whoa— Gotcha. Careful now."

A voice so gentle and so familiar rang in her ears. She felt her body sink into the tender cradle of someone else's.

"...*Eh?*"

She opened her eyes to find...

"Are you okay, Mia?"

Abel's face inches away from her own! But wait! Today, Mia was in mushroom hunter mode. Therefore, she would not be flustered by Abel's embrace. She was mushroom and mushroom was her. Nothing could shake her commitment to Mushrooms First—

Oh moons... He's so dreamy...and so handsome! He was so cute in that apron getup, and now— Ah, the contradiction! It's so good!

...So much for Mushrooms First.

"You're not hurt, are you?"

"N-No, I'm fine. Perfectly fine." She hurriedly pulled out of his arms. "Merciful moons, I've made such a fool of myself..."

As her cheeks filled with color, Abel shook his head.

"That's not true. In fact..."

With a mischievous smile, he reached toward her hair.

"Huh? Wha—"

Her confused gaze followed his hand, which returned from the side of her head with a leaf between thumb and forefinger.

"I'm a little glad that happened," he said with a chuckle. "Now I know you look good no matter what you wear in your hair."

With that, he strolled off. Mia, left to her own bewildered devices, could manage only a fourth "…Eh?"

And so it was proven that despite her espousing the tenets of fungal supremacy, a hug from Abel was all it took to wipe her mind of all mushroom-related thoughts. Mia was a fake Mushrooms Firster!

Chapter 11: Old Ludwig's Theological Inference

"Mr. Ludwig, does God really exist?" asked Miabel.

Soon after arriving for her classes that day, she posed this question to Ludwig, who regarded her curiously through his spectacles.

"Hm? What's this now, Your Highness? Have you developed a sudden interest in the divine?" he asked as he scooped some of the precious tea leaves he'd managed to come by into a pot.

"On my way here, someone was selling something called a Jar of God that gives you the wisdom of your ancestors. It was sort of expensive, but I thought maybe if I used that, I'd be able to borrow some of Grandmother Mia's wisdom…" she said, looking up at him with wide, expectant eyes.

He rubbed his chin, feeling no small amount of concern for her gullibility, and considered what to say. Coming up with an answer wasn't the problem; that was easy. The empire was a part of the Central Orthodox Church's religious sphere. The people living here had a naive and unquestioning belief in the existence of God. Therefore, the straightforward choice was to simply say yes. In the event that she managed to regain her place and power as princess, it'd be better for her to believe so as well.

However, a certain concern kept him deliberating. This was the simple answer. The prescribed one. Giving it to her would be easy, but it would not benefit her down the road. Thinking for oneself was a valuable skill, and he wanted her to have it. To that end, he couldn't just hand her all the answers. His goal was to make her think. So, he composed his answer in the form of a logical exploration.

"Good question… I personally believe that the being we call God does exist."

That was hardly a radical statement, but he followed it up with a basis for his claim.

"Otherwise, there would be too many things in this world we cannot explain."

"What kind of things?"

Miabel gave her head a puzzled tilt. He gestured her toward a chair and repositioned his glasses.

"Let me see… An easy example would be humans like you and me."

"Huh? Mr. Ludwig and me?"

He smiled impishly at her confused blinking and removed his glasses, setting them down before her.

"Look at these glasses. They're very well made, yes? Has Your Highness ever thought about how they make it easier to see?"

Bel picked them up and peeked through the lenses a few times before shaking her head.

"There are principles that govern the function of the tool known as glasses. I won't get into the specifics right now, but suffice it to say, they came about when wise men long ago focused their intellect on figuring out how the human eye worked. They studied its structure and function. Then, they set about crafting something that would correct the eye's faults. They did this by actively applying their will toward a goal. In other words, it was people with great intelligence exercising their intent to create such a thing that gave birth to the object known as glasses. For example, let's say you took the materials used to make these—glass and iron—and placed them outside on the ground.

Would the rain sculpt the glass into lenses? Or the wind mold the iron into frames? They have no will, no intent. Such a feat would be impossible."

Ludwig put on his glasses again and continued.

"What about us humans, then? The humans who make and use these glasses? We are even more intricate, more comprehensively designed than the crafts and artworks we produce. So how, Your Highness, do you think we were created? Do you think we were shaped by rain, wind, and soil?"

"No, I don't think so," answered Miabel with a shake of her head.

Ludwig was convinced that there was a god, that is, an entity possessing greater power and intellect than humans who had designed the world. This was a conclusion he'd reached after copious thought. Though he knew not the method, he believed in its existence—that mankind, along with all of the world, was created by a being of profound intelligence exercising the intent to make the world as it was. To deny this was to be left with far too much that was inexplicable. Not only humans, but animals, plants, and even the minuscule critters of the earth... Someone had to have carefully designed and created them that way. It was, he figured, the only explanation.

Suddenly, the words of his old master floated through his mind.

"To unthinkingly attribute all worldly phenomena to the divine or infernal is an affront to God, who designed us humans to be thinking creatures. That contradicts our faith in the flawless magnificence of God's craft. Yet, to presume that all worldly phenomena have no connection to deities, whether good or evil, is also an act of narrow-mindedness."

Ever since he'd received that piece of wisdom, he'd striven to always view things in a balanced manner as much as possible. It was something he'd committed himself to, and he wished for Miabel to acquire the same habit of critical thinking.

"Then…does that mean the jar is real?! It can really work divine miracles?!" exclaimed Miabel, eyes glittering with excitement.

"No! Wait!"

Seeing her gaze shift toward the door, Ludwig hastily stopped her before she ended up running off to buy the damn thing.

"Please, calm down, Your Highness. God may exist, but whether or not a jar of miracles exists is an entirely different question."

"Huh? Why is that, Mr. Ludwig?" she asked with another puzzled head tilt.

What Ludwig *wanted* to say was "What do you mean 'why?' What part of it doesn't sound like a scam?!" What he actually said, after forcing himself to think of a judicious answer, was, "Though we do not know for sure, let us assume for the sake of argument that the world was indeed created by God. That it was designed with an intricate system of cosmic principles that govern its function. What, then, is a miracle? Wouldn't it be something that defies those principles?"

No one could communicate with their dead ancestors. That was how the world worked; it was a consequence of cosmic principles. The miracle that the jar could supposedly bring about would subvert those principles. Bel considered this line of reasoning for a moment before righting her neck and answering, "Yes, it would be!"

There was frankly a little too much enthusiasm in her voice to believe that she actually understood what he'd meant. Nonetheless, he continued, allowing himself only a brief grimace at the potential futility of his endeavor.

"After so carefully designing the principles that govern this world, would God be so willing to upset them? If it were me, I'd certainly be hesitant to upend a system of rules I'd worked so hard to create."

Miracles were, by definition, rare events. If there was an appropriate time for them to occur, it would, in Ludwig's opinion, be when the world itself was at risk of utter ruin. Had God designed the world with slipshod rules, then those rules might indeed have been easily broken. The more he studied the cosmic principles, however, the more he was awed by their intricate perfection.

By that line of logic though, considering the state of the world, it's arguable that the time is indeed ripe for a miracle... The reckless brutality of Rafina the Empress Prelate... The crises of Sunkland and Tearmoon... When so many have died, and history itself is crumbling before our very eyes, perhaps it's suitable...for a miracle to lend us the wisdom of the Great Sage...

He shook his head and pushed the thought to the back of his mind. Then he looked straight at Miabel.

"Miracles occur when they absolutely need to. They are not something to be obtained offhandedly. That's why you should always be cautious around people who speak of miracles that fly in the face of the principles governing our world. There is never any shortage of people who invoke God's name for the purpose of deception..."

Ludwig's mind wandered as he regarded the familiar sight of Miabel snoozing comfortably in the middle of his lecture. He ruminated on their prior discussion.

"Proposition one: for every phenomenon, a theory can be put forth to explain it. Proposition two: miracles of God do not occur easily. Given these... Hm..." His eyes grew distant. "Miracles are rare... As rare, I suppose, as lands blessed by God..."

He thought of Saint-Noel Island where, due to God's blessing, no toxic flora could exist. Furthermore, it was protected by strict security measures that made it impossible for poisons to be brought in from the outside. Saint-Noel Island, whose land was protected by divine favor. Saint-Noel Island, whose academy was devastated by a mass poisoning. The numerous lives lost in that terrible incident shook the continent, spawning endless theories and speculation. A number of prominent explanations were put forth, such as the potential existence of a security loophole allowing the poison to be snuck in or the use of a special substance that only functioned as a poison under specific circumstances. To this day, however, none had established itself as the widely-accepted answer. Soon after, the continent had been plunged into an ongoing era of chaos, and the incident faded from collective memory. The truth was, most likely, lost forever. Future historians would likely write about it as the mystery of the century. But...

"Assumptions...are terrifying things. That, perhaps, is the true moral to this dreadful tale."

...Not Ludwig Hewitt, for the method that had most likely been employed in the mass murder was already apparent to him. There was no security loophole. No sophisticated, conditionally-activated poison. It was nothing like that. The answer was far more mundane. The perpetrators had merely taken advantage of a simple assumption.

"No poisonous flora can grow in Saint-Noel, where the water has been purified by God's blessing. That assumption was wrong from the start..."

There existed no particular lore or legend suggesting Saint-Noel Island enjoyed divine favor. It was the Holy Principality of Belluga that was said to be blessed by God. Therefore, even if Saint-Noel was indeed blessed, it had to have resulted from the island being a part of Belluga. The reason for its purported holiness could only be a corollary of its encompassing parent. So was the blessed Belluga devoid of poisonous herbs then? Clearly not. The existence of false Belluga mushrooms was evidence enough.

As their name suggests, the noxious fungi were prevalent throughout the principality. In other words, even in a land blessed by God, toxic flora could grow unabated. To then assert that Saint-Noel Island alone was devoid of poisonous herbs would be rather ludicrous.

"Thinking about it rationally...the claim that poisonous plants don't grow in Saint-Noel has to be a lie."

But what *kind* of lie was it? An innocuous superstition? A worthless folktale? Perhaps. It was also possible, however, for there to have been intent behind the lie. For it to possess a goal. In the case of the Jar of God, the goal was to inflate its value for sale. What about the case of Saint-Noel Island then?

"To impair the vigilance of guards...seems most probable..."

Even if no one could bring poisons from the outside in, those precautions would be worthless if poisonous flora and fauna had existed on the island to begin with. Nevertheless, the fact failed to attract the attention of those in charge of security. They assumed that they simply had to stop people from bringing it in. They directed all their efforts outwards, giving no thought to what lay within.

"What blinded them...was their faith in the miracle of the island's blessing."

With the continent in chaos, Ludwig had decided to conduct an investigation into the incident. At the end, he'd come away with a peculiar discovery. The idea that no poisonous plants grew on Saint-Noel Island was surprisingly young. He couldn't determine the exact time of its inception, but when the academy first opened, there had been no mention of such a belief. In fact, there were records of the earliest students being warned that the island's plants were potentially hazardous and to avoid consuming them without ample caution.

Then, at some point, a strange superstition had arisen. What if the one who'd spread the rumor was someone who'd discovered a terrible toxin on the island? A series of minor coincidences could have led this person to stumble upon a place where a potent poison grew. Then, hoping to hide this discovery from the scrutiny of the authorities, that person had intentionally crafted a rumor to focus the efforts of security solely on the dangers of imported poisons.

"The person who oversaw security during the incident was a man named Santeri Bandler. He'd done so for thirty-five years. If the rumor had been spread before he'd been appointed to the post…"

Who could have done so? Needless to say, Ludwig had already researched the matter and developed a hypothesis. When the assassinations occurred, it *just so happened* that a certain man's daughter—born late in his life—had been attending the academy.

"Duke Yellowmoon…the oldest and weakest of the nobles… What in the world had he been trying to do?"

He narrowed his eyes as if trying to peer through the haze of time, then closed them with a weary sigh.

"What does it matter? The man is gone. Even if I uncover the truth, am I to, what, tell Rafina? Will it soothe her rage? No, there's no stopping her now. A shame… What a terrible, terrible shame…"

Bel kept snoozing. She never did hear his quiet lamentation.

Chapter 12: Pure Bliss! At Long Last... Mia Picks a Mushroom!

Now, back to the forest...

After enjoying a bit of flirting with Abel, Mia discovered that even more bliss awaited her.

"O-Oooh my..."

Trancelike, she walked toward the mushroom that had caught her attention. Slowly she extended her arm, only to freeze mid-motion. A sense of conditioned unease washed over her. Surely, someone would get in the way again. In Remno, the hunter Muzic had intervened. On the deserted island, Keithwood had subtly parried all her attempts and, in the end, allowed her to pick only herbs. Even when she was back home, the head chef had emphatically told her to stay away from mushrooms. But now... Now! At long last!

Her hand trembled as it inched closer to the mycologic MacGuffin, only to freeze again a hair's breadth away. She turned toward Citrina, remembering the red-colored menace she'd once seen.

What was that mushroom called? Salamandrake, I think? Apparently, even touching that thing can ruin your day...

She looked hesitantly at Citrina, who glanced down at the object before them. The young girl nodded. Mia's expression promptly blossomed. She pressed her hand to the mushroom.

Ah... So this is what mushrooms feel like... A little chilly to the touch. And coarser than I thought. But...it's a mushroom!

Moved by this momentous occasion, she gently picked her prize from the ground. It was a craggy brown thing bearing more than a passing resemblance to a rock.

"Congratulations, Your Highness. That's a brown rock fungus," said Citrina.

"Brown rock fungus... Is it edible?"

"It's a little bitter, but it's edible."

Mia felt a wave of emotion well up in her chest.

Aaah... I did it... I finally picked an edible mushroom with my own hands!

It had taken more than a year of dogged persistence, but she'd finally gotten a taste of the forbidden fruit that was mushroom hunting. And it was *fantastic!* Profoundly delighted by the thrill of plucking her first fungus from the soil, she exclaimed, "Marvelous! Let's get picking, then!"

Cap after cap she collected, working with the quiet but intense concentration of a master artisan. When she brushed aside a patch of yellow leaves and pulled out a blue mushroom, Citrina chimed in with some advice.

"Ah, that's a similar species to the brown rock fungus. It's called blue rock fungus, and it's very tough. If you stew it for a long time, it should become a little softer. It's edible though."

"Hm, I see. So this is a blue rock fungus. I remember reading about them in a book..." mumbled the self-proclaimed mushroom guide before moving on to her next target.

It was a good thing they had an actual mushroom guide with them. The route Citrina had picked for them proved perfect for the occasion, leading the group through numerous patches of different mushrooms. Mia all but squealed at the sheer variety on display.

"Look! There's a different kind over here!"

The next mushroom she discovered was a gigantic one the size of her hat.

"Wow! Impressive, Your Highness. That's a demonstone cap, and it's rare to find one this big. It's…technically edible, though it's got a touch of acridity and tastes pretty bland otherwise."

Following that, she dashed over to an equally gigantic blue mushroom. Citrina promptly followed, dispensing advice with the accuracy and detail of a true veteran.

"And that's a blue demonstone cap. It's a cousin of the demonstone cap, and it's sort of bitter. Still, it's…possible to make it edible with enough effort."

"Oho ho, what a haul!"

After thoroughly plundering the local mushroom population, Mia was all but walking on air. A thought, however, suddenly occurred to her, dragging her back down to earth.

Hold on a minute… Is it just me, or have I not had any chances to demonstrate my expertise?

Reflecting on the day so far, she realized that she'd done little but run around picking mushrooms. She was supposed to be showcasing the wisdom of the Great Sage of the Empire, but that hadn't happened at all. The cause, she decided, was Citrina, whose commentary kept beating her to the punch.

Hm… As a girl of the forest, I certainly know a good thing or two about mushrooms, but researching them isn't exactly my main job. When it comes to sheer knowledge, I suppose it makes sense that I'd end up playing second fiddle…

Not that it was Citrina's main job either, but anyway… In order to keep her pride as a girl of the forest from suffering any further dents, she turned to Citrina.

"Just so you know, Rina, you don't have to stay with me the whole day. I'm sure the others would appreciate some advice from a knowledgeable guide like yourself as well."

"Yes, I know that, Your Highness."

Citrina smiled her sweet smile. And...just kept smiling. She made no attempt to leave or pick any mushrooms for herself. For some reason, it almost seemed like she was keeping an eye on Mia. Like a guard. Of course, as the daughter of a Tearmoon noble, it was entirely appropriate for Citrina to stay by the side of the Tearmoon princess. The problem was that her constant presence disrupted the whole dynamic, making it seem like Mia was a little rich kid on a field trip, and Citrina was the knowledgeable guardian who had to amuse her while keeping her from hurting herself. Mia considered herself a girl of mushrooms. She did *not* need adult supervision. Her pride would not stand for such treatment.

Not that Mia was actually a girl of mushrooms. Or the forest. But anyway... The thought cooled the mushroom hunting fervor that had consumed her mind. With her wits back about her, she realized something else too.

Hold on another minute... Is it just me, or are all the mushrooms I picked...sort of sketchy? They're all a little bitter or bland or hard to chew.

In fact, upon closer review, Citrina's choice of wording for every single one of her mushrooms had been "edible." That was no way to describe food!

But no, this can't be my fault. It has to be because only sketchy mushrooms grow around here. The location is bad, that's all!

Just then, she heard her granddaughter's voice.

"Rina, how's this one?" asked Bel, holding up a mushroom.

"Ah, nice one, Bel. That's called caviar fungus. They're very tasty, especially when stewed. One sip, and you'll be craving more for days to come."

It's the location! The location is bad!

Grandmother Mia suffered a terrible blow to her pride.

Gah! All right, well, it looks like I have no choice. Time to go deeper into the forest where tastier ones grow. Exquisite mushrooms, here I come!

"Mia, shall we stop for lunch soon?"

Until Rafina's prompting, Mia had been utterly focused on the hunt. As a matter of fact, the extreme concentration she displayed was so daunting that multiple people had already attempted to ask her to stop, only to wither before her silent intensity. Rafina was the only person who dared disturb her. As a result, the basket Anne carried on her back was now overflowing with mushrooms. At least sixty percent of them were the "a little bitter but edible" kind. About twenty percent were straight up acrid. Only ten percent were reasonably palatable. Faced with this highly questionable collection, Mia couldn't help but grimace. As a veteran mushroom guide, this was far from acceptable.

"Hold on… Just a little longer…"

Rafina frowned.

"I certainly understand that as the organizer of this event, you feel a responsibility to deliver good results…but I think a break would do us all some good. Look at poor Anne. She must be exhausted."

Mia froze, eyes widening at the reminder. She'd been so focused on finding mushrooms that she'd forgotten about Anne. Running around picking was one thing, but having to lug her spoils around was something else entirely.

"Moons, you're right… Anne… I've been terribly thoughtless." Mia felt a tinge of regret. "I'm sorry. You must be very tired."

"Nonsense, milady. I can do this for days," said Anne, laughing brightly as she gave her chest a confident thump. Then, her voice grew more sober. "But that's me. I think *you* should take a break, milady. No good will come of you overexerting yourself."

Seeing the concern in her maid's face, Mia found herself moved.

Such devotion... Anne truly is special. I've put her through all this, and she still won't say a single bad thing about me.

She was so moved that...

Anne's a forest novice. It must have been terribly difficult for her to keep up with a girl of the forest like me...

That...

She deserves to be rewarded for her unwavering devotion. And I know just the thing. I'm going to treat her to some exquisite mushroom stew if it's the last thing I do!

...Her resolve to find better mushrooms only hardened.

Mia came to the clearing where the rest of the group had already finished lunch preparations. A mat was spread on the ground, upon which her friends had loosely arranged themselves and were now engaged in friendly conversation. Her pretextual goal of promoting solidarity among student council members through this event was, to her profound surprise, proving remarkably successful. Who would have thought? Not her, at least!

The collaborative cooking episode, in particular, had strengthened the bond between the boys. This was especially beneficial for Sapphias, who'd always had trouble fitting in. Now, he was chatting merrily away with casual confidence. The girls were not to be beaten though. Roused by the forest's enchanting atmosphere, their volume and pace of conversation rivaled if not surpassed that of their counterparts.

"Mmm. Not a bad sight, if I do say so myself," said Mia, regarding the scene.

The organic camaraderie on display was infectious, and she soon felt a growing desire to partake in the fun. Needless to say, her life during the previous timeline had been devoid of such pleasant activities as lunchtime picnics in a forest.

"I couldn't agree more," said Rafina. Her smile was gentle, but her voice was charged with emotion. "To see everyone, nobles and commoners alike, sitting level with each other, enjoying sandwiches in a forest clearing... What a wonderful lunch this is. And it's all thanks to you, Mia."

Bel, seeing that Mia'd arrived, beckoned excitedly.

"Miss Mia, come on! Over here!"

Mia complied, seating herself on the mat. With, by the way, Abel on one side and Sion on the other. What, did you think she was going to sit beside Bel? Of course not. Mia was here to revel in youth. The season might be autumn, but her spring was in full bloom. Positioned comfortably between two handsome boys, she was ready to have the time of her life! Before anyone starts imagining this scene though, let it be restated that Mia was still wearing her peculiar mushroom getup. Therefore, it looked more like Mushroom Princess Mia being waited upon by a pair of handsome human servants who used to be princes of kingdoms that had fallen to her fungal onslaught.

Further down, Bel sat beside Sion, and Citrina beside her. Bel, for her part, was delighted by the seating arrangement.

"Well," Sion quipped at Mia as soon as she sat down, "now that we've waged a good campaign against the fungi, I think it's time to compare our spoils. How's yours, Mia? Will Tearmoon's dignity survive intact?"

Mia regarded him, considered this rare outburst of lighthearted humor from the Sunkland prince, and smirked.

Oho ho. Oh, Sion, Sion, Sion. You try so hard to put on a serious face all the time, but a little picnic, a little atmosphere, and you revert right back to the child you are!

Whether her own mental maturity was sufficient to warrant such a belittling stance was debatable, but in any case, she replied defiantly, "Oh, I don't know, but it's probably in better shape than Sunkland's."

"Oh really? I wouldn't be so sure if I were you..." he said, glancing toward his own basket.

Mia followed his gaze to discover a mound of mushrooms protruding from the top. Most of them, if she remembered correctly, were ones Citrina had deemed "tasty." She growled and looked at the mound of mushrooms protruding from her own basket. Most of them were ones Citrina had deemed "not poisonous."

"I'll have you know... This battle's not over yet. It's only just begun..." she said with a sullen snarl.

Sion chuckled with delight.

"Fair enough. In that case, you'd better rest up and recharge so you can put up a better fight in the afternoon."

Before she could snarl again at his infuriating attitude, a glass of water slid into view before her.

"Here, have a sip, Mia."

"My, Abel. Thank you."

"Yeah, that outfit of yours looks pretty hot. I figured you'd appreciate a drink."

"I certainly would."

Her clothes *were* a little on the hot side. She dabbed some sweat from her brow and took a sip. Refreshingly cool water flowed down her throat. She gulped down a few more mouthfuls and let out a satisfied breath.

I didn't realize before, but I think I'm actually pretty tired. I really should get some rest before going for round two in the afternoon, she thought as she turned her attention toward the food on display. *Before that though...I need to pass some judgment. All right, boys, let's see what you've got.*

She stared at the sandwiches with the kind of intensity usually reserved for protagonists who'd finally found the villain who'd murdered their parents.

"Time to give these a try," she said, picking up one of the sandwiches.

Hm... Shape-wise, there's nothing remarkable. It's just the usual shape of bread... Minus one point for lack of originality.

With that snobbish initial assessment, she proceeded to rip a piece of just the bread off and put it in her mouth.

"Hmm... It's pretty good. There's a gentle sweetness to it that's quite delectable."

Mia's taste buds were generally of the same maturity as herself. That is to say, she had the palate of a child, which bore an unconditional love for all things sweet.

"Ha ha, it's an honor to receive such high praise from you."

Sion flashed a courteous smile her way.

"...Ah, right. You made the dough, didn't you?"

"He sure did!" Bel piped up. "Isn't he talented, Miss Mia?"

She gave her granddaughter an icy look.

All right, simmer down, girl. It's just bread. Ugh, she can be such a fangirl sometimes. I mean, yes, it's pretty good bread, but it's still just bread. I'm eating a sandwich right now. Sandwiches are all about the harmony between the container and the contents. The bread and the filling! It's the sum of the parts that determines the whole!

With the hauteur of an armchair expert and the pretension of an overeager foodie, she mentally pontificated about the essence of sandwiches. Then, she bit into it, filling and all. Her eyes immediately doubled in size!

It's...so good!

The crisp crackle of fresh greens giving way between her teeth was followed by the rich flavor of fried egg, further embellished by a mellow sourness—white sauce, presumably—and the fragrant salty savoriness of smoked meat. The inside of her mouth was transformed into a culinary wonderland.

H-How... How come they can make it taste this good on their first try? This... This is not fair!

"How is it? We tried our best, but..."

She looked up to find Abel's anxious face. Beside him, three others with equally expectant expressions—Sion, Keithwood, and Sapphias—were all waiting with breath bated to hear her thoughts. As she looked from face to anticipatory face, it finally dawned on her that she'd been defeated. It wasn't, she realized, about marriageability. She'd been fighting the wrong battle. They, the ones who were wholeheartedly enjoying themselves, were clearly the true winners of the day. That was why, after a brief moment of contemplation, she said...

"It's...delicious. Absolutely delicious."

Her earnest compliment elicited earnest smiles. She watched as the boys looked at one another, faces all aglow with pride, and found herself a tad jealous. It lit a fire in her that...

Well, seeing as how they worked so hard to provide us with a tasty lunch, I'd better return the favor...by treating them to some exquisite mushroom stew! Delicious mushrooms, here I come!

...Again, only hardened her resolve.

In fact, that reminds me. This mushroom hunting trip isn't just fun and games at all. My life is riding on it...

The steady chewing of scrumptious sandwiches, coupled with the accompanying nutrients, activated her non-fungal thought centers again, causing her to recall a rather crucial fact. Why had she proposed a mushroom hunting trip in the first place? Had it been to enjoy a pot of exquisite mushroom stew? Nay! It was to prevent her from succumbing to the allure of other foods on the night of the Holy Eve Festival. By hosting a mushroom stew party with the student council, she was hoping to protect herself from the Chaos Serpents.

Specifically, she was relying on the stew's mind-melting fungal goodness to overwhelm her enemy's culinary temptations. There was, in fact, a totally serious reason for this trip! She wasn't picking mushrooms *like* her life depended on it. She was picking mushrooms because her life *did* depend on it!

So how, then, did her current finds look from this perspective? If the Serpents assaulted her with exotic sweets, did the mushrooms in her basket possess the fortitude to subdue their saccharine strength? They, with their bitterness and "technical" edibility? What were the chances they could hold her stomach against her foe's onslaught of dangerous delicacies?

Sadly, the answer was zero. Zip, zilch, nada! She was going to need tastier mushrooms. Much, much tastier... The ones that grew deep in the forest. She needed...Belluga mushrooms. The question was how to get to them.

I can't exactly bring up the idea with the others. They'll just shoot it down. And then keep an even closer eye on me. That'll only make things harder. If I go, I'll have to go by myself... In which case, I have to figure out how to sneak away... In particular... She eyed the girl next to Bel. *Unfortunately, Citrina's being a good Tearmoon noble and sticking close to me. I'll have to shake her. But how... Think, Mia, think. What can I do to get my hands on tastier mushrooms? Hm...*

"I'm sorry? What was that, Mia?" asked Rafina.

Too absorbed in her own thoughts, Mia failed to hear.

"Yes, tasty mushrooms... Need more... Much more... Tasty tasty..."

Her mumbling trance brought her to her feet, at which point Rafina asked again, "Mia? What's the matter?"

The second prompt brought Mia back to her senses. She looked around and realized she was the only one standing up, and everyone was staring at her.

"Huh? O-Oh, um... I just, uh..."

She stammered for a few seconds, struggling to find a suitable excuse.

Th-This is bad! I was so focused on getting deeper into the forest that my body just acted on its own!

Panic rose. She could feel it crawling up her increasingly parched throat before ejecting itself in the form of, "F-Felt like going for a stroll. To, um, pick some mushrooms..."

Obviously, that was no excuse. It was the truth, the whole truth, and nothing but the truth. Which was the exact opposite of what she'd wanted!

Gah! I just blurted it out! Now they know I want to go into deeper parts of the forest to pick mushrooms, and they're going to stop me!

The activation of her thought centers proved woefully short-lived. Though the sandwiches were nutritious, they weren't up to the task of powering her brain for long. Presumably, if she wanted to get any real thinking done, she'd need proper Mia fuel—sugar. Sadly, there was none available.

Oh no, this is hopeless... I can't think of a way to talk myself out of this...

Just as she began to give in to despair...

"Pick some mushrooms? What do you— Oh."

Someone—she wasn't sure who—uttered the abruptly truncated question that ended in a realization immediately shared by everyone else present. A unanimous "Ooooooh" of understanding made its way through the group. The boys looked away awkwardly. One of them muttered a "just keep an eye out, then."

"Uh... Okay? Sure?"

Mia scratched her head, not sure what to make of the response. Anne alone made to rise, clearly intending to follow her.

"Wait, Anne, it's okay. Just stay here and get some rest," Mia hastily said.

Unlike me, Anne's a forest novice. It would be unreasonable to make her come with me.

She smiled at Anne to reassure her.

"I'll be fine on my own."

Then, she walked off.

Now, for the slightly obtuse among you, some explanation is likely in order. "Going to pick some flowers" was a common euphemism for ladies who had to answer the call of nature while outdoors. The group had all clued in to what—they thought, at least—Mia meant by her statement, figuring she'd taken advantage of the occasion to engage in some wordplay and enhance the euphemistic nature of the phrase. No one expected her to stand up in the middle of lunch...and *actually run off to pick mushrooms by herself*. That would fly in the face of all common sense—the very common sense that blinded them to her true intention.

"Oho ho! I can't believe how well that worked!"

Mia hummed as she made her way deeper into the forest, delighted by how she'd managed to give the group the slip.

"I have to say though, they sure let me off easy. I wonder why?"

It seemed baffling to her...until she had a flash of inspiration!

"Oh, what am I talking about? It's so obvious. I'm a girl of the forest. I can handle myself out here. They're just finally realizing that now. It must have been the basket of mushrooms I brought back. Taste aside, that was a pretty handsome haul, if I do say so myself."

Motivated by the thought, she nodded to herself and pressed forward.

"Hm, according to the map, going this way from the clearing should..." she mumbled, parting branches from her path like an intrepid explorer.

Soon, she came upon a precipice that prevented further progress.

"Huh. This cliff...wasn't on the map."

Arms crossed in thought, she peered over the edge. Yellow foliage protruded from the cliff side, obscuring her view of what lay below.

"I can't see down. That's a problem. Should I try to get down somehow? Or should I go around? Hmm... Where would those mushrooms grow? Down this cliff...? Or somewhere past it..."

The cliff didn't seem particularly high. With some care, she could probably climb down. After a little thought, she decided to follow her gut.

"The correct choice...is definitely to go around! My veteran mushroom guide instincts say so!"

...It was definitely her instincts. She was just following her heart. It definitely had nothing to do with the climb down seeming like a lot of effort. Just saying.

"All right, let's try going left along the edge..."

She began walking, keeping the cliff to her right. Barely five steps later, she heard someone call her name.

"Your Highness!"

"My, who's that?"

Stopping to look in the direction of the voice, she saw Citrina jogging toward her. Her cover was blown, but there wasn't much she could do about it. She waited patiently for Citrina to catch up. The young girl stopped right in front of her and put on her usual angelic smile.

"Jeez, Your Highness, you can't be running off by yourself like that. Not this deep in the forest..." Citrina said, her lips somehow forming words without ever breaking that sweet smile of hers. "What if something happened to you, hm? What would you do then, Your Highness?"

She just…kept smiling. Even as she spoke. Even as she abruptly gave her head a curious tilt, the motion puppet-like. All the while, her smile remained unchanged. It was so sweet. So endearing. The adorable quirk of a young child. And yet, for some reason…it chilled Mia to the bone.

M-My… Am I getting goosebumps? What's going on? I feel oddly cold…

"Well? What would you do, Your Highness? If something happened to you? Hm?"

Citrina looked up at Mia with her big doll-like eyes. Mia tensed. She felt a primal urge to back away. Just then…

"Miss Mia! Rina!"

…Bel appeared in the distance behind Citrina, hand waving eagerly as she ran toward them.

"Oh, Bel… I told you to wait for me…" Citrina said under her breath. As she did, Mia felt the chill gripping her wane.

Wh-What in the moons was that?

She frowned at the strange phenomenon, but a shrill shriek broke her contemplation.

"Eek!"

Bel lurched forward, slipping on the yellow carpet of wet leaves. "Ah—"

The same shocked sound left the mouth of both observers as they watched Bel take a mighty fall. The motion flung a small object from her, sending it in an arc through the air.

"What's that?"

Mia stared dumbfounded as the object flew past her, revealing itself to be the small troya charm that Bel had put her heart and soul into making. Its trajectory took it out over the edge, but before falling downward, it caught on the branch of a tree growing diagonally outward from the cliff.

"Oh... Thank the moons..."

Mia let out a breath she'd been holding. It coincided with an identical sound nearby. Citrina had evidently done the same.

"Well, how lucky," Citrina said to Bel after quickly recomposing herself. "That's not too far out. We should be able to get it back."

Bel, however, took a look at the protruding tree before giving her head a shake.

"No, it's too dangerous. If we slip, we'll fall off the cliff." She smiled. "It's all right. I can always make another. After all, it doesn't matter how tightly you try to hold on to a thing. When it's time for it to go, it goes. That's just how it is."

Her mask of nonchalance was betrayed by a forlorn glance at the dangling troya.

Mia bit her lip. This would never have happened had she not forced the issue and snuck off into the forest herself. Guilt began to bear down on her conscience. It quivered under the weight. Moreover, she knew that Bel had worked hard to make that pair of charms so that she and Citrina could match. True, she could just make another one. But that wasn't the problem.

That charm is one of a kind. Bel poured her heart and soul into making it. Another couldn't just take its place. Which means it's too soon to give up.

Fortunately, the tree that had caught the charm was thick. It would take some careful climbing, but retrieving it seemed well within the realm of possibility. Especially for Mia, since she was a girl of the forest. Having thoroughly convinced herself of her competence in this matter, she turned to Bel and spoke in an assertive tone.

"You're right, Bel. No matter how much you treasure something, no matter how tightly you hold on to it, when it's time for it to go, it will certainly go. This is true. But." She placed a hand on the charm-bearing tree. "That's no reason to give up without even trying."

"Miss Mia? What are you doing?" asked Bel, eyes wide with shock.

"What I'm doing," said Mia, turning to fully face the tree, "is demonstrating the importance of effort, because the possibility of losing something is no excuse for not trying your absolute hardest to hold onto it!"

With that, she leapt onto the trunk. It extended diagonally outward from the cliff at an angle that wasn't too hard to climb. She wormed her way up, trying not to think about the absence of any visible ground below.

It's okay. I'm a forest veteran. Well, I'm a mushroom *veteran, but that should still mean I can climb trees no problem.*

The logical validity of her mushroom-forest equivalence notwithstanding, she was full of confidence. Flashing an intrepid smile at an awe-struck Bel, Grandmother Mia looked every bit the storybook hero about to pull off an incredible feat that would earn the eternal admiration of her breathless granddaughter.

And then she slipped and fell.

"Gaaaaaaaaaaah!"

Chapter 13: The Oldest and Weakest of the Loyal

Ludwig made full use of all his connections for his investigation. Paying secret visits to his fellow "disciples," he collected every last scrap of information they offered.

"I figured I'd start by taking a closer look at what role the House of Yellowmoon and its associates played. In the process, I received word that a fellow pupil of my master wishes to speak with me. He works in the Azure Moon Ministry"

"Another one? You know, the scale of this pupil cabal of yours never fails to amaze me," said Dion.

Ludwig smiled despite himself.

"They're an eccentric bunch, but they can be rather useful in situations like these."

The two were waiting in a private room of a large tavern on the outskirts of the capital. Soon, their guest arrived.

"Ah, it's a pleasure to see you again, dear elder pupil of our master. It's been too long."

A young man entered, greeting Ludwig with an affable grin.

"Not long enough to wipe that cheeky look off your face, I see," said Ludwig with a grimace. It was in jest, of course. Mostly. "Good to see you're still as infuriatingly sociable as ever."

"It's a curse I endure with great reluctance, I assure you," the young man said, smiling even more broadly than before. "And you, O elder pupil, seem as prone to poking your nose into sticky matters as ever.

Oh? Might that handsome fellow behind you be the sword of Her Highness? The one that's been making the rounds in the rumor mills these days?"

The young man peered at Dion, who shrugged.

"Don't know for how long, but I'm still dangling from her belt for now. The name's Dion Alaia." He shot a sharp, scrutinizing gaze at the young man. "Still figuring out if I'm pleased to make your acquaintance."

"Ha ha ha, you're exactly as intimidating as they say! Ludwig, how do you spend so much time around this fine fellow and not soil yourself every other minute?"

Entirely unfazed by Dion's menacing aura, the young man extended his hand.

"Gilbert Bouquet," he said, with an accented flourish on the soft g. "Call me Gil, if it please you. It'll please me, at least."

Dion shook the hand, glancing at Ludwig while he did.

"Gotta say, Ludwig sure has some interesting friends. Are you as *promising* a young talent as the rest?"

"Oh, you flatter me. I'm but a lowly official of the Azure Moon Ministry."

The Azure Moon Ministry was one of the five main branches of the Tearmoon government and dealt primarily with the administration of the imperial capital. As one would expect from such a broad description of purpose, this ministry's duties were quite diverse. One of these duties was negotiating with the central nobility. It was common knowledge that if one wished to obtain information about the empire's prominent nobles, asking someone from the Azure Moon Ministry was the surest path.

"Man, I have to say though, the last thing I expected was for the Great Detester of All Things Imperial himself to be working for Her Highness. What's behind the change of heart, Ludwig?"

"Hah. You'd understand if you met her. Her Highness is someone who makes you feel like anything would be worth it to keep serving her. Even our master has firmly committed himself to her employ."

"Yeah, that's the craziest part. Not only you, but that old rock of a man too. I didn't think he had it in him to change his opinions anymore."

Gilbert pursed his lips in thought and nodded, evidently intrigued by the topic. And so the Great Sage Indoctrination Campaign sunk its claws into its next victim. As its most ardent member, Ludwig knew no rest. He worked whenever and wherever. Weekdays and weekends, on the clock and off, so long as there was a mind to be converted, he would be there converting it.

"Anyway, back on topic. You wanted to know more about the Yellowmoons?" said Gilbert, as a waiter arrived with a round of drinks.

"That's right. If you have any interesting information, I'd like to hear it."

"Well, I do have something, but it's not so much information as it is…a warning." Gilbert paused to scan the room before lowering his voice to a whisper. "By the way, smart move bringing that Dion fellow with you. If you're sniffing around Duke Yellowmoon, you literally cannot be too careful."

"That bad, huh? I figured I'd need to take extra precautions based on what I've found out so far, but…"

"…Just to be clear, I know your definition of 'extra' is orders of magnitude above most people's, but even so, it probably wouldn't hurt to tighten it another notch." Gilbert leaned back and shook his head. "Honestly, I can't for the life of me imagine why you'd want to pick a fight with these people… Anyway, where should I start? Let's see… By the way, do you know how the Duke of Yellowmoon came to be known as the 'weakest' noble?"

"Of course. Lord Georgia's uprising. It's been so ever since."

The event he spoke of had occurred almost two hundred years ago. It was arguably the largest insurrection in the history of the Tearmoon Empire. At the time, the house's head had been Duke Georgia Etoile Yellowmoon. After conspiring with a number of powerful nobles, he rose up in rebellion against the imperial family. The scale and momentum of this revolt was so formidable that it threatened to rend the empire in two and plunge it into civil war. Despite its thunderous start, however, the uprising had ended with an astonishingly pathetic whimper.

Lord Georgia was killed by his younger brother, Gardier, and the rebel army crumbled soon after. The nobles who'd conspired in the uprising were all put to death, and their families' reputations were ruined. Of particular note was that the younger brother, Gardier, despite his critical contribution to averting a costly rebellion, was placed not under a halo of glory but upon a bed of thorns. Many began to speak of him with disdain, pointing to the fact that the Yellowmoons had been the ones to cause the calamity in the first place, and he'd simply prevented his own treasonous family from doing more harm. Adding oil to the fire was his petition to spare the lives of those whose families were involved in the conspiracy, though the cost of treason was widely accepted to be the death of one's entire house and clan.

In defending those guilty by association, Gardier earned himself no small amount of censure. In the end, public opinion on the two brothers diverged. The older came to be seen as a fearsome, ambitious figure with the heart and nerve to challenge the empire for his own ends. The younger was disparaged as a traitorous coward, betraying the nation and then his own house.

Even so, Gardier's petition saved many lives, and grateful survivors from implicated houses gathered under the Yellowmoon banner.

The entire Yellowmoon faction came to be known as an assembly of losers whose ranks consisted of those defeated in the power struggle. Over time, they were progressively joined by other nobles in similarly alienated positions, such as outland counts who suffered frequent contempt from the central nobility. Thus, a faction of misfits was born, resulting in the Yellowmoons being called "the oldest and weakest of all."

"And that's the gist of the story, which everybody knows. But what if I told you it was all planned? That the whole uprising was a calculated move? What would you think then?" Gilbert asked with the amused tone of a parent riddling a child.

"You mean, if the uprising wasn't a simple uprising but a means to some other end…" said Ludwig, crossing his arms contemplatively. "A lure, then… A lamp for moths…"

Gilbert snapped his fingers at Ludwig's answer.

"Bingo. I knew you'd get it. It's not exactly hard to dig this information up, but some of these nobles in the Yellowmoon faction right now…their ties with the duke go way back. Before they even lost that power struggle. For example, around the time of the uprising, there was a marquess whose power and influence almost rivaled the emperor's, but for some reason, he started losing heirs left and right. Specifically, his sons were succumbing to sickness one after another. Other nobles began looking at him askance, deeming him a source of bad luck, and eventually he was ostracized from high society. That's when an old friend of his, the Duke of Yellowmoon, just happened to show up and invite him to join their faction." Gilbert took a swig of wine and smirked. "Now doesn't that just reek of something fishy?"

"I see. So you're suggesting that the Yellowmoons assassinated the marquess's sons to weaken his influence. Hm… They approach those who are a nuisance to the empire, gain their trust, and then cripple their power.

The fact that they targeted not the marquess directly but his sons, along with the imperial family's ostensible ambivalence toward them, shielded them from any substantial suspicion of wrongdoing."

"And on top of that, the Yellowmoons are experts in botany and herbology. It really makes you wonder, you know?"

"They have a longstanding interest in medicinal horticulture...would be the benign explanation. But no. This is likely a case of medicine and poison being two sides of the same coin."

"Precisely. The House of Yellowmoon is a clan of assassins who use poison to eliminate those who are a threat to the empire. That's my theory," Gilbert declared in a casual tone, completely at odds with the gravity of the subject matter.

Their fall from grace was camouflage. Being labeled "the weakest" hid that they performed a special function for the emperor. At the same time, they still existed as a faction, making their sphere of influence an alluring place for those conspiring against the empire to gather. The role of the Yellowmoons...was to be a lure. They were at once the lamp that drew the noxious moths of the empire in as well as the flame that exterminated them.

Every emperor needed someone to do his dirty work. There was no glory to it, but it was an important role that needed to be filled. It made perfect sense...for a normal empire. But Ludwig knew Tearmoon was no normal empire. When factoring in what he'd learned of the first emperor's intentions...

"Being the weakest and most estranged from the central nobility makes the Yellowmoons an attractive ally...to *new* nobles. Those not affected by anti-agricultural beliefs. It would be easier for, say, outcounts to approach them. And, if said newcomer proved problematic, assassinate them. Is that their purpose?"

If this whole web of intrigue was a deliberate arrangement to help the empire propagate anti-agriculturalism, then the House of Yellowmoon would have played an extremely vital role. And by successfully doing so...

"I see. And that's where the other version comes from. The oldest and weakest of the loyal..."

"The point is, watch your back. The Yellowmoons seem to have, you know, a bit of a knack for assassination," said Gilbert with the same easy smirk.

Chapter 14: Yellow, White...and Red

"Mm... Mmm..."

With a quiet groan, Mia slowly opened her eyes. The world was a blur. She rubbed her eyes, blinked a few times, then rubbed them again. Finally, she sat up and looked around.

"This is... My, where am I?"

The beauty surrounding her took her breath away. Thick yellow foliage swayed overhead, dropping small leaves that gently danced their way to the ground, which was blanketed by a layer of white as even as newly fallen snow.

"Are these...white mushrooms?"

She took another look at her surroundings and gasped at the remarkable sight, realizing that she'd been lying on a bed of white mushrooms. The soft, squishy carpet had broken her fall.

"Yes, now I remember... I fell from the cliff...and these mushrooms saved me from hurting myself," she said, tenderly stroking the cap of one of her tiny heroes.

Only then did it occur to her that her right hand was balled tightly into a fist, and that there was something inside. Uncurling her fingers revealed the horse charm Bel had made.

"Oh thank the moons. I didn't lose it. If I'd dropped it somewhere here, I'd have a terrible time finding it again..."

She gingerly hoisted herself to her feet, bracing for any sudden jolts of pain. None came. As far as she could tell, she wasn't injured.

Her mushroom outfit likely deserved some credit too, seeing as it was thick enough to have functioned as a cushion. Mia had finally come into her own as a maiden of the mushrooms. Favored by their blessing, she was now a true Mushroom Princess.

…What even *is* a Mushroom Princess?

"Well, this is the very definition of a lucky mistake… I've managed to stumble my way to the Belluga mushrooms." She grinned greedily at the vast expanse of white around her. "And sweet moons, there are so many… This is an all-you-can-pick mushroom bonanza!"

Recalling that Citrina had mentioned there was a place in the forest where lots of Belluga mushrooms grew, she figured this was clearly it. She'd struck gold. Well… Let's just say the name of the things *did* include the words "Belluga" and "mushroom."

"Marvelous… Absolutely marvelous! I need to tell everyone…" She looked around and paused, noticing something odd. "My… What's that?"

The white mushroom carpet was dotted here and there with ones that were entirely red. It was an eerie sight, like drops of blood spilled on a field of fresh snow. Upon closer inspection, she realized that the source of the aberrant color was something she'd seen before…

"Your Highness!"

"Miss Mia!"

A familiar pair of youthful voices reached her ears, followed by the sound of people descending the cliff.

"Ah, you came for me…"

Seeing that Bel and Citrina had appeared, she turned her gaze upward.

Hm, if those two can make it down here, then the height can't be much of a problem. The rest of the group should be able to make it down too. The actual picking of the mushrooms won't be any problem. The issue is, these mushrooms here…

Her thoughts were interrupted by a Bel-sized mass slamming into her.

"Oof!"

The young girl all but tackled her to the ground.

"Omigosh, I'm so glad you're okay, Miss Mia."

Bel wrapped her arms around Mia and squeezed.

"Oh, Bel, you silly girl…" Mia gently stroked her granddaughter's head. "Look, it's your charm. I got it back for you."

She softly peeled Bel off her and dropped the troya into her dainty little hands.

"Ah, this is…"

"You worked really hard to make it, right? Next time, make sure you tie a nice strong knot, so it doesn't go flying again. I can't keep diving off cliffs to get it back," said Mia, in a tone far too preachy for one whose dive was entirely involuntary and the result of a spectacular failure of tree climbing.

Her pretentious attitude, however, did not bother Bel in the least.

"…Thank you so much, Miss Mia."

Bel simply wrapped her arms around Mia and squeezed again.

"Aww…"

Mia beamed contentedly at this earnest display of affection. For a good while, Bel kept her face buried in her grandmother's chest. After thoroughly indulging in a long embrace, she finally took a proper look around herself.

"Wow! What a beautiful place this is, Miss Mia!"

She promptly dashed off.

"Wait!" Mia hastily threw out her hands in a halting gesture. "Hold it, Bel. You can't go trampling all these mushrooms. They're supposed to be very tasty."

The thought of losing her hard-found trove of Belluga mushrooms to a pair of tiny rampaging feet gave her a minor panic attack.

"Okay, Miss Mia."

Bel stopped where she was, but continued glancing around with an eagerness that unnerved Mia, who couldn't help but feel that Bel's curiosity might cause her to resume her mushroom flattening spree any second. Suddenly, Bel's eyes widened.

"Look, Rina, do you see that red mushroom? What is it? Is it tasty too?" she asked, having spotted one of the red ones hidden among the white.

Mia felt a pang of disappointment at the fact that her dear granddaughter hadn't posed the question to her.

"Oh, I don't know. My memory's a little hazy, but probably not."

Hearing Citrina's reply, Mia grinned.

"My, Citrina! A mushroom that you're not familiar with? Oh, but I suppose I can't blame you. This one *is* rather exotic," she said with the utmost smugness. Then, she turned to Bel and, somehow managing to make her smug grin even smugger, said, "That's a salamandrake, and it's very poisonous."

She *glowed* with pride. After basking in her own hubris for a while, she remembered to add, "Oh, and by the way, it's dangerous to even touch, so stay aw— Gah! Bel!"

Bel was already walking toward it. Mia yanked the girl back by the collar.

"You need to stop doing that. There are lots of dangerous mushrooms, so you need to listen to veterans like us and follow our instructions. Right, Rina? Hm? Uh…Rina?"

Finding the lack of a reply odd, Mia turned toward Citrina. For some reason, she was just standing there facing the ground, her expression shrouded by her hair falling over her face.

M-My, how odd. Why am I feeling this chill again?

It felt like something cold was filling her bones. But it lasted only a moment, dispersed by a charming giggle from Citrina.

"Wow, it's really impressive how much Your Highness knows about mushrooms. What a *surprising* talent."

What remained was her usual smile. It was sweet, flawless, and... in Mia's opinion, a little frightening.

"In any case, I think it'd be best if we head back."

Figuring they couldn't keep dawdling at the bottom of the cliff, the three of them made their way back to the picnic site. Upon returning, they were greeted with relief by their friends, who'd been looking for them.

"Just so everyone knows, we found some poisonous mushrooms in the forest."

The group's expressions quickly changed to concerned frowns at Mia's announcement.

"...Are you sure, Mia? They really were poisonous?"

The deepest crease touched the brow of Rafina. Though she'd been relieved of her duty as student council president, as Duke Belluga's daughter, she was still responsible for anything that happened on Saint-Noel Island. A safety concern like this was not something she could afford to ignore.

"I'm absolutely certain. Very poisonous. They're called salamandrakes, and they're these beautiful red mushrooms—"

"E-Excuse me, Princess Mia," interjected an anxious Keithwood, "but just to be sure, you didn't bring any back, did you?"

"Of course not. I've been told that it's dangerous to even touch them," she said, remembering Muzic, the hunter she met in Remno, and the look on his face when she'd reached for one of them.

Mia had an affinity for big men, and Muzic was a pretty big fellow, so she was receptive to his admonishment. Judging by how sternly he'd warned her, she figured barehanded contact would not end well at all.

"Ah… R-Right. Of course you didn't. Someone as wise as yourself wouldn't possibly bring back something so dangerous. I don't even know why I asked," said Keithwood in the tone of someone who knew exactly why he'd asked.

Mia scowled, peeved by the sheer relief in his voice.

"Well, I'll have you know that they're very pretty mushrooms, and if I had some gloves, I'd have brought back a bunch," she said facetiously.

"No! For the love of the sun, please don't!"

Keithwood did not take the joke well. His visibly paling face amused her, and a devious smile spread across her lips.

Oho ho, this might be interesting… she thought, delighted by the prospect of teasing a young man about his anxieties. Legitimate anxieties, yes, but still teasable. Mia the Seductress strikes again!

"Oh, I remember now. It was him, wasn't it? The hunter we met that time…" said a nodding Sion.

"Um, I've read about that mushroom in an illustrated reference book," Chloe added. "It's supposed to be really poisonous. It's obviously deadly if eaten, but apparently even just touching one can kill you…"

"A mushroom like that, here on Saint-Noel… But poisonous things aren't supposed to grow on this island…" murmured Rafina, gaze lowered in troubled contemplation.

Keithwood was next to speak.

"In that case, what about the mushrooms we've already picked? Some of them might be poisonous too. We can't afford the risk."

"Those are fine," Mia reassured him. "That's why we have Rina here with us, so she can make sure they're safe. Right, Rina?"

Citrina nodded.

"Yes. The mushrooms we've picked so far don't resemble any poisonous varieties I'm aware of, so they should be safe to eat. As an extra precaution though, I recommend getting confirmation from professional kitchen staff as well."

"I see..." Keithwood inclined his head. "I guess it's fine if we get a professional opinion..."

Mia sighed as she listened to the exchange.

Well, this is rather disappointing. I finally found a place where Belluga mushrooms grow, but it doesn't look like I'll get to go pick any. With the way this conversation is going, we're definitely going to pack up and head back to the academy. This forest will probably be off-limits for a good while too...

She'd come so close. She'd *touched* the things. But unfortunately, the treasure trove of Belluga mushrooms and their purportedly exquisite flavor continued to elude her tongue. It was terribly frustrating. She blew out another discouraged sigh and sat down...only to freeze mid-motion.

Hm? What's this?

One of her pockets bulged unnaturally, as if it held something that was being pushed outward by her hunkering form. She didn't remember putting anything in that pocket though. Slowly, she slipped a hand in to retrieve the offending object.

Oh... Oh my... This is... It can't be...

She could scarcely believe her eyes. There, in her hand, was a white mushroom.

A Belluga mushroom?! But... How? When?

She tilted her head, mentally retracing the day's events.

It must have happened after I fell down the cliff. When I hit the ground, it somehow got into my pocket. But still, it's probably risky to eat this, isn't it? Hm...

A tiny Mia in a white mushroom suit whispered into her ear.

"It certainly is. Rina told us, didn't she? There's a poisonous species that looks a lot like Belluga mushrooms called false Belluga mushrooms... and now that the salamandrake we found has proven that poisonous mushrooms can grow on this island, it's far too risky to eat this."

However, her evil counterpart in a red mushroom suit objected.

"What are you talking about? We finally have it. We're holding the exquisite Belluga mushroom in our hands right now, and you want to just throw it away? Nonsense. Besides, even if it's a poisonous false Belluga mushroom, we'll just have to deal with a tummy ache for a while," argued the tiny pint-sized Mia. She continued to whisper fervently into her master's ear. *"We know what we're doing. We have the knowledge, and we just gained hands-on experience. We're a bona fide mushroom expert now. Not to mention, we found the Belluga mushrooms. And we did it all by ourselves! We're so good at this, we can totally call ourselves the Mushroom Princess! So take a good look at that mushroom… What does our mushroom sense tell us?"*

She stared at the white mushroom, eyes narrowing like an antique appraiser trying to determine the true value of an unearthed artifact.

"Hm… My mushroom sense says… This one's good to eat!"

So decided her gut. Furthermore…

"Also, for it to show up in my pocket like this is nothing short of a miracle. This is clearly God giving me the thumbs up, in which case it's my divine duty to consume this mushroom!"

Somewhere far in the distance, there may or may not have been a faintly Ludwig-sounding voice shouting, "Miracles don't happen that easily!" His ghostly admonition, however, failed to reach Mia's ears.

And so, with an air of blithe innocence, Mia followed her group out of the forest.

Chapter 15: Princess Mia...
Stews It! Then Eats It!

Thus, Mia finally had the ingredients for her long-desired mushroom party.

There were a few private rooms available in Saint-Noel Academy's cafeteria for dinner parties, during which food would be delivered from the kitchen. Any student could book them for their personal use, and one was currently reserved by the student council.

The mushrooms Mia and her friends had picked were brought to the kitchen where, when the time came, they would be inspected for edibility by specialized staff before being stewed. Upon entering, they were greeted by Saint-Noel's chief of security, Santeri. He exuded an air of diligent but stubborn dedication to his duties, and after glancing in their direction, he lowered his head in a deep bow.

"Welcome back. As a supervisor of the island, it pleases me greatly to see you've returned safe and sound. I do hope you found your mushroom hunting trip enjoyable."

"Thank you for your concern, and oh, it was *very* enjoyable," Mia answered on behalf of everyone.

"That is good to hear. Furthermore, allow me to express my deepest thanks for the invitation to this stew party of the student council. It will be my great honor to attend."

"Please, you're far too modest. Without people like you, we wouldn't be able to enjoy our school life with the peace of mind that comes from knowing our safety is in good hands. It's only natural for us to show our appreciation. I hope you enjoy this little party of ours."

After exchanging a series of formalities with Santeri, Mia wandered deeper into the kitchen, making sure the quality of her locomotion was sufficiently nonchalant to not betray any hint of intent or motive.

"Ah, welcome back, Princess Mia."

One of the kitchen ladies she was acquainted with greeted her.

"Yes, the trip was lots of fun. I'm sorry that we brought more work back for you though."

They traded some friendly words. Mia then politely greeted each of the cooks in turn. They all smiled back at her. Thanks to Mia's frequent visits to the kitchen, she was a familiar face to the whole staff by now. It should be mentioned that her visits always resulted in her making off with some food, but her habit of kitchen-lifting was received with surprising warmth by the victims. This was due to the extensive networking that Anne had tirelessly engaged in.

In general, Anne was the only person Mia had no intention of being stingy with. She regularly gave her maid handsome sums of money so she could engage in some therapeutic spending in town. Anne, however, used her allowance for a different purpose. Every time she received money, she'd head into town and pick up a slew of gifts, which she'd then have delivered to various academy staff in Mia's name. As a result, Mia had gained a reputation as a benevolent princess popular amongst the common people.

Anyway, back to the kitchen. After a round of friendly greetings, Mia walked over to her bulging basket of mushrooms on the counter. The lady trailing her grimaced at the sight.

"You've brought us quite the challenge, haven't you? Fitting this mountain of mushrooms into a single stew is going to be tough. Also, a lot of these mushrooms are…a little difficult to prepare."

"Yes, it does seem so. By the way, and I'm asking this purely out of intellectual curiosity... How might one go about preparing a Belluga mushroom?"

"Huh? Did you bring back some Belluga mushrooms too?" asked the lady in a surprised voice.

"No, of course not. Like I said, I was just curious. We'll call it a point of academic interest."

"Oh, okay. Well... Hm..." The lady pursed her lips in thought. "Belluga mushrooms taste very good, so I think if you just give them a quick wash, then cut them into two or three pieces and stewed them for a while, it'd be fine."

"Hm, hm... It's that easy, huh... That's certainly good news. In, um, an academic sort of way. Oh!" Mia, as if suddenly remembering something, widened her eyes in a decidedly artificial manner. "Would you by any chance happen to know where I can wash my hands? They're rather dirty."

She waved them to illustrate.

"Ah, right. After a trip to the forest, they would be, wouldn't they? You can get some water over there." The lady pointed, taking her question at face value.

"How clean is the water, by the way? I have delicate princess hands, and they must be washed with *clean* water. As for how clean... let's say the kind of water you'd usually wash your ingredients with."

"Well, you're good to go then. That literally is the water we wash our food with, so it should be no problem."

"Ah, excellent. Thank you."

She smiled and slipped a hand into her pocket.

Hm, wash it clean, cut it into big pieces, and drop them into the pot... Sounds simple, but easier said than done.

Hiding the mushroom in her palms, she cleaned it in the water while pretending to wash her hands. She carefully scrubbed every inch, aiming to give it such a thorough cleansing that it'd be safe to eat even if raw. All the while she kept it concealed. It was a feat of manual dexterity that rivaled the sleights of veteran illusionists. Mia usually tended to be a tad ham-fisted, but for some reason, when it came to mushrooms, her butterfingers were endowed with a newfound deftness. It was, perhaps, a sign that her powers as the Mushroom Princess were finally awakening.

…Again, what even *is* a Mushroom Princess?

After completing her comprehensive aquatic sanitization procedure, she snuck a few glances left and right before creeping up to the pot of stew. Standing over it, she warily peeked around again.

The one I have to be most careful of is that Santeri fellow. Watch where he's looking… Have to time it… Three… Two… One… Now!

She burst into motion, her form blurring through sheer speed. In the span of a breath, she'd divided the mushroom into four quarters, thrown them into the pot, and left the scene of the crime. Whistling nonchalantly as she walked—rather, blowing breathy hisses out of her mouth, because she couldn't actually whistle—she felt a sense of accomplishment filling her already pounding heart.

With her mission complete, she returned to the private room, where she engaged in a carefully timed interval of conversation before making her way to the kitchen again. There was one final step to her plan. It was time for the master stroke.

If they find it beforehand, they'll definitely stop me from eating it. I know that's a genuine Belluga mushroom, but I doubt they'll listen. I have to make sure that doesn't happen, and there's only one way to do so!

She snuck in again and approached the pot.

"Ah! No, Princess Mia. It's still cooking—"

"Oho ho, don't worry. I'm just having a quick taste. One sip is all. Just one sip," she said as she raised the lid on the pot.

One of the white mushroom chunks immediately leapt into her sight. Before anyone could stop her, she swiftly snatched it up and plopped it into her mouth. Her slightly-enlarged cheeks undulated a few times. Then pure bliss spread across her expression. The mushroom's juicy texture delighted her tongue, and its savory aroma pleased her nose.

"Mmmmm... Now this is some serious flavor... There's a depth to it that I can't even begin to describe. Aaaah, it's so goo— Mm?!"

Abruptly, she felt it—a gastrointestinal disturbance. It hit hard, and it hit fast. Her tummy emitted an unnerving gurgle...before it all but twisted into itself.

"Ow... Ow ow ow! Ah, my stomach! It hurts! Augh! Oooh!"

The sharp pain brought her to her knees.

"Ow! Ow! I can't... This is... Uh oh—"

Her stomach heaved, and she felt the distinct sensation of something flowing back up her throat.

"I-I'm going to... U-Urp..."

The double whammy of nausea and stomachache knocked the consciousness right out of her.

Chapter 16: The Case of Mia,
the Mushroom-Eating Saint

Following Mia's incident in the kitchen, during which she'd eaten a poisonous mushroom and passed out, she was instructed to rest for three days. Fortunately, the prompt application of an emetic had made her retch her stomach clean, limiting the effect of the toxin. Though her dignity suffered gravely, she was nonetheless well on her way to recovery. This allowed her to assert that the entire episode had been the result of her own carelessness, thereby preventing it from blowing up into a major scandal that caused no end of problems for everyone. Had she not reassured Rafina of the incident's accidental nature, there would be an army of anti-Chaos Serpent interrogation specialists marching toward the academy right now.

Which was all well and good, but...

"Ugh, I'm so bored. I'm so so bored," Mia muttered while lying in her bed.

Her fast recovery had the unfortunate side effect of leaving her with far too much energy to be confined to her bed for three days. Making things worse was the fact that her meals had been changed to a bland diet meant for the sick, robbing her of the only thing she could look forward to. There, trapped in her room with nothing but her own good health, she understood what it meant for her world to turn gray.

Which probably painted her in too sympathetic a light, considering this was *entirely* her own fault. She was truly getting a taste of her just deserts.

Her attempt to pass the time by rereading the story drafts her court author, Elise, had sent her had been duly thwarted as well when Anne had discovered her defying her medically prescribed bed rest and promptly confiscated them. In the end, she was left with nothing to do but waste away in boredom.

"Oh, I know… Anne, could you tell me an interesting story?"

Asking someone to tell an interesting story off the top of their head was, frankly, a pretty unreasonable request. Given her circumstances though, she figured Anne would indulge her. Surely, Anne, her most loyal of subjects, would have mercy on her. Which was why…

"A-Anne? Um…"

She was surprised when no answer came. Anne simply kept cleaning the room. After an uncomfortable moment of silence, she stole a glance at Anne, only for the maid to meet it for just a brief second before looking away.

"…Huh?"

Something was clearly wrong. Alarms began going off in her head as she continued to ask with growing unease, "H-Hey, what's going on, Anne?"

Her second attempt failed again to elicit any acknowledgment. She realized that Anne seemed to be mad at her, but she had no idea why.

"Wh-What's the matter? Did I do something to make you angry? I-I don't…"

Though she had no recollection of wrongdoing, she nevertheless got up and hastily rearranged herself into a position of deference with her legs folded under her thighs.

I don't know what's going on! What do I do?

Normally, it would be unthinkable for an attendant to express such blunt displeasure toward their master. Mia and Anne, of course, shared a unique relationship that transcended their relative standings.

Mia cared about Anne. She thought of her as a special friend and never held her to traditional expectations of attendant behavior. An overt expression of disapproval like this was hardly something Mia would take offense to. However, Anne had never indulged herself. Despite Mia's lenience, she'd always behaved with the utmost respect.

Anne was a model attendant. A paragon of stewardly virtue. And she'd just ignored Mia. Twice. She was so mad that she refused to even acknowledge her. Flustered, afraid, and well aware that this was no laughing matter, Mia looked helplessly at her maid. A long, nerve-wracking silence ensued. Finally, Anne spoke.

"You...left me behind again...milady."

Her voice was strained, and her gaze remained averted.

"Huh? O-Oh... Um, well..."

Mia was about to make an excuse about how Anne had looked tired at the time, but those words dove right back down her throat the second she saw the look on Anne's face.

"When I heard you went deep into the forest and fell down a cliff... I thought my heart was going to stop."

Anne turned toward the bed. Her eyes glistened with tears.

"A-Anne..."

The sight flustered Mia even more. This was, she realized, the first time she'd ever made Anne cry, and she had no idea what to do about it.

"And the stew too... I'm sure you have your reasons...and I trust you...so I won't ask why you picked a poisonous mushroom...or why you put it into the pot...or why you had to eat it yourself...but..." Anne's voice cracked, and along with it, her emotional dam. Tears gushed down her cheeks. Her breaths came in sobbing gasps, but she kept speaking. "If... If you ever...do something dangerous again...

I'm going with you… I don't care where…or what…but I'm going. I learned how to ride horses. If I need to use a sword, then I'll learn that too. So…don't… Don't leave me behind anymore…"

Facing Mia, she folded at the waist. Droplets of sorrow fell from her bowed head, splattering against the floor.

"Anne… You…"

Mia bit her lip. Words failed her. She pressed her eyes shut, trying to fight down the rush of emotion pushing against her face from the inside. A few seconds of stillness passed. Then, carefully, so as to not reveal the unsteadiness of her voice, she spoke.

"You…are truly my most loyal and trustworthy subject, Anne."

The deep devotion her maid displayed moved her to the core. But she placed a metaphorical hand on her wavering core and held it steady…

"I…understand now. Your feelings, and the loyalty that drives them, are a gift I will hold dear in my heart for the rest of my life."

She gave a grateful response. But a noncommittal one. No oaths were sworn. No promises made. For she knew that she yet walked a perilous road, and her life was still destined to end this winter. It would, to the best of her knowledge, be a messy death—one that might very well bring harm to all those close to her.

I hope it doesn't happen, but if I do end up dying, I can't afford to drag Anne into it too.

After everything Anne had done for her… After all the love and kindness she'd shown… She deserved better. Mia inwardly shook her head.

And there's Bel too…

If she were to die, who would take care of her precious little granddaughter? A vision of her future self flitted across her mind—

the self that had died of poison. It occurred to her that she must have gone peacefully, physical agony notwithstanding, knowing her children and grandchildren were safe in the care of people she could trust.

Okay, no, enough morbid thoughts. It's not like I'm trying to put myself in dangerous situations. I should be fine. All I have to do that day is hole up in my room. Yes, it'll be okay. I know it will.

Anne, meanwhile, just kept staring at Mia with tear-reddened eyes. There was no way she could have known about Mia's internal struggle, and yet, her gaze was so piercing that…

"Please," Mia said with a nervous chuckle, "don't look at me like that. You know me. I don't make a habit of flirting with danger."

Her placating smile failed to elicit a response in kind.

…Those who found this conversation between princess and attendant to be poignant and heartwarming may wish to *not* be reminded of the fact that the whole affair had resulted from Mia's unadvised enthusiasm leading her to eagerly snarf down a poisonous mushroom. If you are one of those people, consider yourself not reminded. No one was there to remind the two in question, anyway.

Three days later, with her confinement ended and her health restored, Mia thought she'd be ready to charge out and seize the day. Instead, she almost wanted to have another bite of that mushroom. That way, she could stay in bed instead of…attending Rafina's tea party.

Rafina's tea party!

Considering the timing of the invitation, she immediately realized that neither the tea nor the party was the primary purpose of the event; no, Rafina wanted to *talk*. On top of that, the island's chief of security, Santeri, would be present as well. It seemed blatantly clear that she was going to get a serious dressing-down!

"Oooh, I'm in for it now… They must be furious!"

She recalled the sight of Rafina's bloodshot eyes during the election and shuddered. The smooth sailing she'd experienced lately had caused her to grow complacent and forget a crucial fact: Rafina Orca Belluga was, in general, a very scary person. Reckless and arbitrary stunts that caused problems for tons of other people would undoubtedly evoke her unbridled wrath. And Mia had just gone and pulled one of them. To her credit, she'd at least managed to absolve the kitchen staff of responsibility, but that was cold comfort. It couldn't possibly save her from the intense scolding she was about to receive.

"Ooooh, stupid me. Why'd I have to play with fire like that? Ugh… I need to think of an excuse…"

Her anxious muttering continued all the way to the site of the tea party which, strangely, happened to be the same private room in the cafeteria as the one where her ill-fated taste test had taken place.

"Excuse me…Miss Rafina?" squeaked Mia as she slunk into the room, only to stiffen at the sight of those present.

Rafina was accompanied by the ex-Wind Crow, Monica, along with a brooding Santeri, who glared at Mia as she entered.

Nope, this is definitely not going to be a chitchat session… Ugh, my tummy is starting to hurt again…

She reflexively rubbed her stomach, wincing at the stress-induced ache. Rafina frowned at her in concern.

"Does your stomach still hurt?"

"Oh, um, no," Mia responded hastily, "not that much…"

She trailed off as another thought occurred to her.

Wait, maybe I should have said I still don't feel good. That might have earned me enough pity points to avoid a serious scolding. Ah, but then again, saying I'm perfectly fine makes it sound like not much damage was done, so maybe I'll get off easier that way instead? Mmm… A hard call…

As both the offender and the victim, Mia found herself in an exceedingly awkward position. Unsure of what to say, she stared broodingly at the ground. Her silent contemplation was broken, to her surprise, by a gentle prompt from Rafina.

"Please, don't push yourself, Mia. Here, take a seat. I'm terribly sorry to have asked you here today. I know you're still recovering. If it's any consolation, I've prepared some tea and sweets that are easy on the stomach, so feel free to try some of them if you feel up to it."

"A-All right... I think I will, then. Thank you..."

Mia lowered herself into a chair and let out a short sigh. Monica, now a maid, promptly poured out some tea for her. It had a strange, herbal fragrance. She took a sip.

Aaaah... How relaxing...

She let out a longer, more peaceful sigh. Her nerves calmed enough for her to start plotting out a course through the hazard-ridden maze that was the impending conversation.

Okay, first things first. I need to apologize. No matter what I do, there's no way I'm escaping blame. In that case, I should apologize as sincerely as possible. Just keep saying sorry over and over to buy enough time for me to figure out my next move.

With her approach decided, she turned to Rafina.

"I am aware that apologizing will not make my actions any more acceptable, but nevertheless, I am sorry for my irresponsible behavior," she said, lowering her head deeply in repentance.

Rafina listened intently, nodding.

"Irresponsible behavior... Yes, that was certainly very irresponsible of you," said Rafina, nodding solemnly. Then her face contorted with grief. "But it was us who forced your hand...and for that, I am equally sorry."

For Mia, who was preparing to launch her second volley of time-buying apologies, this reaction caught her off guard.

"I can imagine how difficult a decision it must have been," Rafina continued, "and the struggle you must have gone through…"

"Eh? Uh… I, well…"

Mia nodded along, trying to decipher the meaning of this statement.

Well, I mean… It's true that if Rafina or the others caught me doing it, they'd stop me, so I had to work fast to sneak it into the pot and then sneak it into my mouth… In that sense, I guess you could say they "forced my hand." As for the struggle… Well, I did have a hard time deciding whether it was a poisonous mushroom when I found it. Maybe that's what she means?

She couldn't quite figure out what Rafina was getting at. A moment later, however, inspiration struck.

Aha! So that's it! I know what she's thinking now. She's feeling responsible for the fact that in the process of trying to treat everyone to delicious mushroom stew, I had to act on my own without consulting anyone. Obviously, if I didn't think they were going to stop me, I wouldn't have done everything in secret. I would have asked for a second opinion from Citrina, and I wouldn't have needed to be my own food taster.

Mia felt like a path had revealed itself before her. It was a narrow, winding thing, but it was a way out of this maze…

I have no choice! Narrow or not, if this path leads out, then I'm going to charge down at full speed!

She nodded with the weight of hardened resolve.

"As a matter of fact, it *was* a very difficult decision, and I *did* struggle."

First, she made sure to emphasize the fact that her decision regarding the mushroom's potential toxicity was not made easily. It was an *ordeal*. She'd put in a whole lot of pity-deserving effort. Furthermore…

"And I did it with everyone's best interests in mind."

…She drove home the point that her intentions had been altruistic. She'd done it for the benefit of everyone else. It definitely wasn't to satisfy her own cravings! No, sirree! There was no selfishness involved here whatsoever!

Thus she went, playing one pity card after another, hoping to win the "extenuating circumstances" game. It was, frankly, quite shameless. But shame didn't pay the responsibility bills, so she carried on, shooting surreptitious glances at Rafina to gauge her response. To her delight, it appeared to be working.

Miss Rafina doesn't seem nearly as angry as I thought she'd be. I…I think I might actually have a chance of getting out of this!

Just as she began to feel a sense of relief…

"Hmph, all due respect, Princess Mia, but lord knows you've gone and made all our lives harder."

Santeri interjected in a severe tone, fixing her with a frigid look. The attitude he took toward her would have been unacceptable in Tearmoon, but unfortunately, they were in Belluga. Here, the Holy Lady reigned supreme. Not only was Mia's authority limited, but her actions were by all measures deserving of reprimand. Having messed up so badly that there was nothing she could say to excuse herself, she had to humbly accept any criticism thrown her way. So she kept her head down, her mouth shut, and her posture suitably hunched to convey the image of someone in deep repentance.

"Yes, you discovered that poisonous mushroom," he continued. "That's to your credit. Allowing such a vile thing to exist here is an oversight on our part. But your actions have done irreparable damage to the reputation and legacy of Saint-Noel's student council. You do realize, I hope, that had we been less fortunate, this could have blown up into an international incident between Belluga and Tearmoon?"

She accepted his castigation meekly, knowing she was in no position to rebel. Had Ludwig found out about her antics, he probably would have given her an earful as well. Though this had all been kept under wraps, with only a select few privy to the details, it would be nothing short of a disaster if word somehow got to Mia's father. A war or two would be getting off easy. That was why Mia figured her only appropriate gesture was to resign herself slump-shouldered to the fate of being raked over the coals. Which was why…

"As the person responsible for maintaining peace and order on Saint-Noel Island, as well as the one charged with upholding the academy's reputation, I simply cannot overlook such destruct—"

"Silence, Santeri."

…She absolutely did not expect to hear the functional equivalent of "shut your damn trap," least of all from Rafina. A mousy glance toward the Holy Lady revealed a pair of intimidating eyes. Anger flickered brightly in them, and they were locked on Santeri.

"Are you truly so dense? Do you not understand the meaning of Mia's actions?"

"…The what?"

This unexpected outburst sent Santeri's jaw to the ground. Which was nothing compared to Mia, whose jaw went *through* the ground. What in the world was Rafina talking about? If Santeri had no idea, then Mia had less than none.

"Throughout this entire incident, Princess Mia has been the very model of a saint. Do you not see the integrity and virtue with which she conducted herself?"

"…Eh?"

Mia blinked at Rafina, then Santeri, then Rafina again. It didn't help, so she just kept blinking.

"A-A saint? What do you mean?" Santeri asked (unwittingly for Mia's benefit as well).

Rafina regarded the bewildered man and, after a moment, spoke in a quiet voice.

"Santeri, do you truly believe Mia acted out of selfishness? That she did those things with the intention of benefiting herself?"

"Are you…suggesting that she didn't?"

Rafina nodded solemnly.

"Yes, of course. Isn't that right, Mia?"

The sudden mention of her own name triggered Mia's knee-jerk reaction, in which she mimicked Rafina's solemn nod and agreed with whatever had been said. Frankly, she hadn't the slightest clue what Rafina was going on about, but that wasn't important. She was a wave rider, and this was undoubtedly a wave. In classic Mia fashion, she ceded control to the forces flowing around her, allowing them to tug her as they pleased.

Seeing Mia's meek expression of affirmation, Rafina smiled with satisfaction.

"As I thought. Mia wouldn't possibly do something so selfish and foolish. Nor did she mean it as a joke or prank. Think about it. Don't you think it's strange how she just happened to bring us on a mushroom hunting trip, and there just happened to be poisonous mushrooms in the forest for her to discover? Not only that, but she then ended up selecting a weakly poisonous one to bring back with her, dropping it into the pot of stew without any of us noticing, and then *eating it herself*. What are the chances of that, hm? Are we to assume this was a string of coincidences? Does that sound even remotely plausible to you?"

"W-Well, I suppose not… Looking at it like that, it seems… intentional."

"Intentional. In other words, she ate the poisonous mushroom on purpose. Does that sound like a normal thing to do?"

"N-No, I don't believe so…"

With Santeri having admitted that Mia's behavior was peculiar, Rafina gave him one final push.

"Why then? Why would she engage in such abnormal behavior? She had to have a reason. An objective," she declared with utter confidence.

"An…objective? What was it?"

Santeri and Mia both asked the same question, albeit the latter in the form of internal monologue. With bated breath, Mia waited for Rafina's climactic reveal, during which she would—for the first time—learn of her own hidden motive.

"Her objective…" said Rafina, "is the reformation of our security measures for the Holy Eve Festival."

"What?! What do you mean by that? What problem is there with our security measures?" Santeri exclaimed indignantly, his tone projecting unwavering faith in the quality of his own work.

"I do believe Mia has already answered your question. She has, on this island where poison supposedly cannot be brought in, not only acquired it, but added it to a pot of stew in a place that shouldn't allow for such things to happen…and she even managed to *eat it herself.* Does this not seem like a security problem to you?"

"It…"

He hesitated for a moment, then promptly shook his head.

"Very well. I will acknowledge the value of her discovery. We did not expect there to be poisonous mushrooms growing on the island. However, even accounting for the possibility of obtaining lethally poisonous mushrooms here, overcoming the guards and protocols we implement on the day of the festival to actually use the poison is a different story. I don't believe the two to be comparable."

Santeri's counterargument failed to move Rafina, whose expression remained grave.

"True... Adding poison to the banquet feast is likely impossible. The food there will be consumed by our students, and we have strict measures in place to ensure their safety. But...what of their attendants? Is *their* food safe?" Rafina's contemplative eyes fixed themselves on Santeri. "Between the food served to us student council members today and the food that will be served to attendants on the day of the Holy Eve Festival, which of them is subject to stricter scrutiny?"

Potential assassins did not limit themselves to operating solely on the day of the festival. To account for this, stringent security measures were always in place to ensure the day-to-day safety of people like Rafina and her council members. Therefore Santeri had no choice but to admit that the latter—security around food served to attendants—was lax in comparison.

"But... Hm, attendants, you say?" He frowned, puzzled by the suggestion. "I suppose it's possible to add poison to the food prepared for attendants...but for what purpose? What assassin would bother to do something like that?"

"If the assassin's motive was the murder of influential authority figures to incite chaos in a nation, then you would be right. Targeting attendants would be meaningless. What if, then, their motive was instead the defamation of the academy? To do, as you so aptly said, 'irreparable damage to the reputation and legacy of Saint-Noel'?"

Indeed, like Santeri had said himself, a scandal of this nature would leave a lasting stain on the student council's image.

"Suppose that a number of attendants from various nations were killed here in Saint-Noel," continued Rafina. "What would happen then? Belluga is currently rallying neighbors to fight against the Chaos Serpents. Such a grievous blunder seems liable to severely fracture our unity, does it not?"

She closed her eyes. Her voice grew quieter, but firmer.

"Mia saw the danger, but she knew she had to demonstrate it. Prove it. So she did…using her own body."

"What? Impossible… An imperial princess wouldn't go to such lengths to…"

Santeri, eyes wide with shock, spun toward Mia, who did not expect the conversation to veer so suddenly in her direction. She froze for a second, trying to decide how she should respond. Figuring it was safer to err on the side of honesty, she began to wave her hands in denial, only for Rafina to answer in her place.

"She would. Because she's Mia. If someone had to get hurt, she'd rather it be herself. That's just the kind of person she is…"

As someone who definitely wasn't that kind of person, Mia sort of felt like she should say something to the effect of "You give me far too much credit. I'm not like that at all." What she actually did, though, was keep her mouth shut and hands off. Being pulled along by forces greater than her, after all, was the foundation of Mia's tactical philosophy. If Rafina said that's how she was, then that's how she was! No ifs, ands, or buts!

"As I'm sure you're well aware, Santeri, it is stated in the Central Orthodox Church's Holy Book that there is no greater love than the willingness to forfeit one's life for a dear friend. We preach this teaching day after day, but how many can put it into practice? How many, when faced with a security flaw that can lead to fatal poisonings, would without the slightest hesitation choose to expose its danger by personally eating a poisonous mushroom? And for whom? Attendants. Commoners. Those whose interests are so often neglected… Who, Santeri? *Who* would do that?"

As someone whose purported virtue and integrity was reaching incredible new heights, Mia sort of felt like she should get off this dangerously tall wave. What she actually did, though, was keep her tongue still and mouth closed. If Rafina said that's how she was, then by the moons, that's how she was!

Mia is someone who would gladly eat poison mushrooms to keep others safe. She's selfless and kind. I never knew this side of me existed, but Rafina said it's there, so it must be!

In order to keep her thoughts in line with Rafina, Mia began engaging in self-hypnosis. She wasn't particularly good at it, but she was trying.

"The truth of the matter, Santeri...is I actually brought up this issue with the student council. I explained that I have some safety concerns about the Holy Eve Festival, at which point Mia told me to leave it to her. As soon as we returned from our trip, she suggested that we invite you to our stew party, so I asked you to join us in the kitchen." Rafina placed her hand over her heart. A sense of quiet acceptance entered her voice. "That's why...this whole incident is my fault. If anyone deserves to be blamed...it's me."

Selflessness, huh... Now there's a word that brings me back...
Rafina's voice began to grow distant as Santeri felt himself pulled into the past. Old memories of his days spent in the military began to resurface.

Ever since he was a child, he'd been a devout believer in the Holy Book. Those around him, impressed by the piety he displayed, had great hopes for him as a future member of the clergy. The path he eventually chose for himself, however, was that of a guard in the Belluga army. Guards, whose duty was to use their own bodies to shield dignitaries from harm, were in his eyes the very embodiment of the Holy Book's teachings on the spirit of self-sacrifice.

So he devoted himself to his duties, and his diligent efforts ultimately saw him promoted to the prestigious position of Saint-Noel Island's chief of security. He could in perfectly good conscience say that for the past few decades, not a day had gone by when he hadn't striven for excellence. He took pride in his work. But when… When had that pride begun to take on a hint of arrogance?

I see now… I see where I went wrong. I'd always considered my job of protecting people as my way of following God's teachings. But what began as the means…has turned into the ends. I used to see my work through God, but at some point, I started to see my work as God…

Which, to his profound dismay, had led him—Santeri Bandler, devout observer of the spirit of selflessness—to force a young girl who hadn't even come of age yet to sacrifice her own health for their interests. The shame that accompanied this realization was crushing. He hung his head under its weight. Turning toward Mia, he said, "I see now that I've been a stubborn fool, and my stubbornness has forced you to endure much suffering, Princess Mia. There are no words to express the depth of my regret."

Then he turned to Rafina, and lowered his head in an equally deep bow.

"Lady Rafina, I ask that you formally dismiss me from my post as chief of security… I am also ready to accept any and all punishments you deem appropriate."

"I'm sorry, Santeri, but there will be no such thing. Your request is denied."

His solemn resolve to face the consequences of his failure was, to his bewilderment, rejected.

"…Why? It was due to my actions that Princess Mia was forced to eat the poisonous mushroom. For that, I must take responsibility—"

"I do commend your willingness to accept responsibility and resign. If you feel guilty for what you have done, then the desire to seek punishment is certainly understandable. But punishment is not what Mia desires."

Then Rafina turned her gaze toward Mia.

"Huh? Uh… That's, um, right…"

A bout of panic gripped Mia, who hadn't the foggiest idea what anyone was talking about. The conversation had left her so far behind that its form had long since disappeared into the horizon of discourse, leaving her floundering for direction. In an attempt to calm herself down, she picked up the cup of tea in front of her and took a slow sip. The soothing liquid helped her flittering thoughts gather into coherency.

Well, I guess I would feel pretty bad if this fellow got fired because I decided to munch on a poisonous mushroom… Especially if people found out that I actually did it for a pretty stupid reason. That would make me feel very bad…and look even worse.

Coward Tactics 101: always prepare for the worst. If Rafina ever discovered that there was, in fact, no grand plan of selfless altruism and she was made to fire one of her loyal subjects entirely because Mia had pulled a brain-dead stunt, there would be…consequences. Angry Rafina consequences. That was the stuff of nightmares! Just thinking about it made her tummy ache again.

I need to set things up so it won't be too bad even if I get exposed. Otherwise, the sheer stress of worrying will probably do me in. At the same time, I do want to keep a lid on the whole thing if I can. After all, if I can get away with not being found out in the first place, then that's even better…

After a quick bout of mental calculation, she put on the gentle smile of a saint.

"Miss Rafina has forgiven me for my sin of deciding at my sole discretion to eat a poisonous mushroom."

First, she went for a classic fait accompli opening; by preemptively stating that she'd been excused for her behavior, she hoped to establish it as fact and remove any incentive to pry further into its motivation.

"Though I do not believe she has wronged me in any way, Miss Rafina nevertheless seems to be burdened by a sense of guilt. Therefore, I feel it necessary to formally address the matter. I hereby forgive Miss Rafina for whatever she feels she has done to cause me harm."

Next, she began sealing off her opponent's potential moves. In particular, she wanted to make sure Rafina didn't spend too much time dwelling on her supposed transgression and end up getting some weird ideas. This matter was done. Dead and buried. Under no circumstances should it be exhumed for further scrutiny. It was the equivalent of sweeping the elephant in the room under the rug, but by the moons, she was going to get it done! When it came to covering up inconvenient truths, Mia was second to none. Then, as the final stroke of her three-hit combo...

"And if both Miss Rafina and I are to be forgiven, then it is in no way fair for you alone to shoulder your sins unabsolved. We should, in my opinion, all share in this forgiveness."

Concluding this affair by shoving all the blame onto Santeri was a great way to sow the seeds of trouble. Those made to take the fall would harbor resentment. It would fester within them, nourishing those baneful seeds, until one day, when the conditions were right, they would sprout. That revitalized resentment might then push them to dig up the inconvenient truths of the past.

In other words, it could come back to bite her, and she did not much appreciate the sensation of figurative teeth on her delicate rump. Explicit elucidation of truths was the opposite of what she wanted. Mia's ideal was for everyone to engage in collective fudging, covering the truth with so much buttery obfuscation that nobody could pick fact from fudge if they tried.

Sitting atop the elephantine bulge under the rug, she nodded with satisfaction to herself. Then she turned to Santeri, only to realize that his face looked…strange. Like the rare melting of snowy permafrost, his frigid expression gave way ever so slightly, ceding a glimpse of the soft earth underneath. Smelling a whiff of opportunity, Mia hastily added a few more words.

"There's one thing I'd like to make clear though. I have nothing but the utmost respect for your work…"

Flattery first. Always flattery first.

"And I look forward to seeing your continued dedication to your work as you strive for even higher peaks of excellence."

Then, the seeds. Not of trouble, but hope. Santeri's job was directly connected to Mia's life. Its importance could not be understated. The more passionately he felt about it, the better.

It feels like he's a little more willing to listen right now. I think I might actually be able to convince him to keep taking good care of the island's security. In fact, if I can get him to be even more motivated, maybe he can prevent me from getting assassinated…

Coward Tactics 102: prepare early and prepare extensively. Anything that could increase her chances of surviving the Holy Eve Festival was worth doing, and she made sure to do it.

"You…look forward… So I see…" For a long moment, Santeri's expression was distant, almost blank. Then he said, "I see that you do indeed deserve to be called a saint. I shall take your words to heart and draw on their virtue to further fulfill my professional duties."

He took a knee before her and solemnly made this oath.

Santeri Bandler ultimately devoted the entirety of his life to the security of Saint-Noel Island. The chief of security, though aged, was known for his eagerness to solicit advice from younger colleagues, and always gave their words serious consideration.

"I've been made aware that there exists those with more wisdom than me. I also know that at my age, experience often works against one by stiffening the mind. That's why I must seek the advice of the young. Though they have less experience, their minds are more flexible, and what they have to say is worthy of serious thought. By considering every viewpoint, I expand my own field of view. Only then can I hope to prepare for all possible eventualities."

The old man's creed became the guiding principle of Saint-Noel's security force, resulting in an island safer and more peaceful than ever before.

Chapter 17: Citrina Has No Friends

Citrina Etoile Yellowmoon was a sweet little girl.

Her smile bloomed like a flower, her voice rang with the pleasing timbre of chirping birds, and she was a charming converser who always knew what to say. Precious and beloved, she was always surrounded by lots of people. Any appearance she made in mingling events of high society was sure to draw a crowd of adoring onlookers.

Nevertheless, she had no friends. Why, you ask? Well…

"What a surprise that was to Rina. I didn't expect Her Highness to eat the false Belluga mushroom herself."

At the brink between day and night, when light gave way to darkness and sun-shy wrongdoers prepared to go about their wicked ways, Citrina sat in her room having her hair combed.

Fwish. Fwish.

The rhythmic friction of teeth on strands filled the room with their faint sound. Her beautiful hair was the handiwork of her attendant, Barbara, whose deft motions bespoke her age and experience as a maid.

"Ugh, this is the worst. I can't believe she found the salamandrakes…"

Citrina observed the combing of her hair in a hand mirror as her thoughts began to wander. Recently she'd been bathing more often. In order to approach Princess Mia, she'd gone looking for herbs that were good for baths. Frequently, she'd taken baths herself, which she did with Bel, a girl that Mia seemed to treat like a younger sister. Her frequent cleansing had imparted an unprecedented luster to her hair.

Not that it matters…

She closed her eyes and continued.

"Has there been word from father?"

"I've been told that the princess's people have been posting more eyes around us lately. Correspondence has been paused as a precautionary measure, as letters may be a target of their scrutiny."

"My, so rude! How dare they peek at private letters written to a father from his darling daughter."

Of course, whenever sensitive content had to be written in a letter, she'd encoded the message using an ancient Yellowmoon cipher… Still, no amount of caution was too much, for they were dealing with the subordinates of the Great Sage of the Empire.

"I guess there will be no letters for Rina until father does away with these people. Ah, what a bother."

A sigh escaped her dainty lips.

"Why did you not eliminate the princess right there and then?" asked Barbara in a voice devoid of expression.

"In that place? Are you saying Rina should have tried to kill both of them on my own?"

"With your skills, milady, I do believe that should have been possible."

Barbara glanced at her questioningly. In response, Citrina smiled.

"I suppose so. Killing them would have been possible. But if I killed them there, people who came looking would have discovered the salamandrakes, you see? And it'd make them think of Rina as a suspect. Considering what we're trying to do, that seems a little backward, doesn't it?"

There was almost nothing Citrina could have done at the time. She had to stop the members of the student council from finding the salamandrakes. Failing that, she needed to keep them from learning how deadly the mushroom's toxin was. That was the only way to ensure their act of mass-poisoning on the day of the Holy Eve Festival would be successful.

Killing Mia would be like lighting a massive signal fire. Her death would draw abundant attention. Even if her death were faked to look like she accidentally fell off a cliff, an exhaustive investigation would be still conducted on the premises. The emperor, overwhelmed with rage and grief at the loss of his *precious* daughter, would undoubtedly demand that Belluga dig up every last detail concerning her death, even if it meant flipping the academy upside down. In the process it was by no means impossible that suspicion would fall on Citrina...and if it did, it would mean the end of their plot.

"Given the circumstances, I didn't see any point in killing her. Was I wrong?" she asked with an inquisitive tilt of the head.

Barbara regarded her silently.

"I see. I would have expected no less from you, milady. You were prudent in your judgment, and I stand corrected."

The maid inclined her head. Then, without another word, she circled behind Citrina and continued combing her hair.

"This does prove, however," Barbara said after some time, "that Princess Mia is a serious hindrance to our plans, and, sooner or later, she's going to become a serious nuisance."

"True. That occurred to Rina as well. We'll have to do something about her," Citrina responded, her voice as melodious as ever.

"Oh? So you agree then, milady?" said Barbara, her eyebrows shifting upward ever so slightly.

147

"Hm? Of course I do. Is that strange? She's reforming the empire. First she stopped the revolution in Remno, and now this. She's ruined so many of our plans that I'd be surprised if anyone didn't see her as a problem."

"I see. That is certainly good to hear. In that case, do you have any objections to changing our operation during the Holy Eve Festival to a targeted assassination of the princess?"

That took Citrina by surprise.

"Wow, you sure make it sound easy. And how exactly do you expect me to go about killing her? We just lost access to our poison, in case you've forgotten," she said, craning her neck to scowl over her shoulder.

Barbara placed an arm behind Citrina's shoulders, as if she were leaning in for a sideward embrace.

"By using…this."

She tied a length of string behind Citrina's head, then pulled away, leaving a small item dangling from the girl's neck. It was…the troya Bel had given her as a present.

"That girl…" said Barbara. "The princess is particularly fond of her, isn't she? I recall you saying yourself, milady, that you intend to use her. Show her then. Have her see you wearing it. Please her… Then, *control* her. Make your way into her heart using those sweet words of yours. We Serpents are manipulators. Smiths of the mind. Words are our tools, and hearts are our ore."

"But—"

Citrina attempted to protest, only to be cut off after a single word.

"You've done this enough times before, haven't you? This time is no different…"

As if on cue, emotion faded from Citrina's face, and a slow, viscous smile crept across Barbara's.

"Don't worry. Everything will go as planned. I will make sure of it, milady," she hissed in a sibilant whisper.

Citrina Etoile Yellowmoon was a sweet little girl.

But she, who should have been loved and adored by all those around her, had no friends. Why, you ask? Well… Because all her friends—friends her father had instructed her to make—had had their lives ruined. Sometimes, their fathers died. Sometimes, their mothers died. Sometimes, they themselves…

But Citrina wasn't sad. Everyone she'd befriended was the same as her. They were all nobles. They should have known that every bond was a strand in a web of intrigue. Every present was given with calculation. They knew what they were getting themselves into. They had to… So, she didn't mind, even if they were gone. She felt no sorrow. Her heart didn't ache.

Over time, she developed a habit. Whenever one of her friends disappeared from her life, she'd throw away all the presents she received from that person.

I've done this plenty of times before… I'll just throw it away again. I don't mind.

Her hands closed tightly around the small horse charm dangling from her neck.

Chapter 18: Mortal Combat!
...Mortal Combat?

While Mia's brain was taken over with poisonous mushroom-related affairs, Ludwig and Dion were traveling. Their meeting with Gilbert had allowed Ludwig to fully appreciate the danger posed by the House of Yellowmoon. With this realization, he decided that intelligence alone wasn't enough; he'd pressure the foe with a divide-and-conquer approach while simultaneously continuing to gather information. This was a common trick to use against large organizations. The greater their number, the more fragmented their allegiance. No faction of great size could be a monolith. There were always members that could be pressured, tempted, or otherwise persuaded into breaking from the group.

If the House of Yellowmoon was meant to function as a lure for those harboring hostile sentiments toward the empire, then it would be foolish of him to assume everyone under its banner was his enemy. The first potential non-enemy he set his sights on were the outland nobles, who were shunned by the central nobility. If they'd sought the Yellowmoons because they were lacking in allies, then he should be able to peel them away by offering a second option. With that thought in mind, Ludwig had decided to pay a visit to Outcount Rudolvon in the hopes that he would assist in persuading the other outland nobles.

"The sun's already down…"

Sighing, he observed the darkening skies from the window of his carriage. Though the path to his destination was not exactly perilous, traveling by moonlight would nonetheless entail a degree of danger. Normally it would be time to make camp for the night.

"Slow down a little, but keep going. Time is of the essence right now," he said, instructing the driver to continue.

Dion concurred with a nod.

"Yeah… Best to keep going. In fact," he said, eyes narrowing, "best to keep up the speed too."

"What do you mean?"

Mere seconds after Ludwig frowned at this, the feral howl of a wild animal echoed in the distance.

"What in the world was that?"

His answer came in the form of a guard riding up to the window.

"Sir."

"Situation?" Dion asked.

"Wolves, sir. They seem to be coming after us."

The mounted soldier's reply was equally terse. Terse but clear, leaving no room for misinterpretation. Still, Ludwig couldn't help but doubt his ears.

"Wolves? Out here?"

The soldier nodded before loosing a fire arrow into the darkness behind them. It traced a glowing arc through the air. The instant it touched the ground, it exploded with light that repelled enough of the surrounding gloom to reveal the forms of black wolves. They were massive, and there were three of them.

"Impossible… I've never heard of any wolf packs that attack people within the empire's borders…" insisted a bewildered Ludwig.

"…These aren't regular wolves." Dion opened the carriage door and leaned out, squinting into the darkness behind them. "I can just barely make out the sound of hooves."

In a fluid burst of motion, he readied his bow and pulled the string taut, its creaking tension echoing the high-strung atmosphere in the carriage. A breathless moment passed. Then...his fingers twitched, and his arm became just a blur. Three sharp twangs sent three arrows streaking brightly through the night. They were met with a dim crescent that flashed amidst the wolves. It was, Ludwig realized a beat later, the moonlit glimmer of a blade.

The guard shot another fire arrow at their foes, only for another swing of the blade to split its shaft in two mid-flight.

Dion whistled.

"Hey, not bad."

"Is that...a man on a black horse?" murmured Ludwig, peering backward from inside the carriage.

"A man on a black horse who can smack arrows out of the air in the dark." Dion grinned. "I think I like the guy."

"Is he alone?"

"Probably. Well, depends on if you count the furry buddies he's got protecting his flank, I guess."

"A wolfmaster, then? Not something you see every day... Still, I assume this means we've become enough of a nuisance for them to start sending assassins. Granted, it seems a bit odd to send only one person, but..."

Ludwig's puzzlement was not shared by Dion, who simply shrugged.

"Not really. We've only got about a dozen guys with us right now. If it were me, I could definitely cut them all down and ride off with your head. Wouldn't be surprised if our enemy sent someone of equal capabilities."

He then signaled to the three guards riding closest to the carriage. They were all exceptional soldiers who'd served under him since his imperial army days. Even so...

"You three stay with the carriage. Make a beeline for Outcount Rudolvon's domain and request his protection. Ludwig is your sole priority. Ensure that he arrives without a scratch."

"What about you, captain?"

"Me? Ha ha, I'll be having the time of my life keeping our fine assassin busy. Oh, gimme one of your horses."

"By yourself, sir? Are you sure? We can—"

Dion silenced the concerned soldier with a shake of his head.

"The enemy is an expert. Frankly, no one else stands a chance."

After appropriating a steed from one of the guards, he let out a laugh.

"Well then. It's farewell for now, good Ludwig."

"Knowing you, I'm sure you'll be fine, but…"

"Of course I will. Look, just between us, the truth is that carriage rides aren't really my thing and I've been itching for some exercise. This guy looks like he'll fit the bill," Dion said before flashing a smirk. "You should be more concerned about your own head. Make sure it stays on your shoulders while I'm gone, yeah? It'll be hard to work with you otherwise."

With that, he drew his blade and reversed his horse with the enthusiasm of a child who'd found a new toy. A few moments later, the three wolves charged down the path and pounced at him.

"Sorry, doggies, but I've fought too many wild beasts to find your kind interesting. Out of the way."

He glided through their snapping jaws with ease and shot straight toward the dark figure who, after siccing his wolves on Dion, was in the midst of circling around to catch the carriage. Both steed and assassin were clothed head-to-toe in black, the former of fur and the latter as mask and robe.

Dion took aim at his masked foe and swung. His blade split the air with a deadly swish, threatening to rend whatever stood in its way, be it metal or be it bone.

The assassin abruptly angled his body, somehow managing to hang at such a precarious angle that it seemed he should've fallen off, and evaded the strike by a hair's margin. It was as if horse and rider were truly one.

Dion whooped in delight at this display of equestrian prowess.

"Bloody good show! Also, smart of you to dodge my sword. We'd be done if you tried to meet it."

Laughing, he drew his horse around again. The assassin did the same, man and mount performing a perfect pirouette. They clashed, once, twice, thrice, four times. Sparks lit the air amidst a series of heavy clanks, and Dion immediately realized he didn't have the upper hand.

Huh. Bugger me sideways. He's better on horseback. I've got him beat in strength, but he's winning in speed. And he rides like a bloody acrobat—

The point of the assassin's sword flashed in a fierce thrust. A breath later, it slid straight through Dion, half its length jutting out behind his back. The motion was fluid, almost beautiful. And, as Dion's sly grin revealed, ineffective.

"No reason to keep fighting on your turf now, is there?"

In truth, the blade only grazed his side, passing by with little harm. But now Dion had the assassin's arm locked in his elbow.

"Care for some exercise? A big guy like you won't mind a little fall from a horse, right?"

He leapt off his horse, launching himself backward with his foe's arm held firmly in his grasp. There was a brief sensation of weightlessness...

Their forms fell from their steeds tangled, but did not remain so on landing. The pair instead parted in midair, each twirling away to land on their feet and lash out in a spinning strike, clashing once more before backing off.

"All right. Enough four-legged shenanigans. Let's fight like proper two-legged men with our feet on the ground. Pace yourself now. We've got all night to bleed each other dry, and I want to savor every second," said Dion, grinning as he drew his second sword. "Before we dive in, would you like to tell me your name?"

The masked killer answered with a sudden thrust. Dion slapped away the straightforward strike and whistled.

"That was a pretty boring thrust. Too obvious. Which, of course, is the point, since you're trying to shift my attention away from the wolves circling behind me. Good for you. Points for having an actual plan."

A flurry of pawsteps sounded behind him, growing rapidly louder. He laughed, hearing their feral breathing as they closed in.

"Bloody hell. Coordination, eh? Honestly, I'd love to know how you're commanding the furballs."

Without warning, he kicked his opponent and used the impact to launch himself backward. Twisting in midair, he whipped his sword around in a horizontal swipe. The blade flashed menacingly in the moonlight. Vicious beasts though they were, the wolves couldn't help but flinch from his deadly aura. He landed in a crouch before them and shot their intimidated forms a dismissive glance before shrugging.

"Well, well, well, looks like beasts will be beasts, for better or for worse. Smart of you to keep out of my range. That said, had you all charged me, one of you might have actually landed a bite. Missed opportunity there. Instinct can tell you when to dodge a sword to the face, but it can't teach you when to take one.

And that, I suppose, is why you're only beasts." With the sword in his right hand resting on his shoulder, he gave the one in his left a twirl. "Of course, even if you'd come at me, I might have just cut you all down instead."

He glared at the wolves, causing them to shrink away. In that moment, the alpha had been established, and it was him. For beasts, that hierarchy was absolute. To challenge a definitively superior foe through pure will was the kind of folly only humans engaged in.

"Now then, with that out of the way, let's resume our conversation," Dion said, turning back toward his bipedal foe.

The assassin abruptly took a step back.

"Hmm?"

Dion lifted an eyebrow, only to smack his forehead in realization when a black horse raced past them, and the assassin flipped onto its back.

"Ah, forgot about the bloody horse... Should have seen that coming. If he can get the mutts to do his bidding, he obviously knows a trick or two with horses as well."

A quick glance around revealed that the wolves had vanished.

"A clean retreat. Pretty impressive. I probably bought everyone enough time though. Ludwig should be safe now. But I gotta say, that fellow sure wasn't talkative. I was hoping to hear his voice at least, but he literally didn't speak a word. Also..."

He craned his neck from side to side and shrugged his shoulders.

"Now where the hell did my horse go?"

Chapter 19: The Confessions of a Foolish and Cowardly Conman

To the east of the central nobility domains, on the outskirts of the imperial capital, was the domain of Duke Yellowmoon. His manor was situated in a secluded corner of his lands. For the residence of one of the Four Dukes, it was a little on the small side, but the structure nevertheless dwarfed the mansions of lesser nobles. Its courtyard was home to a flowering garden and, standing in the center, amidst the abundant flora, was a man. He looked to be in his mid-fifties and had the waist circumference to match. His mildly rotund form resembled what might have become of a certain princess who failed to stave off her encroaching F.A.T. There were dark bags under his eyes, which darted about with the anxious energy of a small animal.

"No, but… Not like that… Still, the poisonous mushrooms… Augh…"

Duke Lorenz Etoile Yellowmoon paced nervously around his garden, muttering to himself. Suddenly, there came the sound of approaching footsteps. They rang with a steady rhythm, though he didn't seem to notice. An old butler appeared, who walked up to his master with the stately posture of a career attendant and respectfully bowed his head.

"Pardon the intrusion, milord."

The deferential greeting nonetheless caught Lorenz off guard, and he flinched before glancing in its direction.

"O-Oh, it's you, Bisset," he said with relief upon determining the identity of the speaker. "You surprised me. I was…absorbed in my thoughts."

The old butler was unmoved by his embarrassed smile.

"I apologize for disturbing your contemplation, milord. I have, however, urgent news that requires your ear… Pardon my curiosity, but have you been here since last night?"

"H-Hm? Oh, yes, I suppose I have. It's…a crucial matter, after all. I can't afford to sleep," Lorenz answered timidly before yawning.

"Then allow me to prepare some tea to help you ward off the drowsiness. The report can wait until after that…"

"Ah, very well. That would be good. Thank you, Bisset…"

As he watched Bisset turn and go, Lorenz let out a deep sigh.

Upon returning, Bisset promptly admonished his sleep-deprived master. "But please, milord, you must sleep. Even if only for a few hours. Your strength will not last like this."

Lorenz, however, only grimaced in response. "I'd love to, Bisset. I really would… But I'm a conman, you see, and not a particularly good one at that. It takes every ounce of my wit for me to obtain the things I want," he lamented as he pressed his fists into his face and gave his weary eyes a rub. "The Holy Eve Festival draws near. There's not much time left for me to wring what few ideas I have out of this cursed head of mine."

"That is, in fact, the subject of this report."

Lorenz's shoulders twitched uneasily.

"Th-The Holy Eve Festival? What's the matter? Has the situation changed?"

"Yes. The poisonous mushrooms in the forest… The salamandrakes. They've been discovered by Her Highness."

"Aaah…"

Lorenz leaned backward, his face tilting toward the sky. What little strength remained seemed to ebb as his arms fell helplessly to his side.

"So she has… Ha ha… How unfortunate. The Great Sage of the Empire indeed. Her Highness does not bear the title in vain…" Slowly, a smile spread across his lips. It was a resigned smile, the kind produced when all other emotions had been exhausted. "That girl really is something. It took every last drop of my wisdom to do what I did, and I still only managed to *delay* things a little… And I had to get my daughter to clean up after me… I had to do the demons' bidding, Bisset, to accomplish this much. Meanwhile, she just goes and… A marvel of a girl, truly… But I digress. Did any other information come in? Do we know what happened afterward? And what does Barbara intend to do?"

"Unfortunately, we know none of these things. Her Highness's retinue is proving exceptionally capable. The purging of Wind Crows from the empire has dealt us a heavy blow. Our eyes are limited."

"A-Ah, right. Of course. That was Her Highness's doing as well, wasn't it? Remarkable. Truly remarkable," mumbled Lorenz, who shook his head as he breathed out a long sigh.

"I have received word, however," said Bisset, "that the wolfmaster has failed."

"Moons, we're on a fine losing streak, aren't we? Then again, I suppose this particular piece of news isn't too surprising. We already knew Her Highness is accompanied by an exceptional sword. I must say though, the Serpents are supposed to be quite proud of this *wolfmaster* of theirs. For him to have failed… Well, I can't imagine they're taking this news very well either."

"They seem quite flustered, yes. Apparently, he almost lost his own life in the process… I've been informed that they wish to recall him for the time being."

"I…see."

Eyes still nervously darting about, Lorenz let out a sigh, but this time in relief.

"So be it then. It's certainly not something we have any say in. Offer them whatever aid they require in getting him out—" His expression abruptly sobered. "Recall… Which means the direction is… From Saint-Noel, through Belluga…"

His muttering resumed. Bisset made no attempt to stop him, choosing only to watch in silence. After a while, Lorenz paused as if noticing his butler's patient gaze and reverted to his timid smile.

"Ah, look at me. Lost in my thoughts again… Apologies, Bisset. I must be no end of trouble for you. Which reminds me, you've been here a while. Don't you miss home? You could have gone back with them."

"Your consideration is deeply appreciated, milord, but I do not see myself returning until I've repaid your kindness. Moreover…" Bisset paused. Then, as if changing his mind, his expression softened. "Rather, I ask that I am allowed to remain. It is an honor to serve you, milord."

"Come, man. Enough with the flattery. I am foolish, cowardly, and a liar. That's why, even if it's to obtain the most trivial thing, I need to wring my brain dry of its limited wisdom."

Lorenz fell into another bout of thought. After some time, he spoke again.

"Alas, my mind is proving insufficient… The streams are too many, their flow too complex. I can't read the state of affairs. But…something might happen at Saint-Noel. Let us do what we can to prepare…"

Chapter 20: The Melancholy of Mia
—Princess Mia...Resolves to Reach Peak Decadence!—

As the cold of winter crept up on the cheery briskness of fall, the Holy Eve Festival was at last only a week away. On this day, Mia was paid a visit in her room by her friend, Rania Tafrif Perujin.

Every year, Perujin would supply the Holy Eve Festival with delicacies made from the fruit they'd grown. Saint-Noel gathered a large number of highborn youths from a variety of nations. There were also many students who, like Chloe, came from merchant families. If any of them took an interest in Perujin goods, it could lead to significant business opportunities. So, every year around this time, Perujin princesses would try extra hard to market their new confections to their peers.

Today, Rania had arrived bearing a type of pastry she planned to display at the Holy Eve Festival. The official reason for her visit was to have Mia sample them and procure some preliminary opinions about their quality. Her *actual* reason, though...

"Um... Anne, do you have a moment?"

The tasting session had gone smoothly, and Rania had just exited Mia's room when she paused to whisper to Anne, who was seeing her out.

"Sure. What is it?"

Rania, visibly hesitant, took a few seconds to work up the courage to speak.

"I just thought that Princess Mia looks, um, a little down. Is something wrong?"

The real cause for her visit had, in fact, been concern for Mia, who'd been looking rather glum lately. She wore a somber expression wherever she went and was prone to melancholic sighs. Rania had brought her finest selection of delicacies in the hopes of cheering up her dispirited friend, but…

"She didn't finish all of it. I've never seen her do that. It was so shocking, I could barely believe my eyes…"

Indeed, Rania had just witnessed an extremely rare sight. Mia, faced with a yummy pastry, had *left it unfinished*. This was unthinkable by the princess's usual standards, which involved dutifully consuming every last morsel on her plate.

It should be noted, however, that the pastry Rania had brought today was a fruit pie. What Mia had left unfinished was not the soft, sweet filling but the crust, whose tougher texture was presumably less appetizing. Even in despondency, her sweet tooth reigned supreme.

Regardless, the fact that Mia's appetite had been poor for the past while had already been widely observed. Her recent trips to the cafeteria had always ended with a bite-sized portion of food left on every plate, leaving the kitchen staff deeply concerned.

"The poisonous mushroom did give her stomach a lot of trouble. Maybe there are still some lingering effects?"

A cook had suggested this after one of her visits, and the kitchen staff promptly tweaked her meals to include extra recipes that were more easily digestible. To their dismay, their stomach-friendly additions all met with the same bite-size fate. For Mia, who'd ostensibly always held herself to strict standards of meal-finishing-ism, this was extremely atypical behavior.

Now, the astute may have already noticed that the math in this situation is actually a tad odd. Assuming a bite-size portion is ten percent of the total, leaving the same amount of food on *every* plate when "stomach-friendly additions" had been introduced meant Mia was eating ninety percent of the extra recipes on top of ninety percent of her usual meal, sending her well above a hundred percent of how much she normally ate. Nonetheless, the sheer impact of seeing her leave food on her plate was so great that this mathematical truth escaped the notice of everyone involved.

"Thank you very much for your concern, Princess Rania," Anne said with a deep bow before her expression grew pained. "But the truth is… I'm not sure what's going on either. It's shameful, I know, but I don't know what to do… It's clear that milady is troubled by something, but she won't tell me anything…"

Rania regarded the maid with empathetic concern.

"I'm sure she has her reasons. This is Princess Mia we're talking about, after all. So don't be too hard on yourself. I'll keep looking for ways to cheer her up too. Let's just do what we can."

Angle deepened by gratitude, Anne bowed again as Rania departed.

Upon returning to the room, Anne found Mia gazing idly out the window. The maid, already saddened by Mia's troubled mien, felt her heart seize as a mournful breath escaped her mistress's lips.

"Milady…"

That terrible scene flashed across her vision again. Once more, she couldn't help but see Mia collapsing after eating the poisonous mushroom.

That day, when we talked, she refused to promise me… She didn't say she'd take me with her if she ever went to risk her life again…

Anne had been listening carefully during their conversation. She'd committed to memory every last word Mia had spoken. That was why she was painfully aware that nowhere in those words was a promise to be found; Mia had intentionally avoided it.

She might be expecting something to happen soon... Something dangerous like that terrible incident with the mushroom, and she's probably worried...but she doesn't want to drag me into it, so she's trying to shoulder it all herself.

Furthermore, Anne had noticed something else.

Lately, her skin hasn't looked as healthy as it should. It must be the stress. She's probably not sleeping well...

Ever since this realization, she'd been checking in on Mia multiple times throughout the night, but she always seemed to be soundly asleep.

It's her *though. She might just be putting up a brave front so she doesn't make me worry. I know she tends to do things like that...*

...Does she? Mia's behavior in front of Anne was frequently neither brave nor a front, but perhaps that is a matter of perspective. Even if Mia was trying to be a stoic hero, it wasn't working, because Anne was worried. Deeply and genuinely worried.

As for whether Mia was, in fact, troubled to the point of losing sleep... Well, no. Not really.

The truth of the matter...is that Mia's melancholy, which had been a profound source of anxious concern for her friends, was, in fact...not existent at all! She wasn't losing sleep. She wasn't putting up a front. Heck, she wasn't even glum to begin with. Her ostensibly mournful sighs were in no way related to any mental anguish. Their source was actually more physiological. Gastrointestinal, to be specific. Those who observed this princessly specimen more closely would have noticed that every time she engaged in her exhalant respiratory behavior...

"Phew..."

...Her hand would go to her abdomen and give it a rub. In other words, she was suffering from chronic hyperingestion—that is, over-snacking!

165

Admittedly, she wasn't *completely* free of concerns. The knowledge of her potentially impending demise had weighed on her mind, but she'd soon gotten over it, figuring it wasn't worth living in constant fear of prophetic doom.

Why bother thinking about it all the time? Plus, I've already done basically everything I planned to do to make sure I don't die.

On the night of the Holy Eve Festival—the time and date of her foretold death—the student council party would, by her design, be in progress. She'd gotten them to beef up security too. She'd done what she could. Since the rest was out of her hands, she'd convinced herself to stop thinking about it altogether. Mental flexibility was, after all, one of Mia's strong points.

So why was she behaving so strangely then? Simple.

In the extremely unlikely event I don't survive, I need to make sure I don't go with any regrets. If I'm going to die anyway, then why bother holding back anymore? I should be living it up!

Thus, she'd decided that until the day of the Holy Eve Festival, she would engage in a celebration of life so extravagant that it would put lifelong hedonists to shame. Basically, she'd shifted to "if the world's ending tomorrow, then I can do whatever I want today" mode. Mia, you see, was now *living in the moment*. And the moment decreed that she should begin by debauching her brains out at every meal.

Eat only the best bits and leave the rest! That's the plan! Forget about wastefulness. Just take one bite of the yummiest part of everything. That…is the ultimate form of luxurious eating!

Many of you might have forgotten, but Mia was, in fact, the princess of a mighty empire. Sure, she hadn't exercised her rich girl muscles in a long time, but it wasn't like she'd forgotten how to. When it came to sensual gratification, she was a pro.

Oho ho, it's time to reach peak decadence! Watch out, yummy foods, because I'm coming for you!

And so, true to her word, she went after said yummy foods, only to realize...

B-But, hnnngh...not eating this would be such a waste... Maybe I can take one more bite? Ah, but this one's really good too. Okay, two more bites, then...

...That one did not simply walk away from frugality. Her penny-pinching had become a habit, and she now had a deep, psychological aversion to wastefulness. She'd intended to eat only a small bite of everything. Instead, she ended up *leaving* a small bite of everything. As a result, the meal she'd ordered, which consisted of more food than usual to account for her nibbling approach, proved to be far too much.

And she kept doing this too, thinking she'd be able to stick to the plan next time, only to fail over and over, resulting in the kitchen serving her even more food on top of her order in the form of special stomach-friendly recipes. She ate so much that she started developing acute F.A.T., which was a little worrying.

Her dietary chaos was reflected in her skin, whose luster began fading under the effects of her unbalanced diet. The phenomenon was similar to people used to bland diets suddenly gorging themselves on luxuriously rich food and suffering an all-out stomach revolt. Only now did Mia realize all that healthy eating had robbed her body of its capacity for debauchery, leaving it with nothing but...well, healthiness.

"Okay, when it comes to eating, normal is best. I should just stick with my usual diet..." she concluded after her failed attempt at culinary excess. "I'll have to reach peak decadence some other way then. What else can I do? Hm..."

She mulled over her options. The first thing that came to mind was to run through the academy, scribbling nonsense on every surface like some sort of graffiti lunatic—a magnified application of the propensity of young children to deface school property. She quickly discarded the idea, deeming the cost of such an act too terrifying in the case that the Princess Chronicles' prophecy proved unfounded.

Though she was acting on the assumption that the world—her world, anyway—was ending soon, she was acutely aware of the possibility that it also might not. In that case, even if the Chronicles didn't kill her, a furious Rafina would after seeing the mass property damage she'd committed. However she went about seizing her remaining days, it couldn't be *too* crazy.

"Scribbling on things doesn't even seem that fun... Hmm... You know what? Having fun doing bad things is harder than I thought."

It took courage to do evil. For Mia, who was a chicken at heart, deriving pleasure from misdeeds was too tall an order. After much contemplation, she finally clapped her hands in inspiration.

"Oh, I know. If I'm going to die anyway, I might as well flirt with Abel to my heart's content! I want to go on horseback dates, and forest strolls, and trips to town..." The idea excited her. "Actually, that just made me realize something. I've been too focused on trying to survive lately. There's been no gratification in my life. I should have spent more time with Abel and gone on more mushroom hunting trips! Ugh, what a terrible mistake. I need to make up for lost time..."

Just as she was about to rush off, a thought gave her pause.

"But Abel probably has things he needs to do... I wouldn't want to be a nuisance by dragging him around with me."

Another bout of thought resulted in another flip-flop.

"No, I don't need to worry about that. I'm going to die on the night of the Holy Eve Festival anyway, so I'm just going to do whatever I want!"

Having found the perfect way to reach just the right amount of peak decadence, oxymoron notwithstanding, she grinned.

"Oho ho, nothing can stop me now! I'm invincible!"

So, Mia, proud liver of moments, went looking for Abel.

Chapter 21: The Man Who Vanished in the Empire...and the Invasion of Mia the Moment-Living Princess!

"Mia…"

A deep sigh escaped Abel as he walked down a hallway. With the Holy Eve Festival around the corner, the academy was astir, but the festive atmosphere did little to elevate his mood.

"I wish I knew what was wrong…"

He'd also noticed her recent forlornness. How could he not have? For a long time now, his singular wish had been to catch up. To be a good match for her. And he was willing to do whatever it took. He tirelessly trained with the sword, hoping to become a dependable man who could protect her. He buried himself in books, hoping to match her boundless wisdom. Not a day went by when she was absent from his thoughts, but no matter how hard he tried, he couldn't figure out what was troubling her. And that wasn't the worst part.

"…She's dealing with some sort of problem, but she won't say a word about it to me. I think that's what hurts most."

It was a realization that hit pretty hard. Mia did have a tendency to act suddenly on her brilliant whims. The poisonous mushroom stunt she'd pulled a few days ago—that had given everybody a minor heart attack—was a good example. She was undoubtedly a genius, but that genius was accompanied by a propensity to neglect explaining her thoughts to those around her.

He knew that was simply a part of her character…but it still hurt. Perhaps he was disappointed that she didn't trust him enough to seek his help.

Or...perhaps her reserved attitude had left him feeling lonely and he was simply wallowing in self-pity. He hoped it wasn't the latter. Being forced to acknowledge that he harbored such petty sentiments might be more painful still.

After struggling with his feelings for days, he finally worked up the resolve to seek Sion's advice.

"Just because I can't figure out what's troubling her doesn't mean no one can. Maybe Sion noticed something I didn't."

In Abel's eyes, Sion Sol Sunkland was a wall. A towering barrier to be scaled, but one whose crest remained far beyond his reach. Every time he looked up toward its invisible apex beyond the clouds, then down at the meager progress he'd made, he felt like giving up right then and there. The gap seemed so vast, the distance so insurmountable, that holding onto the mere desire to one day become his equal was a herculean feat in and of itself. His ego groaned in agony at the thought of asking this overwhelmingly superior rival for advice, but he mentally beat it into submission. His pride could wait; Mia was more important.

Upon arriving at Sion's room, he was greeted by an unexpected voice.

"Ah, Prince Abel. I hope you've been well."

"Hm? Who's—" He turned toward the speaker to discover a woman in a maid uniform. "Oh, Monica. I didn't expect to see you here."

He and Monica had been well-acquainted during her time in Remno as an undercover agent. Ever since she came to Saint-Noel, however, they hadn't run into each other much.

"Yeah, I'm fine. Same goes for you too, I hope?"

"Yes, Lady Rafina has treated me very well."

"I see. Good, good... But, uh, what are you doing here in Sion's room?"

Sion, half hidden behind a disorderly heap of papers on his desk, raised his finger.

"That was me. I asked her to help me with something," he said before gesturing at the documents, "and she kindly acquiesced. A better question is what are *you* doing here, Abel? Not that you're unwelcome, but you're not exactly a frequenter of my quarters."

"Yeah, about that. The reason is, uh…I noticed that lately, Mia has been looking sort of down, and I was wondering if you might have any idea why…but if you're busy, then I'll come again some other time."

"No, it's fine. Good timing, actually. I was just thinking I should take a quick break."

Sion leaned back and stretched his arms as he yawned.

"Really? All right then. But, uh…" Abel's brows furrowed in bewilderment at the papers. "What *is* all this? And why do you look so tired?"

"Because," said Sion, giving his face a quick rub before holding up one of the pages, "I've been looking into this."

Abel took the page and read it over.

"Hm… Jason, Lucas, Max, Thanasis, Bisset…" He raised an eyebrow. None of the names sounded familiar. "Who are these supposed to be?"

Sion did not answer directly. Instead, he shrugged and said, "I, you see, have also noticed that Mia hasn't been in the best of moods."

Abel eyed him, puzzled by this reply.

"So I have been worried as well," Sion continued, "but despite my best efforts, I cannot think of a way to cheer her up. Therefore, I have decided that my time would be best spent doing what I can."

"Doing...what you can?"

"That's right. Over the past couple of days, I've been taking another look at the Wind Crows. Ever since I made a mess of things in Remno, I've been thinking long and hard on how I can redeem myself. This would be part of that effort."

Abel was reminded of what Sion had said during the student council election. When urged by Mia to run in the election, Sion had declined, insisting that he'd earn the chance to redeem himself on his own terms.

"What you see there," said Sion, pointing at the paper in Abel's hand, "is the list of names a Wind Crow agent had used while undercover in Tearmoon."

"A Wind Crow agent?" asked Abel. "You mean one of the agents you recalled?"

"No. They were used by an agent who went into hiding."

"...Went into hiding?"

Suddenly, something clicked in Abel's head. He lowered his voice.

"Wait... I remember you saying you had a contact who gave you information about the Serpents. That's how we learned that one of Tearmoon's Four Dukes is connected with them. It's that person, isn't it?"

"Ah, very sharp of you. That's him."

"This man was also my mentor," Monica added. "It was him who laid the groundwork for the entire intelligence network that operated in Tearmoon. As the chief intelligence operative, he coordinated all on-site collaborators and was referred to as the spymaster."

"If that man is still alive, then he doubtlessly has information that would be useful to Mia. So, I figured I'd track him down, but..." Sion shook his head. "I'm coming up frustratingly empty."

"You think someone offed him already?"

"Maybe. The thing is, I don't know. There's only so much I can find out from here. We recalled all the Wind Crows from Tearmoon, after all. For what it's worth, I also asked Monica to try the Wind Crows' emergency contact method, but we haven't received any response at all yet."

Sion spread his hands helplessly. Despite the gesture, Abel found himself impressed.

Sion...has his feet on the ground. He doesn't have all the answers, but he's doing what he can to help Mia, one step at a time. Meanwhile, I'm... Ugh, what am I even doing...

He combed his fingers through his hair as a frustrated sigh escaped his lips, moments before he felt a smack on his shoulder.

"Chin up, man," said Sion. "If Mia's feeling down, then it's your job to cheer her up."

"Ha ha, frankly that's a pretty tall order for me right now... but you're right. The least I can do is try."

Understanding what was going through Mia's mind was difficult, if not impossible. He wasn't even privy to her troubles. And might never be, by her choice. He could neither solve her problems nor share her burden. But surely, he could at least be a source of emotional support...

"Doing what I can, huh... Yeah, that's a good place to start."

With the boys engaged in such sober conversation, the room had become a bastion of *serious business*, complete with hardening resolve and contemplative introspection. It was this introspective atmosphere that Mia barged in on.

"Oh, finally. There you are, Abel. I've been looking all over for you. Hey, listen, I need to talk to you for a bit," she said, wading in with all the delicacy of china-busting bovines.

The invasion of the Moment-Living Princess had begun! Would the delicate sensibilities of these sentimental young boys stand up to her assault?

"What are you doing here in Sion's room, by the way?" she asked.

"...What are *you* doing here, Mia?" asked Abel in response.

For those who have yet to identify the social faux-pas in this situation, some explanation is likely in order. A quick analysis of the situational context would reveal the anomalous nature of Mia's cavalier manner. They were in Sion's room, which was located in the boys' dormitory. Though there wasn't a strict rule, the boys' dormitory was generally understood to be off-limits to girls. At the very least, you weren't supposed to stroll in just to take your sweetheart out on a date.

Debauchee Mia, however, couldn't care less about social norms. After all, she was currently invincible! Nothing—well, *mostly* nothing, aside from inherently scary things that would go unmentioned—could stand in her way! At last, her chicken-heartedness had ascended to a higher state. It had leapt for the peaks of lionheartedness, scraped the edge with its feet, failed to hang on, and tumbled back down to an intermediate ledge. She was now...pig-hearted! Not as prone to squawking as before, but it couldn't quite manage a majestic roar either. It simply oinked. Hopefully, her newfound porkiness would remain an attribute of her heart and not an adjective for her tummy...

In any case, that explained Abel's surprise at seeing Mia, who grinned playfully.

"I'm here because I need to borrow you for a bit. Will that be okay?"

"Huh? U-Uh, sure, I guess?"

Abel glanced at Sion, who held up his hands in a "this one's yours" gesture.

"The princess demands, and the princess gets. It is, I believe, the duty of a gentleman to ensure the causal link between the two," Sion said with a wink.

"In that case… Sorry for cutting our conversation short, but I guess I'll excuse myself."

After Mia escorted a hesitant Abel out of the room, he asked, "So, what exactly do you need me for?"

This time, it was Mia's turn to hesitate.

"Mmm, well, you know…"

Turns out, she didn't know either! Had she written her plan down on paper, it would have read "Step One: Find Abel; Step Two: ???" She considered heading out to town on a confectionery tour, but the moment she stepped out of the dorm, a chilly breeze made her reconsider.

This…isn't exactly going outdoors weather. Too cold.

Mia was the kind of person who preferred to spend cold days inside. Braving the frost to go on a date outside was not even close to being an option.

Which leaves us with…somewhere inside the academy?

Just then, her ears picked up a faint music in the air. It was a lively sound, and it was coming from the grand hall. Before she knew it, her feet were pulled in its direction.

In the hall, preparations were underway for the grand banquet that would follow the candlelight mass to celebrate the Holy Eve. The decorating was almost complete, and the hall was looking magnificent. Stately wooden walls were adorned by sacred paintings in gilded frames. They were displayed only during special occasions like these. Brilliant red cloth hung down from where the ceiling met the walls, further embellishing the festive air. Arranged at the front of the hall were rings of musicians currently rehearsing pieces for the upcoming ball.

The sight brought forth a memory in Mia's mind.

"Holy Eve Festival... Dancing... Oh, I know."

She was reminded of the welcome party for new students. She'd danced with Abel that day, and for a variety of reasons, hadn't been able to do so again since.

"We should dance. I want to see how good you've gotten before it's time for the ball."

"Huh? What do you—"

"Excuse me," said Mia, addressing one of the staff, "but we're going to borrow that spot over there for a while."

"What? Mia, wait—"

Ignoring Abel's reluctance, she firmly clasped his arm and pulled him to an empty corner of the hall. Undaunted by the astonished gazes around her, she stepped close to him.

"All right, Abel. Let's dance."

With a graceful flourish of her skirt, she signaled for him to begin. He stared dumbfounded at her for a few seconds before conceding a wry smile.

"Well, someone's a little pushy today, isn't she?"

The comment elicited a defiant grin from Mia.

"Oh? Someone else is a little out of the loop then. Haven't you heard? I've always been said to be a particularly selfish princess."

"Have you? So this is the real you? Well, in that case, I guess I have no choice but to oblige."

He moved his body close to hers as well, and they began gliding about their makeshift stage. Amidst the hustle and bustle of festival preparations, the pair danced...as though the figures rushing to and fro around them were but a backdrop to their romantic moment.

They weren't though. They were people with jobs to do, and an amorous couple twirling about the venue while they were trying to get work done was nothing but a major nuisance.

More than one person likely hissed a private "Oh get a room already. You're getting in the way." Faced with this inconsiderately public display of affection, the members of the orchestra proceeded to jibe.

Not at them, but *with* them! They'd always been good sports, as evidenced by the impromptu accompaniment they'd provided for Mia during the welcome party for new students. Having seen her take over the dance floor that night, they were more than willing to provide the pair with some ad-lib music.

"My, it seems like we've made the orchestra our own," said Mia, giggling as she began dancing to their lively tempo.

Her motions were graceful and executed with expert precision. They were also matched by Abel, who kept up without missing a beat.

"Well, you've sure gotten better at dancing, haven't you?"

"Ha ha, it's an honor to receive your approval. I never had a chance to show you, but swordsmanship isn't the only thing I've been practicing," said Abel, a touch of pride in his voice.

"Have you now?" replied Mia, a touch of provocation in hers. "Impressive. But can you keep up with more difficult steps?"

Her motions intensified. The increased challenge was thoroughly absorbing, and she lost herself in the moment as they moved from step to step as one. One second, she'd pull away, only to press herself against him again in the next. Round and round she went, twirling about him like a fairy at a woodland revel. She lost track of time and place. It was like a dream. The best kind of dream, where all she knew was delight.

Suddenly...

"Mia, tell me something..."

She heard Abel speak.

"Am I...somehow not good enough?"

His expression was serious.

"Not good enough? What do you mean?" she asked.

"I know you've been troubled by something lately. And I'm worried. I don't know what it is. Sion doesn't either. As far as I know, you haven't told anyone. It feels like you're trying to keep it all to yourself. Shoulder it alone..."

"Abel..."

Moved by his concern, she momentarily found herself without words. All she could do was hold his earnest gaze.

"Is there any way for me to...share your burden? I know I'm no genius. I know I probably can't solve your problems for you. But if it's possible for me to lighten your load by even a little bit, then I'm willing to do whatever it takes."

His words were so tender that she almost swooned. It took every ounce of restraint she possessed to stop herself from spilling every last bean right then and there. Through sheer will, she forced out a mischievous smile.

"Are you now? Well then...how about this? If you ever become as good as I am at dancing, then I'll let you in on the precious secret I've been keeping."

She knew that telling them wouldn't solve anything. She could spill her heart, confiding in them everything she knew, and she'd still sneak off Saint-Noel Island when the time came. And were she to divulge her secrets before doing so, the Princess Chronicles foretold that a far more tragic future would come about.

The loss of Mia would push Abel past the brink of sanity. Forsaking his own well-being, he'd ultimately meet a catastrophic end. Sion, likewise, would be gravely affected, and his actions would eventually topple the whole of Sunkland. Her death would cast a long shadow, weighing down everyone she knew. No one would be spared, and no one would ever escape the all-consuming grief.

179

The passages in the Princess Chronicles detailing these events had been written to underscore the sheer magnitude of her influence, but their bleak consequences had robbed her of words. Indeed, they'd taken from her any possibility of divulging the contents to her peers.

Telling them would only make things worse. If they know it's going to happen, they'd only regret it more when they realize they couldn't keep me away from harm. I'd be dooming Abel to suffer... I wouldn't be able to die in peace if I did that.

It occurred to her that despite the numerous steps she'd taken to prevent her death, she was nonetheless starting to accept her grim fate. That proved to be a terribly unpleasant thought, and she shook it out of her mind.

"...Don't think about anything else right now. Just focus on enjoying the dance."

The time she spent dancing was deeply fulfilling. It felt like the first time in ages she'd been able to laugh from the bottom of her heart. She had such fun. So much that she felt like she wouldn't mind dying right this moment. Delight permeated her body, filling every corner... except a small nook in her heart of hearts.

For some reason, I feel like there's still something I haven't done yet... Something I might regret... I wonder what...

It would be a little later when she'd realize what she'd left undone. After thoroughly relishing every sinful indulgence she could think of (snacking, pastries in bed, sweets for breakfast, etc), there was but one entry left on her bucket list. Little did she know, it was this final item that held the key to her surviving the Holy Eve Festival.

Chapter 22: Under the Banner of Princess Mia −Forged Friendships−

One day, Ludwig visited Outcount Rudolvon in his manor. Having previously asked Rudolvon to persuade other outland nobles, he'd come to see how things were going.

"Ah, it's good to see that you're in good health, Ludwig."

Outcount Rudolvon greeted him with a smile that radiated warmth and earnest consideration. Technically, there was a significant discrepancy in status between Ludwig, a commoner, and the Outcount. Outland nobles were shunned by the central nobility, but they were still nobles. While Ludwig was a central government bureaucrat who enjoyed Mia's unconditional trust, he was by no means this man's equal.

Their demeanors, however, showed no signs of the reservation one normally expected to see between men of their respective standings. Rather, there was a peculiar bond between them. It resembled friendship, and it transcended age and status—a sense of camaraderie shared only by those who rallied under the banner of Princess Mia. They traded a firm handshake before Ludwig seated himself in a guest chair.

"Again, I apologize for burdening you with such a request," he said.

"Not at all. I owe Her Highness a great deal. A task from her is one I accept willingly and shall make every effort to tackle."

"I'm most obliged. Hearing that certainly takes some weight off my mind…"

Ludwig's efforts to divide the Yellowmoon faction from within were slowly starting to show results. With the Outcount's cooperation, they'd succeeded in convincing a number of outland nobles to realign themselves with the Rudolvons. Though their numbers weren't large enough to be called a "faction," Ludwig hoped that this would lead to the eventual rise of a new independent group of nobles who weren't under the influence of any of the Four Dukes. This new group could then function as the core of a faction loyal to Mia personally—the princess faction, so to speak. Suffice to say, all sorts of gears performing all sorts of calculations were currently turning in his head.

All of that can come later though. For now, the problem is…

"Judging by that frown on your face, I assume you've run into some trouble?" prompted Rudolvon.

Ludwig grimaced.

"The outland nobles are coming around, but trying to peel away the rest of them is proving much harder than expected."

Usually, the larger the organization, the more fractured its internal politics and loyalties. With a faction like the Yellowmoons, which consisted of many members who aligned themselves out of desperation more than anything else, that should be doubly true. They couldn't possibly enjoy much unity. And yet…

"Well, yeah. Knowing you'll be killed for your betrayal generally makes you think twice about flipping sides. Seems pretty reasonable to me," suggested Dion, who'd been listening to the conversation.

Ludwig eyed his nonchalant partner and shook his head.

"Not necessarily, no. Those bound by fear should also harbor a subconscious desire to escape from that fear. Therefore, when offered a way out by someone with the power to offer protection, the chances of them taking the offer should be favorable."

He'd subtly leaked the fact that he'd been attacked by an experienced assassin a few days ago. The point was to propagate the narrative that he, a loyal subject of Princess Mia, had been targeted by *someone*, who'd sent a deadly assassin to kill him, only to have the attempt foiled by the efforts of his friend, Dion. It functioned as a veiled message. Though crucial details were kept secret, those in the loop would understand that a statement was being made—they had the means to repel attacks from the Yellowmoon faction.

The rumor would inevitably have made its way into the ears of the Yellowmoon's nobles, and yet, no deserters had appeared.

"Her Highness's forbearance and wisdom are already common knowledge. I made sure of that. Noble houses with power and pedigree would surely see her as a nuisance, but those of shakier standing and loyalty should be practically drooling at such a perfect opportunity to defect…"

In fact, Mia's current situation should be speaking for itself. She'd forged a strong friendship with Duke Greenmoon's daughter, pulled Duke Bluemoon's son into her camp by personally inviting him into the student council, and even went so far as to recruit Duke Redmoon's daughter into her personal guard.

Sure, none of them were the head of their houses, but that didn't change the fact that three of the Four Houses could now be interpreted to be on friendly terms with Mia. On top of that, she had the Princess Guard, a small army of elite soldiers she could deploy at will. With this powerful piece at her command, together with the support of three factions of dukes, albeit indirectly, she was steadily becoming a pivotal figure in the empire whose clout one ignored at their peril.

"And yet, it's still like shouting into the void with these Yellowmoon nobles. *Something* isn't right here…"

Ludwig fell into a silent bout of cross-armed rumination. After some time, Rudolvon coughed politely to pull him out of his thoughts before speaking.

"By the way, Ludwig, about that…*prediction* that Her Highness made…" he said in a hushed voice. "It seems to have come true."

Ludwig looked up with a start, blinking as he processed the implication of this revelation.

"You mean… You're seeing the signs here too?"

Rudolvon took a sip of tea before answering.

"The wheat harvest in my domain is poor. I asked the other outland nobles, and they all seem to be in the same boat as well. Our crop yields going into the next year are definitely going to drop. Of course, there's no telling how long this trend will last, but…"

The future was always a mystery, but for this year at least, Mia's prediction of poor wheat yields had proved true. She'd also given Ludwig and his peers strict orders to make absolutely sure that they were prepared for this eventuality. And now…

"If we're prepared for the worst but it doesn't come to pass, then that's certainly for the best. But if it *does* and we *weren't* prepared, then we'll have to weather a whole lot of condemnation," Ludwig mused.

"Her Highness chose to entrust us with her prediction. And asked us to prepare accordingly. Then let us live up to the trust she has so graciously placed in us," said Rudolvon.

Thus, the two spent some time working out the finer details regarding emergency supply protocols in the case that dwindling provisions led to a full-blown famine, along with the necessary convoys for such routes. After that, Ludwig departed the Rudolvon manor and headed straight for Mia's academy city to check on its progress. It was there that he received a message, and when he saw who had sent it…

Chapter 23: That Which a Lounging Mia Forgot —So That This Time, We Can Finally Be Good Friends—

"Hmm… I feel like I've done everything on my list…but I also feel like I'm forgetting something…"

The Holy Eve Festival was two days away. There wasn't much time left, and the list of things she could plausibly do was growing shorter. As what were potentially the final hours of her life waned before her eyes, Mia rolled from one side of her bed to the other, then back again. In other words, she was lounging the day away. Was it because she'd decided to live in the moment? No, not really. That was just her behavioral pattern. When presented with downtime, the creature known as *M. Princessus* would always choose to lounge.

There was a knock on the door, Sion's voice followed it.

"Mia, do you have a moment? I'd like to talk to you about something."

"My, Sion coming to the girls' dorm? That's not something you see every day."

In one smooth motion, Mia rolled across her bed and leapt off, sticking a solid landing on the floor. Then, she looked down at herself and her wrinkled roomwear.

Hm… Ah, who cares. It's just Sion.

So much for marriageability. Regardless, she opened the door and greeted him with a bright smile. Sion jerked back a little, momentarily astonished by her attire.

"I…see that you were getting some rest. Do accept my apologies for intruding," he said, lowering his head.

He'd obviously mistaken Mia's somewhat disheveled appearance for a sign that she'd just gotten out of bed. Which wasn't *wrong* per se, but incorrect in his assumption that "just got out of bed" meant "had been sleeping and was woken up."

"Oh, don't worry about it. You've come all the way here, so it's clearly something important. Anne's not here today though, so you'll have to do without tea, I'm afraid." She bid him in. "So, what did you want to talk about?"

"It's about one of your subjects, actually. Ludwig, specifically. I'd like to ask him to do something."

"Ludwig? What do you want him to do?"

"Long story short, I'd like him to see if he can locate that Wind Crow agent I mentioned before. The one who disappeared while operating in Tearmoon."

"A Wind Crow who disappeared in the empire…"

She didn't say it, but her expression all but screamed …*Eh? Who are we talking about again?*

"Even you don't remember, huh. I guess it's not exactly surprising, considering it was just a passing mention. It's the person who informed us that the Serpents are in contact with one of your Four Houses."

"…A-Ah, right. That person. Yes, I remember now."

She nodded vigorously to give the impression that it was all coming back to her. Of course, nothing actually came back. Nothing *could*. Mia's brain was really good at forgetting things she didn't have to remember, and her bar for "have to remember" was pretty high.

"But why look for this person now?" she asked.

Sion proceeded to explain his reasoning, which she found convincing.

"I see… It'd definitely be a big help if we could get someone like that on our side. Good idea, Sion. Brilliant as ever, aren't you?"

"Ha ha, remember how I said I'd earn the chance to redeem myself on my own terms?" He grinned playfully before dismissing his own facetiousness with a shrug. "Which is certainly a suitably lofty goal, but here I am asking for your help again. Frankly, it's embarrassing how little I can do on my own, and being stuck here in the academy isn't making it any easier…"

"Well, that seems a tad harsh on yourself. I think you should give yourself more credit. Anyway, what exactly do you want Ludwig to look into?"

"These."

Sion handed her a piece of paper. She read it over and frowned.

"…Hm? Max, merchant… Bisset, butler… Thanasis, local official… What are these supposed to be?"

"These are the fake names and identities our man has used before."

"Huh… Interesting. This is it though? Don't you have a description of what he looks like?"

"Unfortunately, no. He's known to be a master of disguise."

"Ah. Well, I guess that's to be expected…" murmured Mia as she regarded the page.

I have to admit, this is pretty impressive. What Abel said was true then. Sion really has been working out a way to fight against the Chaos Serpents. Oh!

She clapped once as a thought occurred to her.

"Sion, do you mind if I pick your brain about something?"

"Hm? Sure. If you think I can help you figure something out, then by all means," he said, one eyebrow raised in interest.

She nodded in satisfaction.

"This is purely to fulfill my own intellectual curiosity, all right? It's entirely hypothetical. But let's assume you only had two days left to live. What would you do with them?"

Hit with this zinger of a philosophical question, Sion nevertheless crossed his arms and made a sincere attempt to formulate an answer.

"Two days, huh… That's not much time, so there's not much that *can* be done. Let me think… First, I'd probably formally thank the people who've obliged me with their assistance before…" he said in a soft, contemplative voice. "After that… I think I'd go to the people whom I, through my own immaturity and stubbornness, have caused trouble for, and apologize to them."

"My! You have people like that in your life too?" exclaimed an astonished Mia.

Sion grimaced.

"A couple, yes. If, in the course of life, one feels they owe no gratitude or apology to anyone around them, it is surely a sign of profound conceit," he said before qualifying his stance with a shrug that said "That's the way I see it, at least."

I see… Well, in his case, I guess that's true. She found herself concurring with his statement. *Unlike me. I haven't caused trouble for anyone, so I don't have to do any apologizing.*

Correction: she concurred with his statement with respect to him. Profound conceit indeed.

"Hm, but… I suppose that *is* a way to look at things."

She turned to face him and straightened, then inclined her head in a deep bow.

"Allow me to express my gratitude for you, Sion."

"Hm? What's this now?"

"I heard from Abel that you were concerned about me, and you're doing all sorts of things to try and lighten my burden. I do appreciate it, and I'm sorry to have made you worry."

With a *tsk*, Sion averted his gaze and scowled at the wall.

"Damn it, Abel and his big mouth…"

He let out a defeated sigh before turning back toward her.

"Okay, look, just so you don't get the wrong idea, this is all part of my effort to redeem myself for my past failures. In other words, I'm doing this for myself—"

"I completely understand. You're doing this solely because you want to. Still, I must thank you, because I'd feel very bad otherwise. And so, I have done so. You did your thing, I did mine. All for our own sakes. That's all this is." Then, she smiled. "I'm just doing what I want to do too, so don't mind me, all right?"

For what seemed like a long moment, Sion observed her without a word. Finally, he exhaled. It was a soft breath, but long, coming from the bottom of his lungs.

"Ah, damn it… Why'd I tell Abel it was *his* job to cheer her up…" he muttered in a voice inaudible to all but himself.

Little did Sion know…

Owing Sion a favor makes me nervous. Tilting my head and saying thanks, meanwhile, is totally free! And it makes us even! Of course I'd thank him! I'd thank him every time!

…Mia's thoughts on the matter were far less sincere. Moreover, he also didn't know that a few of the words he'd spoken would etch themselves into her mind. Was there truly no one to whom she owed gratitude or apology? If not in this life, then the past? The question would remain with her, looming over her mind like a faint beacon whose light would eventually lead her to the one thing she'd forgotten.

After seeing Sion off, Mia penned a quick letter to Ludwig before diving back into bed.

"Oof, I'm pooped."

The heavy labor of filling half a page with words had left her exhausted. She stretched her limbs, then sank into her mattress like a limp noodle.

189

"Apologizing to people I've caused trouble for, huh…" she murmured with her face buried in her pillow. "I guess he has a point. That does feel like something I have to do if I want to die without any regrets. The problem is, I don't have anyone like that…"

The previous timeline was one thing, but in the current one, Mia had been living a life of continuous redemption. The chef who was supposed to be fired was now happily working as head chef at the imperial court. She'd even put in a good word to her father for his faithful service. Newmoon District, which had previously gone completely neglected until it was too late, was now benefiting from constant reformative efforts. The once-desolate townscape was steadily showing signs of renewed life. One by one, she'd fixed the mistakes she'd made in her past life. Once, she might have sinned, but she'd now redeemed herself.

So why, then, did Sion's words gnaw at her conscience?

"Eh, it's probably just me. If anything, I probably have way more people I have to thank. There's Anne and Ludwig… Abel and Sion… Chloe, and Miss Rafina too… And I guess Tiona counts—"

She froze as a realization suddenly dawned on her. These thoughts she was having felt strangely…foreign. She was at the end of her life, and of all the things to pop into her mind, it was saying thanks to all her dear friends? It happened so naturally too, as if it was simply a part of who she was. Heck, even Sion's name appeared in the list, and he'd been her archnemesis! She no longer felt even a speck of animosity toward him. The same was true for Keithwood and Liora. What bad blood there had once been between her and them, it was all gone now. Well, Dion was still as scary as ever, but ignoring that one anomaly…she'd managed to forge genuine bonds with everyone else. They'd become good friends.

But for some reason, there was one relationship among those that felt a little different, as if there was still some lingering friction there. A sense of distance. They were friends, yes, but not quite good ones.

Tiona… Something didn't feel right between her and Tiona, and it was keeping them from forging a proper bond. What was it…? The answer came in an instant. It took the form of a memory she'd long forgotten. Visions flashed before her eyes, accompanied by phantom sensations. Her palm stung. A girl stared at her, eyes wide with confusion and shock. There were the grating jeers from her obsequious entourage as well as…

"You pauper of a noble! Who do you think you are, getting so chummy with Prince Sion, huh? Learn your place!"

…Her own voice, so scornful and cruel. It was a scene from her past life. She'd forgotten it for so long, but it had come back to her at last.

"Aaah… Yes, now I remember. There *is* something I need to apologize for. What I did to Tiona before… I have to say sorry to her…"

In the previous timeline, Mia had witnessed a burgeoning friendship between Tiona and Prince Sion. Her loneliness and frustration, deepened by Sion's total disregard for her, had led her to act on her worst impulses. She'd struck Tiona. Across the face. She could almost still feel the stinging in her palm. It was, she realized, the one thing she hadn't yet been able to make up for. A mistake yet unamended, because…

"It's something that went away on its own. Without me doing anything…"

It was an incident lost to time. Swallowed by the current of history, its absence left her with one sin that her temporal reset couldn't wash away; there was nothing left to wash. Of course, objectively speaking, Tiona *was* one of the people who'd sent her to the guillotine. It could reasonably be argued that a smack across the cheek was fair payback. At worst, they were even.

Unfortunately, it wasn't about reason. Mia was acutely aware that what transpired that day had embedded itself into her heart like a thorn, and no amount of logic could take it out. What hurt, hurt. Especially with her death drawing near, what she could feasibly do in the time left to her was quickly growing limited. This was not the time for fragile egos. She needed to act.

"Now that I think about it, I never did manage to develop a genuine friendship with Tiona, and I feel like it's all because of that incident."

If her second chance at life had for all practical purposes nullified that sin, then her successful avoidance of her guillotine fate should have signaled the end of her antipathy toward Tiona as well. Mia no longer felt any ill will toward the girl. If anything, Tiona had given Mia a lot of help both in Remno and during the election.

"It wouldn't have been the least bit surprising if we'd become really good friends, but somehow, somewhere, it felt like there was a rift between us. And now that I've figured out why, I need to do something about it, because I won't be able to die in peace otherwise."

At long last, she'd found the answer. Of course, she'd never be able to apologize to the Tiona she'd actually wronged. Doing so to the present Tiona, who had no recollection of being slapped, would probably just confuse her.

Well, so what if it did? That didn't matter. After all, when it came to Mia, it was always Mia First, which was currently amplified by her commitment to living in the moment. Moment-living-Mia-First-ism didn't give two sticks about how other people felt. She was going to have her way.

"I need to make proper amends for what I did to Tiona, because that way… If I do die on the night of the Holy Eve Festival…and by some miracle, I get another chance at life… That's when I'll be able to say with confidence, 'this time, we can finally become good friends.'"

Mia nodded, feeling a long-teetering weight settle into place at last. "Well, now that's decided, there's no time to waste."

The next day, she promptly went to see Tiona, bringing a big box of fancy pastries with her as an apology gift. Let it be known that she definitely, absolutely, *indubitably* did not do so because she wanted to eat them herself.

Chapter 24: A Regret Etched into the Soul
–Words Delivered, and a
Wish Unheard–

Throughout the duration of the revolutionary war in the Tearmoon Empire, Tiona Rudolvon, saint and champion of the revolutionary army, never once stood on the front lines of battle. Part of the reason could certainly be attributed to her outsized significance for the army; as a military leader and a living symbol of the revolution, her life was simply too important to risk. Mostly though, it was because she wasn't particularly skilled when it came to wielding a sword.

Despite this, she was not content to stand by and keep her hands clean while others did the dirty work of bathing theirs in blood. She wished to be useful. To fight alongside her people. So, she gave the issue serious thought, and the answer came to her in the form of archery.

Apprenticing herself to the master Lulu archer, Liora Lulu, her skill with the bow flourished. Eventually becoming a top-class archer in her own right, her arrows claimed the lives of numerous enemies throughout the revolution.

Then, the war ended. The imperial family had fallen. The emperor had been put to death. Mere days remained until his daughter, Princess Mia, would meet the same fate. The fighting was over at last. Tiona, however, did not allow her bowmanship to dull, shooting no less than several hundred arrows a day at practice targets. She displayed a diligence so intense that it bordered

194

on compulsion, as though every arrow she loosed was a desperate attempt to strike some invisible vessel of miracles that, when shattered, would allow her to retrieve something lost. Something forever out of reach. Day after day, week after week, her bowstring would continue to thrum.

One day, upon the conclusion of her practice, a man came to her.

"Ludwig Hewitt… You…are the person Prince Sion mentioned. I believe you used to serve Princess Mia?"

"Yes. I thank you for permitting my visit, Miss Tiona."

"You were given a terrible task during a terrible time. Prince Sion spoke highly of your political acumen. I do hope you will assist in rebuilding this empire of ours. Please, have some tea," she said, gesturing to a nearby table.

Ludwig did not move. Still and silent, he held her gaze and regarded her for a moment before speaking.

"The purpose of my visit today is to ask a favor of you."

Tiona responded with an equal span of silence, slowly picking up her cup for a sip. Her eyes closed as she drew in a breath, ostensibly enjoying the tea's aroma.

"You come bearing a request, then… I will gladly convey it to Prince Sion, if that is your wish," she said in a probing manner.

"I ask that you speak with Her Highness."

His words were simple, and there was no deceit in his tone.

"To what end? What is there to speak about at this point in time? I cannot imagine such a meeting would be fruitful…"

Her voice grew stiff at this request. His reply, however, took her by surprise.

"It is my understanding that when you attended Saint-Noel, there was a time when Her Highness struck you on the cheek."

195

"…Excuse me? Wha—"

"I've been told by Her Highness that she has always desired to apologize to you for her actions that day. I ask that you grant her this chance."

"I…am not sure what you mean. Struck me? When?"

She frowned as she searched her mind for a matching incident.

Indeed, as the victim of countless episodes of harassment during her time at Saint-Noel Academy, Tiona had long forgotten about this particular offense. Mia's feeble slap hadn't even managed to commit itself to her memory. Considering how much Mia hated pain, she could hardly have been expected to put much force behind such an act when it was her own palm doing the striking. The truth was that at the time, as the person on the receiving end, Tiona had felt not rage or shame but confusion at how she was supposed to react to the equivalent of a slightly forceful pat on the cheek.

Her unexpected surprise then baffled Ludwig, and the two engaged in a momentary exchange of perplexity. Finally, he coughed and said, "In any case, would it be possible for you to see Her Highness? And speak to her in person? It would—"

"Change nothing."

Like an arrow splitting the air, her words severed his hopes. She glared at him.

"So what if she does? What am I to do with her apology now? What will it change? What *can* it change? It cannot bring back my father, nor the countless souls who perished under the blightful rule of the imperial family and the old noble houses."

Then, she took another sip of tea.

Mia Luna Tearmoon…must not *be forgiven.*

She repeated the cautionary thought in her mind, etching its pattern deeper into her soul.

There's no need to see her. No need to trade words or understand her character. There's no need...so I won't.

Tiona...feared what would come of such a meeting. If they were to speak, she would learn what kind of person Mia was. What if she began to feel sympathy? Or a desire to forgive her?

What of my father's death, then? Am I to overlook it? That is too much to ask.

Yes, the princess might be repenting. Yes, she might turn out to be a decent person if they spoke. She might even be someone who could make amends for wrongs. But not only could that not breathe life back into her father, it would orphan the unfairness of his death. If Tiona faltered, how would her poor father's soul seek justice? Therefore, she could not allow herself to forgive Mia.

"I will not forgive her," she declared adamantly. "Nor will I ask Prince Sion to spare her life. But..."

At that, her stony tone wavered.

"But...if you wish to speak with Prince Sion, I won't stop you."

Was it a parting mercy? No, it was an escape. She didn't want to face Mia as a person or wield any power over her life and death. So, she fled, choosing to put Mia out of sight and out of mind. That way, her heart would remain calm. She couldn't be tempted by the allure of mercy.

Which was why...

...Some time after Mia's execution, when it was discovered that the assassination of Outcount Rudolvon had not been done under the emperor's orders, she tasted the bitter sting of regret.

"If I'd...spoken to her then, maybe it would have..."

The rational part of her mind reminded her that the execution was inevitable. No matter what she did, it was all but clear that she had no way of saving Mia. But despite that...or, perhaps, *because* of that...

197

Because she knew beyond a shadow of a doubt that she'd never have another chance to speak with Mia… The fact that she refused to trade even a single word, even when it was the last wish of a condemned woman, became a deep-seated regret. It was a regret that etched itself into her very soul, right on top of her own cautionary words— *Mia Luna Tearmoon must not be forgiven*—overlaying the previous pattern with its own, forming a newer, more bitter wound that would never heal.

"…What a weird dream that was."

A day before the Holy Eve Festival, Tiona stood in the archery range of Saint-Noel Academy. Having been made painfully aware of her inadequacy with the sword during the Remno incident, she had, after no small amount of brooding reflection, decided to take up the bow. Fortunately, her attendant, Liora, was an expert archer. Under her mentorship, Tiona quickly discovered that she had a knack for archery and began to steadily improve. After finishing her practice that day, she was in the middle of dabbing the sweat off her forehead when someone approached her.

"Tiona, do you have a moment?"

"Huh? Y-Your Highness?"

The situation bore an uncanny similarity to her dream, except the person to appear was Mia herself.

"I'd like to speak to you about something. Are you free at the moment?"

Overcome by the peculiar coincidence, Tiona could only nod.

"Um, I'm terribly sorry, Your Highness. I just finished archery practice, so I probably smell of sweat… If, um, this involves a tea party or something, I'll go clean up and change first…"

"My, I do seem to have come at a rather inopportune time."

Mia looked Tiona over and pursed her lips. Tiona's hair did glisten slightly with sweat. It would probably be uncomfortable for her to stay like that.

"Hm, in that case, why don't we go take a bath together?"

"Take a— Huh?"

The suggestion clearly went right over Tiona's head. Mia giggled at the look of bewilderment on her face.

"It just so happens that Chloe recently gave me some interesting bath herbs. Apparently, they're good for healing fatigue. Since you just finished practice, why don't we go try them out?"

Like Rania, Chloe had been worried about Mia, and the bath herbs were her way of showing concern. Mia figured she'd better try them today, because she might never have another chance.

"Yes, I think this is an excellent opportunity," she said, ostensibly to herself as Tiona showed no sign of comprehension, and began making her way to the communal baths.

The early afternoon timing worked in their favor, as the baths were conveniently empty when they arrived. Delighted by this discovery, Mia promptly dumped the whole bag of herbs into the water.

"Y-Your Highness? Are you sure you should just throw them all in like that? Sh-Shouldn't we ask for permission—"

"Oho ho, don't even worry about it!" said Mia with an abundance of confidence.

She was, after all, living in the moment. A lack of permission wasn't going to stop her from turning the communal baths into her personal spa. Or so she thought, until the herbs promptly began to emit *smoke* after hitting the water. Her heart almost leapt out of her mouth at the startling phenomenon. Soon, white smoke had filled every corner of the chamber, swirling so thickly that she couldn't even see Tiona a few paces away.

"Y-Your Highness?"

"D-Don't worry… Th-This is fine. Probably."

What had been an abundance of confidence immediately shriveled to a sliver, and the quality of her heartedness reverted from swine to fowl. Just as thoughts of *Oh, I've done it now* and *I'm in so much trouble* began to fill her mind, the smoke thinned at last. It was still a tad thick to pass off as regular steam, but she would probably get away with it with no one the wiser. After a few more murmured recitations of *this is fine*, her inner chicken finally stopped quivering. As she drew a relieved breath, it occurred to her that she recognized the scent emanating from the water.

"My, isn't this lucioluna grass?"

"Yes, I think so. It smells so nice."

Tiona visibly mellowed at the pleasant aroma. The two of them quickly rinsed themselves off and waded into the bath. As the warm liquid enveloped her, Mia sighed in comfort.

Aaah… Chloe did say it's supposed to be a calming scent. Well, she was right about that.

She could feel the tension draining out of her body. The turbulent storm of worry that brewed within slowed to a pleasant lull.

The water's nice, the herbs smell great, and we're both relaxed. Naturally, it's time to chat now. Good going, Chloe! This is exactly what I was after.

With a guttural *hmmm*, she stretched out her limbs before sinking deeper into the water. A giggle entered her ears. She gave Tiona a puzzled glance, wondering what had amused her.

"Hm? What is it?"

"Oh, nothing much," she answered with a smile. "I just noticed that you filled out a little."

"…What?"

Mia froze. The pleasant lull within immediately reverted to a turbulent storm of worry. But…

"I was a bit worried about you. We all were, after hearing that you hadn't had much of an appetite recently," Tiona added as clarification.

"O-Oh, that's what you mean. You were worried I wasn't eating."

Mia nodded. She wasn't quite sure if the clarification made it any better, but she nodded anyway. Then, she regarded her upper arm. Frowning, she pinched the meaty part.

Did I put on weight? I don't think I did. Hmm… It doesn't feel any jigglier. It's always been this jiggly, I'm pretty sure. Even before summer… Wait. Doesn't that mean—

"So, um… What was it you wanted to speak to me about?"

Mia was on the verge of an important realization when Tiona pulled her out of her thoughts, forcing her to abandon the train of thought.

"Oh, right. That. Uh…"

Mia straightened slightly and took a deep breath.

"There's something I need to apologize to you for."

"Huh?"

The statement was so out of the blue that the only response Tiona could manage was a series of bewildered blinks. Mia continued undeterred.

"I…did something to you, a while ago. Something terribly mean."

Her voice echoed quietly in the bath chamber.

"Wh-What are you talking about? I don't… You've always been nothing but kind to me, Your Highness. How could you have ever done something mean to me?" said Tiona, flustered by Mia's bizarre confession. "That's…completely unthinkable."

"Oh? Is it? I can be mean from time to time too. When someone tries to flirt with a boy I've got my eye on, for example…"

"B-But, I've never done anything like that to Prince Abel…"

Just then, a scene from last night's dream flashed across Tiona's mind. Mia had said she wanted to apologize. Tiona had pushed her away, refusing to talk, only to be left with nothing but regrets afterward. It was, of course, just a dream. A mere figment of the imagination. Her heart, however, felt the dull pain of bitter patterns etched into its spiritual flesh. So she gathered herself.

"…I don't know what you speak of, but if…if Your Highness truly has done something mean, then as long as you've apologized, which you did just now, I'm sure…"

Somewhere, sometime, there had been a version of herself that believed she must not forgive Mia. Not couldn't, but *must not*. And she'd suffered for it.

How awful it must feel…to keep hating someone like that…

Tiona reflected on the rest of her dream. She thought of her ensuing life of hating Mia, and in doing so, how much light and joy had been lost from her days. She thought of the moment she realized her hate had been misattributed, and afterward, how desperately she'd wished she could speak to Mia. Driven by those thoughts, she turned toward the presently-living Mia, and looked her in the eye.

"I'm sure that you've been forgiven. I'd forgive you, at least. I…already did, in another life…"

Her last few words, though murmured, seemed to reach Mia, whose expression shifted.

"You…did…"

What tension there was in Mia's expression seemed to melt away. She stared blankly for a moment, as if the weight that had been lifted from her was so profound that she wasn't sure how to handle her newfound levity. Then, emotion returned to her face in the form of a relieved smile.

"Aah... Wonderful. That's...truly wonderful. Now I have no more regrets."

This time, it was Mia's final words that unsettled Tiona, who felt a stirring unease in her chest.

"Um, Your Highness, I want to speak to you too. Talk, I mean. I want to spend more time talking with you."

She put to words the wish that had been etched into her soul. A wish that, in her dream, had been impossible, but now...might yet come true.

For a second, Mia's face was unreadable. Then, she said, "I see... In that case...once the Holy Eve Festival is over, let's talk. We can spend all the time together we want then."

"...The Holy Eve Festival?"

"Yes. The Holy Eve Festival. If I manage to survive it in one piece, we'll get together and chat the night away."

It made sense. As a member of the student council, their myriad duties during the Holy Eve Festival likely made it difficult for them to relax before it was over. Waiting until then was perfectly reasonable. But for some reason...the sense of unease in Tiona's chest only tightened its grip on her.

"Well, I think that will do it for now. Thank you very much for your time today," said Mia as she smiled and rose from the pool.

Tiona looked up at her departing form...and felt her heart skip a beat. There was an eerily ephemeral air to the princess, as if she were the moon who, though once the protagonist of the sky, was now being relieved of her role as the night waned. Perhaps it was simply the faint haze of the bath chamber obscuring her form, but...

"Y-Your Hi—"

The feeling was short-lived. Tiona's cry was cut off by the entrance of Bel and Citrina.

"Ah, Miss Mia. What a coincidence."

"Greetings, Your Highness."

"My, are you two here for a bath?" asked Mia.

"Yes we are…but why is it sort of foggy in here?" asked Bel, who glanced around curiously.

"I tried using some bath herbs that Chloe gave me. It was actually pretty fun. So much smoke came out when they hit the water."

Mia laughed. She was back to her usual cheerful self, the ephemeral aura about her all but gone…

And then, the day of the Holy Eve Festival arrived.

Chapter 25: A Conspiracy Is Set in Motion —Grandmother Mia's Do-or-Die Resolve—

Day of the Holy Eve Festival, Hour of the Eighth Bell (8:00 a.m.)

The day that would decide Mia's fate arrived with little fanfare. A quiet morning greeted her as she sleepily wriggled out from under her bedcovers. Accompanied by Anne, she made her way to the communal baths. There she cleansed herself of night-time perspiration, washed her face, and gave her cheeks a firm smack to wake herself up. It was a rare sight to see Mia so sharp and ready to roll in the morning.

"Hm, I think that about does it…"

"Wow, you're certainly fired up today, milady," Anne commented in a tone of mild surprise.

"That I am," said Mia with a soft smile. "Today of all days, I figured it'd be a good idea…"

Breakfast followed, after which she headed to the student council office.

"Ah, Mia. Good morning."

Rafina greeted her as she walked in.

"Miss Rafina? My… Is there some work we need to get done in the office today?"

From checking security protocols to preparations for the celebration banquet, even the procedures for checking the traffic going in and out of the island… The student council had already reviewed every process the day would entail. In fact, on the day of the festival, the council wasn't supposed to be doing much at all.

"Oh, no. If anything comes up, I'll ask everyone to come by..." Rafina let out a quick giggle. "But I doubt that will be necessary. Ever since our discussion, Santeri has been working so hard that there's hardly anything left for us to do."

She smiled before adding, "And it's all thanks to you."

"That's not true! You give me too much credit."

She certainly did give Mia too much credit. Mia had just been following her stomach, which happened to tell her to snarf down a poisonous mushroom.

"What are you doing here then?"

"Oh, just...reflecting." A tender smile graced Rafina's lips. "A year has passed since I relinquished my authority over this room. A whole year... It's a thought that still amazes me at times."

Rafina proceeded to seat herself on the top of her desk. The gesture surprised Mia, who had always considered Rafina to be a paragon of proper etiquette. Sitting on a desk was certainly not dignified behavior.

"I always come here on this day, you know?" she continued. "Every year before the festival, before I cleanse myself and don the holy garments, I'd come in here and give myself a little pep talk. You might not realize, but the Holy Eve Festival's ceremonial ritual can be pretty nerve-racking."

"I...can imagine."

"But this year is a little different. It still makes me nervous, but just thinking about how we're going to have a party with all the council members afterward makes me so very excited." Rafina's smile glowed with the innocent enthusiasm of a child. "Well then, I think it's time for me to go. But, just so you know, I'm really looking forward to tonight's stew party, okay?"

Mia watched Rafina leave the office before letting out a quiet murmur.

"Tonight, huh… That's right. It's tonight…"

She still didn't know what was going to happen. But one thing was for certain—there was a stew party waiting for her. All her dear friends were going to come together, and they were going to have a wonderful time. On top of that, there would be *mushrooms* in the stew. Exquisite mushroom stew! Exquisite! Mushroom!! Stew!!!

It's okay. Surely no temptation can lure me off the island tonight. It simply isn't possible.

Buoyed by that thought, Mia left the office as well.

Day of the Holy Eve Festival, Hour of the Tenth Bell (10:00 a.m.)

"Ah, Princess Mia!"

A voice called out to Mia as she passed by the grand hall that would soon host the banquet. She turned to find Rania Tafrif Perujin waving at her.

"Ah, Rania. Good day to you."

Smiling affably, Mia walked over, only for her eyes to affix themselves to the items on the table beside Rania.

"My! Those look delicious!"

A mouthwatering display of confections, each the pride of Perujin's best artisans, left her licking her lips. Having learned from the poison mushroom incident, Belluga guards had been posted around all edible matter. Under their careful watch, sneaking a bite was probably unfeasible…

"They look…so very delicious…"

Rania laughed.

"Then make sure you come by later. I'll be waiting to hear what you think of them."

Mia favored her invitation with a gentle smile.

"Thank you, Rania. For everything. I've always had nothing but wonderful experiences with Perujin food. I'll…certainly make every effort to come by."

She left her answer noncommittal. Why, you ask? Well…

I've got mushroom stew lined up tonight, after all… I can't guarantee I'll have enough room…

…She'd run the numbers on her tummy budget, and it was going to be tight, because tonight, she was going to feast on exquisite mushroom stew! Exquisite!—everyone together now—Mushroom!! Stew!!! With that on the list, fitting anything else in would be a challenge.

Rania, meanwhile, studied Mia for a moment before abruptly taking a cupcake from the table and handing it to her with a spoon.

"Here you are."

"My, what's this?" asked Mia.

"A sample. Try it."

"Huh? U-Uh, thank you?"

Though puzzled by this gesture, Mia obliged. She promptly tried a spoonful.

"Mmm! This is—!"

"How is it?"

"It's melting in my mouth, and all the flavors are coming out… So rich… Wait, is this…honey chestnut flavored?"

"It is. Behold, our new creation. Honey chestnut cake."

"Aha, so I was right. It's been so long since I've tasted honey chestnut, but it's still every bit as delicious as I remember," Mia said as she handed back the cup.

Now, described in this manner, it might sound like she simply sampled the cupcake and handed the rest of it back, but all good Mia scholars should know that would run counter to her nature. Indeed, what she handed back was an *empty* cup. During their brief exchange, she'd deftly maneuvered her spoon around the cup, scooping up every last remnant of the cupcake and shoveling it all into her mouth. Never let it be said that Mia was a wasteful eater.

"Keep this up, and Perujin will be sleeping easy for years to come. I'd wish you good luck at tonight's banquet, but honestly, I don't think you'll even need it," she said with a smile.

Rania did not return it in kind. She continued to study Mia for a few seconds before saying, "Um, just so you know, we'll have lots more during the banquet. Lots of delicious things. Not just at my table, but all the others too. Everyone has brought their best. So..." There was a subtle desperation to her voice. "Do come and try them. We all wanted to cheer you up, so we prepared lots of tasty things. Make sure you come, okay?"

She spoke as if begging for a promise. As if...without that promise, Mia would drift away, never to be seen again.

"Well, if it means so much to you..."

Mia decided that she could perhaps afford to slightly reduce the tummy space she'd reserved for the mushroom stew.

Besides, they do say you always have room for dessert, and idioms don't come from nowhere. I should be fine.

Day of the Holy Eve Festival, Hour of the Fourth Bell Second Sequence (4:00 p.m.)

After touring the whole of the academy, Mia went back to her room and proceeded to stay there like a good little doom-evading girl. Some time later, to her surprise, there was a knock on the door. Anne went to answer it but soon returned with a frown.

"Milady, I'm sorry, but may I be excused for a bit?"

"Sure. I don't mind. But what for?"

"Apparently, they need more people to set up tonight's banquet, and they asked if I could help."

"Ah. Well, today's a special day, after all. It's hard to blame anyone for needing a couple extra pairs of hands. Hm... In that case, go do me proud, Anne. Show them what Tearmoon attendants are capable of."

A hint of anxiousness flitted across Anne's expression.

"Understood. But, um, milady…"

She trailed off hesitantly.

"Hm? What is it?"

"Never mind," she said with a shake of her head. "It's nothing. Off I go then."

"All right. Oh, if you happen to see Bel, could you tell her to come back to our room? For some reason, I don't think I've caught a glimpse of her the whole morning."

Bel was a grade lower than Mia, so it wasn't exactly rare for the two of them to go an entire day without seeing one another. Today, however, her absence was oddly discomforting.

"Miss Bel?" Anne's puzzled frown lasted only a second before she nodded. "Understood. I'll see you later then, milady."

After seeing Anne off, Mia looked around the empty room before going over to Bel's bed. She took out the copy of *The Chronicles of Saint Princess Mia* hidden underneath and flipped it open to check its contents again.

I doubt any of it has changed, but just in case… I'll take one last look at the Chronicles to see if— Hm?

She was interrupted by a light knock on the door.

"Huh. I wonder who that is. Did Anne come back, maybe? No, I doubt it…"

Perplexed, she walked over to see who it was. Just as she was about to unsuspectingly open the door, she noticed a piece of paper at her feet that had been slid under it. Her eyes scanned the first few words on the page…

Your dear sister, Miabel, is in our custody. If you wish to see her alive, come alone to the place stated below.

Thus began the ransom note.

"O-Oh moons…" Her voice trembled. "So that's why…"

The sequence of events described in the Princess Chronicles fell into place.

"I see now… This is what made me leave the island and ride off into the night."

The letter included meticulous instructions for her, describing which merchant had been bribed to ferry her off the island, and where she was to go to obtain a horse. Having heard Santeri explain his new security measures, she knew that while entering the island was difficult, leaving was relatively easy, especially during a busy time like the Holy Eve Festival when traffic in and out was far greater than usual. It simply wasn't possible to carefully scrutinize every departing individual. Therefore…

"It's hard to pull off an assassination on the island, but getting someone to leave the island is simple."

A straight-up kidnapping would of course still be difficult. It seemed unlikely that any merchant willing to assist such an effort would be granted entrance to begin with. But what if there was no sign of wrongdoing? What if it was only a slightly unreasonable request from a princess…demanding to be taken off the island for a quick horseback ride to enjoy the night air, for example? Noelige Lake and its surroundings were known to be a safe region, largely free of criminals and aggressive wildlife. How dangerous could it be to enjoy some light riding there?

It was easy to imagine that some people would answer "not very." The perpetrators had created a situation that lay right on the line of what was acceptable, and because it was on the line, there were doubtless many who would be willing to cross it for monetary reward.

"I doubt many would knowingly participate in this sort of conspiracy, but I can definitely imagine that there are those willing to comply with a selfish demand from a young, powerful noble…"

The essence of merchants, after all, was a willingness to place one's own interests at risk so long as there was money to be gained. Those driven by mere monetary greed would, upon discovering that they'd been complicit in an assassination, likely hold their tongues; their motivation reflected the extent of their resolve, neither of which would be sufficient for them to choose truth over self-preservation. That explained why the Princess Chronicles said that she'd left of her own willful accord. Those in the know had probably all agreed to push a story that was more convenient to them.

Mia carefully read through the letter again, checking each proposed step that would lead her off the island. She let out a breath, realizing that should she follow these instructions, it was definitely possible for her to make her exit with almost nobody noticing. There was nothing to stop her.

"…Which means there's only one question left. How much is Bel's life worth to me?"

There was no room for excuses. She couldn't blame the letter for providing an unfeasible plan. It was perfectly possible for her to leave the island. Ergo, the situation had been reduced to a simple yes or no question—was she willing to trade her life for Bel's?

"This is ridiculous. Of course I'm not going to leave the island," she muttered. "That's almost like asking to be killed. In fact, that's exactly what it is, considering they *did* kill me."

Her enemies didn't know about the Princess Chronicles. She was aware that leaving the island would mean her death, but they didn't know that.

"If I go, I die. And judging from the fact that there's nothing written about Bel in the Chronicles, she probably died too, so going didn't even make a difference."

Mia shook her head at what was looking like a no-win dilemma and took off her dress.

"Besides, if I die, wouldn't Bel end up not existing? That'd defeat the whole point. There's literally no reason to go. What a stupid plan. I've got better things to be doing. Like changing into my ceremony uniform. Now, where'd I put the thing…"

She muttered dismissively as she dug through her wardrobe and pulled out an outfit that was decidedly not ceremonial.

"Nonsense… Such nonsense, honestly…"

She closed her eyes, riding clothes in hand, and a vision of Bel appeared in her mind. Bel, who'd said that this world was like a dream…a *wonderful* dream…which was why she was going to enjoy it as best she could, so when she woke from it, she'd have no regrets. Mia watched as her vision of Bel smiled, her expression innocent and full of joy. She heard an echo of her own voice telling her dear granddaughter *"It's okay. This dream won't end. The grandmother you always so respected… She won't let it."*

"I'll just be dying in vain. It's complete nonsense… But hnnnngh, I'll probably feel *really* bad if I don't go…"

There was also another concern that began to gnaw at her. What would happen if she didn't go and kept quiet about the incident? Sure, she'd almost certainly survive, but whoever these assassins were, they'd still be in the academy. Going forward, she could be killed by any one of them at any time. Worse yet, she couldn't imagine them not announcing the fact that she'd abandoned Bel and left her to die. And when they did she'd surely lose the trust of those around her. Her loyal Anne, in particular, would probably be deeply disappointed in her.

In that case, the assassins might even be doing her a favor if they showed up quickly to finish the job. Otherwise, she'd have to suffer both the resentment of others and her own guilty conscience for the rest of her life.

And how would I face Abel after that? How can I look him in the eyes and tell him I abandoned my— our granddaughter…

And what if she went to save Bel? What would happen then? Well, she'd be killed. Though Mia could be rather full of herself at times, even she hadn't reached the levels of delusional grandeur necessary to believe she could rescue Bel from a situation like this and get back with both of them in one piece. However, there was one thin sliver of hope… She'd certainly die. But…what if she leapt back in time again?

There's no way that kind of thing can happen on a regular basis, but…if it could happen just one more time…

She gulped.

…Then going would actually be a viable option. I'd get a lot of information about the enemy that way.

If Mia showed up completely alone, her would-be killers would probably lower their guard and reveal themselves. She'd find out as much about them as she could, then die and bring all that knowledge back with her to the past. The more she thought about it, the more it seemed that if she wanted to save Bel, she'd have to swim back up the stream of time again. Eventually she became convinced that it was, in fact, the only possible way of doing so. In essence, she had to stop this kidnapping *before* it happened.

"Ugh, if there was *any* other alternative…"

A quiet sigh escaped her as she did up the last button on her outfit.

"But… I guess there isn't. The only way I can do this is to die and go back to the past…"

Mia always looked out for number one. That was why, in an attempt to avoid a second encounter with the guillotine, she'd gone so far as to devise a method to flee the empire. On the day she'd escaped that fate, however, her goal had shifted ever so slightly.

Now, Mia sought her own happiness, and she didn't want to compromise. What she desired was grade A pure, unblemished happiness. In pondering how she could obtain such a thing, she'd come to the conclusion that it would require the people around her to be happy as well. Her bliss alone was insufficient; it was through their combined happinesses that she would fully realize her goal.

This was, objectively speaking, a profoundly exorbitant wish— one in which the fates of everyone around her would have to bend to her arrogant will. And she didn't give a rat's rump! Mia was a selfish princess, after all. Exorbitance and arrogance were just business as usual for her.

"The ransom note says I'm supposed to go alone. I can't ask anyone for help, then…"

There was no way to tell if she was being watched. If the enemy saw her with guards, not only might they kill Bel, they might never reveal themselves. Actions that could impede her ability to gain information should be avoided.

"But…they didn't say anything about asking non-people."

She grinned deviously as she made her way toward the stable. There waited a companion with whom she'd arguably spent more time this autumn than anyone else.

"I mean, I'm definitely going to die…but I'm not making it easy for them. If you thought you could kill me for cheap, Chaos Serpents, then you'd better think again."

Thus, Grandmother Mia strode off to battle to save her granddaughter.

What Mia didn't know…was how the resolve she mustered in this very moment had altered the writings in the Princess Chronicles. The step forward she took was like the flap of a butterfly's wings. The tiny current of air it generated would, through coincidence and consequence, eventually make its way around the world and give rise to a towering tornado. Unbeknownst to the snakes of the earth, this towering hydra of the sky would soon consume them in its whirling jaws.

Chapter 26: Two Silvers' Worth of Loyalty

Day of the Holy Eve Festival, Hour of the Seventh Bell (7:00 a.m.)

Rewinding the clock a little…

"Good morning, milady Bel."

"Ah, Miss Lynsha. Good morning."

On the morning of the Holy Eve Festival, Bel was visibly brimming with excitement.

Can't blame her, really. Every kid looks forward to the Holy Eve Festival, thought Lynsha as she regarded the excited child fondly.

She didn't have any younger sisters, but if she had, this would probably be what it felt like.

I do wonder though. What exactly is her relation to Mia?

According to Mia, they were half sisters…but Lynsha wasn't convinced.

They do look pretty alike though. Maybe a distant relative with a bit of a complicated story?

The thing Lynsha particularly appreciated about the girl was how low maintenance she was. In general, noble children were a handful to take care of, requiring their attendants to tend to everything from changes of clothes to preparing baths. Bel, meanwhile, did everything herself.

And it's not like she's a bad girl or anything, though I wish she'd shake that habit of handing out money to everyone who's ever helped her…

That kind of behavior rubbed her the wrong way. Expressing thanks through the hard, pragmatic utility of cold cash felt too much like settling debts or squaring accounts, as if whatever goodwill the other party had bestowed upon you was, with this gift of money, done and cleared. Relationships were developed through a continuous exchange of kindness and favors. If someone treated you well, you should just treat them well in return. Repay kindness in kind. Love with love. Whether between friends, parents, or colleagues, that was how Lynsha believed it should always be.

What would happen when money was thrown into the mix? If kindness was repaid with cash? It would signal the end of the relationship by forcing upon it a transactional nature. Transactions, after all, ended. All that would remain was one party who'd offered money, and another who'd taken it in exchange for something they deemed of equal value. She just couldn't see how that kind of interaction could lead to lasting bonds.

What bothered her even more, however, was...

It almost feels like there's some sort of underlying fear...as if she thinks she won't always be here, so she's constantly preparing for that contingency by repaying every kindness as soon as possible so she can disappear at any time without anyone losing out. And she treats every relationship that way...

It was, perhaps, a legitimate life philosophy. Stoic, certainly, and maybe even admirable in some ways. No one could know for certain if a person they met today would still be there tomorrow, so always thanking them at the first opportunity was...arguably a commendable way to live.

The thing is, in her case, it feels more like giving up. Like she's accepted that she could die at any time, and she's organizing her whole life around that.

There was a sense of fatalistic resignation to it all, and Lynsha didn't like it. Children, in her opinion, should be doe-eyed believers in the possibilities of tomorrow. If not everywhere, then at least here, on Saint-Noel Island. And yet...

That's fine though. If she tries to hand me money when it's time for us to say goodbye, I'm stuffing it right back in her pocket. And then I'm going to give her a stern lecture about how you should say thanks with your mouth and not your wallet. As a final lesson, that ought to leave an impression.

With that thought in mind, Lynsha huffed out a satisfied breath.

Day of the Holy Eve Festival, Hour of the Eighth Bell (8:00 a.m.)

"Good morning, Bel."

Citrina appeared behind Bel, who was currently having breakfast in the cafeteria. Lynsha studied the young Yellowmoon's face and frowned.

Something about her smile is off. It's always so sweet and charming, but today, it seems a touch stiff...

"Hm? What's wrong, Rina? You look a little down," asked Bel, who seemed to have noticed the discrepancy as well.

"Down? No, I'm perfectly fine. More importantly, look, Bel." Citrina gestured at a small item hanging from her neck. "It's Holy Eve, so I figured I'd wear it. What do you think?"

Bel beamed at the dangling horse charm she'd made.

"Ah, it's the troya! Heh heh, I'm so glad you're wearing it."

"That's right, and I'd like to show my appreciation. Do you have time around noon today to go out for a walk with Rina?"

"Go out?"

"Mmhm. Remember the picnic in the forest last time? That was a lot of fun, so I'm thinking it'd be nice if we did it again. It's not like there's anything to do until the candlelight mass anyway."

"I don't mind going, but isn't the forest off-limits now?"

"The place where the poisonous mushrooms grow is, but we can still get into the clearing near the entrance. I actually went not too long ago to make sure."

219

Citrina smiled the sweetest of smiles.

"It's *such* a beautiful clearing, Bel. Don't you want to go see it? Don't you want to go right now?"

"Mmm, okay! Let's go then. Heh heh, this sounds fun." Bel smiled too.

Lynsha did not. The exchange between the two girls made a slow chill crawl up her spine. In fact, it had been making its way up her back ever since she'd first met Citrina. She *recognized* the girl's tone. Rather, she recognized its essence. It was uncannily similar to the seductive tone her provocateur of a brother Lambert used when he was talking someone into something. Driven by a subconscious sense of dread, she spoke up.

"In that case, I'll accompany you, milady."

She looked from Citrina to her attendant Barbara, as if trying to deter them through her gaze.

"That would be much appreciated. It just so happens that I will be occupied in the afternoon."

Barbara made no attempt to object. This lack of concern took Lynsha by surprise.

"I leave milady Citrina in your care then," the older woman said as she lowered her head in a respectful curtsy.

Day of the Holy Eve Festival, Hour of the First Bell Second Sequence (1:00 p.m.)

After lunch, Lynsha accompanied Bel and Citrina to the forest. Like the latter had said, the woody entrance was unguarded, and the three of them gained easy access to the clearing beyond. She'd been here not long ago, but the season had turned fully to winter in the interim, and the scenery had taken on a frosty quality.

Maybe it's just because there's nobody here. The town is bustling with activity thanks to the festival, after all. It's hard to imagine anyone coming to a place like this today.

"Hmm, it feels a little lonelier here than the last time we visited," said Citrina after glancing at the surroundings. She sighed. "What a shame. What do you say we go a little deeper into the forest, Bel?"

"Hm? Deeper? But won't we get in trouble if one of the patrols finds us?"

"Oh, don't worry. We'll be fine. It's not like we're doing anything bad, right?"

Citrina took Bel's hand and gave it a pull. Bel hesitated at first but eventually gave in with a smile. Lynsha watched the pair run toward the woods with an air of blithe excitement.

That's more like it, she thought, letting out a small breath of relief. *Children should always have innocent expressions like that.*

She called out to the two girls.

"Milady, Miss Citrina, don't go running off too far now. It's—"

The world shuddered. A split second later, she felt the pain. Whatever had hit her head, it was heavy, and it robbed her of her strength. Her knees buckled.

"Ah… Ah…"

She didn't even have time to scream before her vision faded to black.

"Miss Lynsha!"

Bel's voice came to her as if from a great distance.

"Milady…run…"

Rallying every last fiber of consciousness left to her, she managed but a hoarse whisper. It fell from her mouth and sank to the earth, far too weak to reach Bel.

"I won't let you kill Miss Lynsha!"

The next voice she heard…was still Bel's. But it came from right above her, and it rang with a furious intensity, sharper and bolder than anything she'd heard from the girl before.

A second voice followed. It was the dismissive laugh of an old woman.

"Ba ha ha, you won't *let* me? Who do you think you are? A princess? Do you think you can simply order me to stop?" The old woman let out a muted chortle. "Silliness. Such silliness. What do we have to gain from not killing her, hm?"

There was a constricting, viscous quality to the voice. Like tendrils of tar, it coiled itself around the listener. Bel's, in comparison, was clear as crystal.

"…If you don't kill Miss Lynsha, then I'll go with you without making a scene. Your goal isn't to kill me here, right? You want to use me as a hostage to get to Miss Mia."

"…Oh? You're smarter than I thought, little Miss Bel."

"If you kill Miss Lynsha right now, I'm going to fight you with everything I've got. What are you going to do then? You can knock me out, but I think that would cause other problems for you…"

The old woman's voice cackled.

"Very smart indeed. Obnoxiously so, in fact. You surprise me. The plan was originally to drug you…but it's true that having your cooperation would make it much easier to get out of here." After a brief silence, she continued, only to use her words as a whip to lash Bel's conscience. "Very well. This girl shall live. For now, anyway. Given that wound, she can neither move nor call for help. She will likely die anyway. The more she struggles, the more she suffers. A quick death right now might in fact be a mercy, but, well, as you wish… A pity though. Such a pity. Had she not involved herself with you, she would never have gotten into such a pickle."

An agreement had been reached, and Lynsha heard what sounded like Bel crouching down beside her.

"…Thank you for everything, Miss Lynsha."

There was the light rustling of fabric, followed by the sensation of something being stuffed down her collar. It was cold. Metallic. And she knew at once what it was.

Two silver coins.

"This is…the most thanks that I can give right now. I'm sorry. I'm really sorry this happened. That it had to end like this. I truly hope you'll be okay."

There was a light pattering of footsteps that got farther and farther away.

Then, the last vestiges of her consciousness left her as well.

"Stupid girl…and her stupid coins… Freaking hell…"

Lynsha woke to the sound of her own swearing. She had no idea how long she'd been out. An attempt to open her eyes ended in failure. And pain. They were glued shut by the trails of crusted blood that had run down her forehead. The pain kept coming. Her head throbbed, causing her to grit her teeth.

She forced herself up to her knees, only to feel an abrupt floating sensation before collapsing back down onto her side. She tried again, only to hit the ground even harder. A third attempt took her to her feet, but three steps later she stumbled, falling hard. Lying there disoriented and with yet more bruises, it occurred to her that trying to move was really only making things worse.

She might be better off waiting for someone to find her. There were patrols posted to guard the poisonous mushrooms. When they changed shifts, there was a good chance someone would see her.

But that wasn't fast enough.

So she advanced. On and on she went, dragging her body along the ground. She partly climbed, mostly crawled up the thick, protruding root of a tree. Resting breathlessly atop it, she felt rage bubble in her chest.

"Give…thanks? To hell…with your thanks. If you want to…thank me…then do it…properly. I don't want…your silver. I didn't…take this job…for your damn coins…"

The rage thrashed against her sternum, pushing her forward. Her consciousness ebbed and flowed. She growled, and it stilled itself as if in fear. Anger alone kept her going, so she fed it. Fury flared. At Bel, yes…but more than anything, at herself for failing to protect her. She pressed on.

"I was there…with her…and it still turned out…like this…"

She was supposed to be the guardian, and yet, it had been Bel who'd shielded *her* from harm. To be protected, then be given money for her trouble… It infuriated her.

Suddenly, she let out a humorless laugh.

"Hah, but then again…serves me right. I'm the one who let her get kidnapped… Maybe I *am* worth exactly two silver coins…"

She clenched her teeth. Her head spun and her jaw ached, but she did not stop. Inch by laborious inch, she dragged herself along the forest floor, fueled by a furious loyalty—not love, perhaps, but no less powerful—to her young mistress.

"So you're telling me my loyalty is worth two silvers… All right then… I'll show you what two silvers buy in this business…"

Steadily, she vanished into the thicket, heading toward Saint-Noel Academy and help.

Chapter 27: With Her Beloved Steed...

Day of the Holy Eve Festival, approximately half-strike past the Hour of the Fourth Bell Second Sequence (4:40 p.m.)

The location specified in the ransom note was a little ways away from the shore of Noelige Lake.

"Past the grassland area, in a small abandoned town... No surprises there. That sounds like the perfect place for this sort of thing..."

Presumably, the idea was to get her far from Saint-Noel so no one could intervene in the proceedings.

"Judging by the map, there's quite a bit of distance... I'll definitely need a horse."

The result of the horsemanship tournament in the fall must have prompted the kidnappers to factor into their plans the fact that Mia knew how to ride. After all, if their ultimate goal was to abduct her without anyone noticing, the easiest method would be to make her voluntarily head out to meet them. The average princess would require the use of a carriage, which risked drawing attention, but Mia could handle a horse on her own. It was therefore possible for them to direct her to far more distant locations.

"They've apparently arranged for a horse to be somehow delivered to me as well, but I see no reason to follow their playbook *that* closely," Mia mused as she entered the stable.

She made a beeline for Kuolan's stall and peeked in.

"Anybody home?"

Kuolan was indeed home. He turned his head and greeted her with his customary nostril twitch. She braced on reflex, but the hail of mucus didn't materialize.

"My, that's rare. I thought for sure you'd sneeze on me..."

She walked up to him and quietly began to put his harness on, the motions fluid and familiar. It was something she'd made a point of practicing in case she ever needed to make an emergency getaway by herself. She didn't think much of it, seeing it as a simple survival skill, but unbeknownst to her, Malong actually held her ability to outfit a horse on her own in very high regard.

Kuolan was giving her a look that seemed to say, "What, heading somewhere far?" She held his gaze for a second before inclining her head.

"I'm sorry, Kuolan...but I need you to lend me your strength. And, depending on how things go, maybe even your life..."

She had no idea if Kuolan could make it back alive after her death. It wasn't hard to imagine a horse running off to save itself if its rider took a tumble, but for some reason...she had a feeling Kuolan was made of truer stuff. Something told her this particular horse wouldn't abandon her. So she gently stroked his neck and spoke as earnestly as she could manage, hoping to convey her message through tone if not through language.

"Listen, Kuolan. Right now, I have no one else to turn to. You're the only one I can rely on. So I must ask you for a special favor... Will you come with me?"

Faced with this plea, Kuolan huffed out two long breaths from his nose. Then his lips spread into one of his signature grins, almost as if he understood her and was saying, "You betcha, boss. I'll get you through whatever they throw at you."

"My... How promising! I'll leave myself in your capable hooves then." She chuckled softly before turning to another steed. "And Kayou, please accept my apologies as well. I'll be borrowing Kuolan for a bit."

The mare made no perceptible reply. It simply gazed at her silently, eyes radiating intelligence.

With Kuolan by her side, Mia made for the harbor. Along the way, nobody paid any attention to her. With the festival under way, the streets were packed with people, and plenty were merchants whose horses were loaded with wares. Despite the natural camouflage, she couldn't help but worry about being found and stopped, so she ended up adopting a sneaking gait the whole way there. Frankly, her skulking only drew more attention to her, but regardless, she made it to the harbor without incident. Once there, it didn't take long for her to find her prescribed boat. It was of modest size but more than enough to ferry both her and Kuolan.

"Are you the merchant who's supposed to take me off the island?" she asked the man standing in front of the boat. He was middle-aged, and wore the textbook definition of a merchant's smile.

"That's me, miss. But uh...what's with the horse, if you don't mind my asking?" He cocked a brow at Kuolan.

"For riding, of course. He's my beloved steed, and he's going to take me on a long run."

That flustered the merchant.

"Wait a second, miss. Taking you off the island is risky enough, what with you being a princess and everything... Besides, I was told they've already got a horse waiting for you on the other side."

"My, whoever said so must have assumed I would ride any old horse, but that's simply not the case. The only horse I will ride is him, my own trusty steed," she said, glancing up at Kuolan, who in that moment did the unthinkable and *worked with her*, standing quiet and proud like a mount meant only for royalty.

"But still... Ferrying a horse is..."

"No problem, I'm sure. Especially if it will add some weight to your coin purse. Feel free to go to the people who arranged this deal with you and request a surcharge for this service. A full bag of gold sounds like reasonable compensation."

Never one to pass up a chance to pester her enemies, Mia promptly appropriated their coffers for her negotiation, in which she employed the highly satisfying tactic of parting with vast amounts of money that didn't belong to her. Just for good measure, however, she added the threat of a stick to her carrot.

"Or...would you rather defy me? In that case, I do hope you understand the consequences of doing so. Just so you're aware, I'm a very close acquaintance of Miss Rafina."

She went full high-and-mighty-Tearmoon-princess on the man, and felt not a shred of remorse doing so. This was, after all, someone who'd agreed to play a part in a wicked conspiracy. She had no sympathy for such individuals.

"Well? Which will it be? Forfeit the money and have your involvement in this reported to Miss Rafina, or ferry me and my horse across the lake?"

Thus, Mia departed Saint-Noel Island with Kuolan at her side, unaware that her peculiar behavior was, in fact, being watched...

Chapter 28: The First Loyal Subject and a New Friend

Asked to help with the preparations for the Holy Eve Festival, Anne was diligently hauling boxes to the cathedral.

I need to finish this quickly and go back to milady…but goodness, how is there so much still to do?

Saint-Noel fell under the jurisdiction of Belluga, so in general, it was rare for her, a Tearmoon maid attending to Mia, to be called upon to accomplish tasks for the academy at large.

I mean, with it being the Holy Eve Festival, I can understand how they might be short on hands, but…

In her eyes, the preparations Mia and the student council had made for the day were impeccable. It therefore seemed strange that there was such an urgent need for her help. Furthermore…

"Ugh, what rotten luck. I can't believe we're stuck doing stuff like this on the day of the festival. Hey, did you hear? Apparently, this is all because someone wrecked the candle stands in the cathedral or something, so we have to bring in replacements."

The grumblings of a fellow maid working with her only deepened her concern.

Wrecking things in the cathedral? Who in the academy would do such a thing?

The more she thought about it, the more she felt a rising sense of apprehension.

Whatever the case, let's get this done quickly...

Just as she quickened her pace, a familiar figure crossed her vision. "Huh? Is that...Mia?"

She spotted Mia, who'd for some reason left the dorm and seemed to be heading for the stables. Though she caught only a brief glimpse of her face, the expression it bore was unmistakably weighty.

"What could be troubling her...?"

Though she was Mia's maid, they weren't together every hour of every day. There were plenty of times when Anne would be busy with something, or Mia would be out with her classmates. Saint-Noel Island was an environment that provided sufficient safety to allow such behavior.

Moreover, Mia was a rare example of a powerful princess with common sensibilities. She could, for example, do her own shopping. Every so often, in an attempt to avoid Anne's scrutiny, she'd sneak off to town on her own to buy snacks. Anne was well aware of this, of course, but she let it go, judging the frequency low enough to warrant a blind eye.

Due to this, seeing Mia make a solo trip out to town was no real reason for concern. It was perfectly possible that she just wanted to do some quick shopping. But that didn't explain the outfit.

"...And why is she wearing riding clothes?"

Considering she seemed to be headed to the stables, her attire did make sense. What didn't make sense was the timing. It would be evening soon, and the candlelight mass was about to start. Students were supposed to be changing into their ceremonial uniforms and gathering at the cathedral. Mia was doing neither of those things.

"She can't possibly be going somewhere far. It's too late for that..."

Anne continued toward the cathedral, but she felt increasingly uneasy. Mia had refused to promise that she'd take Anne with her if she was ever headed into danger. An image of Mia riding away into the distance, never to return, flashed across her mind.

"That…won't happen. It can't."

By all reasonable measures, the thought was nonsense. Mia wouldn't simply disappear. Nonetheless, something about this felt off. For the past few days, she'd been possessed by an odd aura. On top of that, yesterday, she'd abruptly thanked Anne for her services… Granted, it was a Holy Eve tradition to give thanks to the people who've helped you in your daily life, so the act alone was no grounds for suspicion, but when viewed in context…

"Mia…"

A dark dread began to fill Anne's heart. She jogged to the cathedral, dropped off the box, and then made a beeline for the stable.

"Mia…"

Her quiet repetition of her mistress's name soon rose to a frantic cry. "Milady! Mia! Where did you go?!"

"Wow, we're really late."

Tiona walked with hasty steps to the dorm. Finishing her archery practice had left her with little time to prepare for the ceremony.

"We won't make it in time for the mass at this rate. Let's run."

"Okay." Liora nodded. "Let's—"

Contrary to her words, she stopped dead in her tracks.

"Liora? What's wrong?"

"A voice…"

"What?"

"I hear…a voice…" Liora eyed the surroundings. "That way."

She broke into a run.

"Wait! Liora! What's going on?"

The clear sense of urgency in her attendant's pace convinced Tiona quickly to follow. Soon, the two came upon Anne, who was about to dash out of the academy's gate.

"Anne? What are you doing here?"

"Miss Tiona! Miss Liora!" exclaimed Anne as she ran toward them.

Tiona stiffened. Anne's face was shockingly pale, and tears glistened in her eyes.

"Did either of you see milady? She should have come this way... With a horse, probably..." she asked, sounding on the verge of panic as she held her hands before her.

The sight lit an anxious fire in Tiona as well, who'd been burdened with a similar kindling of unease ever since her dream in which she regretted not speaking to Mia once it was too late. Its smoldering had been steadily subsiding over the past few days, but now it burst again into flames. She'd told herself to relax, to wait until the festival was over, because they'd have plenty of time afterward to talk... If she really couldn't wait, she could even do so at the stew party the student council was hosting tonight.

Why the rush? asked her mind.

This is why, answered her heart.

Reason bowed to unease, and she acted on the latter.

"Come on, Anne. We'll look for her together. Liora, go tell Miss Rafina— Actually, she's probably busy. Prince Abel and Prince Sion then. Keithwood too. Whoever's free. Grab everyone you can find."

"Got it... You be careful too, Miss Tiona," Liora said before dashing off.

Tiona turned back to Anne.

"All right. We should get moving."

She led the way, forgetting in her haste to take off the quiver and bow she was carrying.

Chapter 29: She Who Believes in Citrina's Pure Heart

Bandoor Village was an abandoned settlement in the Holy Principality of Belluga. The scarlet light of sunset filtered through the rows of crumbling buildings, painting the area in a forlorn hue. It reminded Bel of home. Her real home. That alone seemed to herald the end of this wonderful dream.

In the center of the empty village was a clearing, likely a square where the people once gathered. A masked man stood there alone. Well, not completely alone. Laying obediently by him was a wolf.

Is that...a big dog? But I don't remember dogs having such scary-looking faces...

Bel's pondering was interrupted by a throaty chuckle.

"We do very much appreciate you keeping your word, Miss Bel. Your cooperation has allowed us to arrive here without any trouble," said a gleeful Barbara from behind her.

It reminded her of Lynsha, left for dead in the forest.

"I hope Miss Lynsha is okay..."

Her quiet murmur surprised Barbara.

"Oh? Worried about your attendant? Why bother? You won't ever see her again, so what happens to her shouldn't matter to you anymore."

Bel shook her head.

"It does matter to me. Even if I won't ever see her again, if I'm worried, then I'm worried. Isn't that how people should be?"

Her teacher, Ludwig, had told her to afford every courtesy to those who'd devoted themselves to her. Moreover…

That's how Miss Mia would feel. I know it is.

Her swift and resolute response made Barbara wrinkle her nose in disgust.

"Ugh, spare me your platitudes. Honestly, it's as if *you* were a princess too."

Then, the old woman's lips curled back into a grin, somehow even more sadistic than before, and she cupped Bel's face in her palms. The way she stared gave Bel the impression of a snake about to descend on its prey.

"So noble… So righteous… You sicken me, cursed girl."

Bel felt a sudden pressure on her shoulders. It took her a second to realize that Barbara had seized them. The force pushed her off balance and, with her hands tied behind her back, she fell painfully backward.

"Look at you," hissed Barbara. "Where's all your class now, hm?" Malicious sarcasm dripped from every word. "All the sublime dignity bestowed upon you by the order of this world? What a sorry sight you are. Or was all that regality an act? Are you…a fake princess?"

A cruel smile on her lips, Barbara pressed her face close to Bel's. Then she lifted her hand, primed to strike.

"Stop it, Barbara."

"Ah, Rina…"

Citrina stepped up to them, almost in defense of Bel, and glared straight up at Barbara.

"Don't do anything to hurt her."

"Oh? What's this, milady?" Barbara lifted an eyebrow. "Are you intending to maintain this facade of friendship?"

The old woman put a hand to her mouth in feigned surprise before snickering.

"Do you mean to play her *dear* friend right to the very end? Even after bringing her here?"

Citrina's shoulders twitched at the remark. Then, erasing all emotion from her countenance, Barbara brought her face close to Citrina's. With wide, monstrous eyes, she observed the girl for some time before whispering in her ear.

"Of course, we still have some time before Princess Mia arrives. Until then, go ahead and enjoy your little game. But I believe in you, milady. I believe that you're a splendid Serpent who won't hesitate to kill even her 'friends.' So long as you remember that, you can amuse yourself in whatever fashion suits."

She clapped her hands once, as if she'd just come upon an excellent idea.

"In fact, why don't I give the two of you some alone time."

"Huh?"

"I need to go discuss how we're going to kill the princess. In the meantime, I think you'll appreciate a chance to chat with your *friend*. After all, this will be your last chance. Then I think we'll have you kill her yourself. That should make for a nice little memento."

"W-Wait—"

Citrina reached out as Barbara turned to leave, but her little hand caught only empty air. Her attendant traded a few words with the wolf man before they walked away, leaving her alone with Bel. Her lips trembled, and she regarded Barbara's departing form with the helpless expression of an abandoned kitten.

That is a very nasty person, thought Bel, who puffed out her cheeks at Barbara. *I bet she's doing this because she knows it'll hurt Rina. She left us alone just to be mean to her.*

Seeing this, Bel decided to speak in a perfectly casual manner.

"Mmm. Hey, Rina, is it just me or is it getting sort of cold this evening?"

She shuffled toward the small bonfire burning in the center of the square. After a moment of appreciating its crackling flames, she turned toward Citrina.

"Heh heh. I was looking forward to seeing the Holy Eve Festival's bonfire, but this is a pretty good replacement," she said with the same bright smile she always wore.

Her blithe tone shocked Citrina, who fumbled for a response.

"That's...nice, I guess," Citrina said with a confused nod.

Then she regathered herself and put on her own usual sweet smile.

"Say, Bel, how about some tea? I'll go make some for us."

"Oooh, that sounds perfect. Now that you mention it, we were supposed to go for a picnic, weren't we?" Bel gazed up at the night sky, before continuing with a depth of emotion that sounded like it belonged to someone much older. "The moon's out...and it's so very beautiful. You know what? Picnics at night might be more fun than I expected."

For some time, she continued to gaze wordlessly at the cosmic canvas, turning only when Citrina returned.

"Hm? Rina?"

The young Yellowmoon stood beside her, a small knife in hand.

"Don't move..." she said, crouching down behind Bel. "You can't drink tea like this, after all."

With a smile, Citrina cut the ropes binding Bel's wrists.

"Why, thank you. They kept rubbing my skin and were starting to be a bit of a nuisance. You're so thoughtful, Rina," said Bel as she massaged her reddened skin.

Citrina gave a curt nod.

"That's good. The water's heating up right now, so why don't we chat for a bit?"

She lowered herself beside the bonfire and tossed the knife onto the ground nearby.

"Hey, Rina," Bel said with a frown, "you can't just leave knives lying around like that. It's dangerous."

Despite this admonishment, Citrina made no attempt to retrieve the knife. With a resigned shrug, Bel walked over and picked it up instead, holding it out for Citrina to take.

"Listen, Bel…" Citrina said, still refusing to even look at the small blade. "I want to give you…a chance. Because you're my friend. Go ahead and use that knife."

"…Eh?" Bel blinked, puzzled. "Use it how?"

"Like this, for example…"

There was a bewitching, almost feverish, glitter in Citrina's eyes as she turned toward Bel. She closed her hands around Bel's—around the hand that held the knife—and brought the blade to her own neck.

"You can take Rina hostage…and run away."

With doll-like charm, she tilted her head in a wordless *Well? What are you waiting for?*

"Um, you're joking, right?" asked Bel, stiffening at the proposal.

"Not at all. It's a long shot, but it's better than twiddling your thumbs and waiting, isn't it? Or maybe you'd rather just push it into my chest. I did something terrible to your attendant, after all. It'd be fair payback."

The eyes that looked up at Bel were large, endearing, and entirely serious.

"Either way could work. Better than nothing, anyway. So, what'll it be?"

"Hmm…"

Bel looked from her friend's face to the knife. With her other hand, she carefully pinched the flat of the blade between her fingers and held the handle out to Citrina.

"No thanks."

"Oh? Why is that? Didn't Her Highness tell you to hold tight the things you cherish? Should you be letting go so easily then? Giving up just like that? You do realize you'll be dead long before Her Highness gets here to save you."

However slim, it was still Bel's only chance to survive. To refuse the opportunity, then, was to surrender her life. Or so it seemed to Citrina. Bel only shook her head.

"It's not giving up." She closed her eyes. "And I'm not letting go."

There was no deception in her voice. No bitterness. Her words were honest and pure. She knew that she had not given up, for Citrina's palm remained clasped in hers. She still held tight to that which she cherished.

"Then why won't you take arms and fight back?" asked Citrina, still puzzled. "If you take Rina hostage, you might be able to escape."

"Because I feel like if I do that, I won't ever get you back."

"...What?" Citrina all but froze. "Get...Rina back?"

She stared blankly, confused by the statement's meaning. Bel looked her in the eyes.

"I've been thinking, Rina. For a long time now. About how best to hold on to the things that are important to me. Because you're my friend, Rina, I've been thinking about how I can get you back... Get our friendship back. I thought really hard, but..." Bel let out a bashful laugh and scratched her head. "I'm not very smart, so I still don't know. If it was Miss Mia, she'd probably figure it out in a snap, but I still have no idea."

Citrina's expression faded, her face becoming an unreadable mask.

"Friendship... Seriously, Bel? Do you even understand what is happening? I was just pretending to be your friend. To get close to you. To manipulate you."

"You say that, but I know it's a lie."

"Why? What makes you so sure?"

Bel, not breaking her gaze, placed her hand on Citrina's chest.

"Because of this, Rina. You're still wearing the charm I gave you."

The troya Bel had given her as a gift did indeed still dangle from her neck.

"...That's it? Are you really that dense, Bel? This was just a trick to get you to trust me."

Citrina smiled her best villainous smile. It was a pale imitation of both. It was betrayed by the tightness with which her fingers wrapped themselves around the charm. The protective motion was subconscious, urgent, and revealing.

"Even so, it still makes me happy."

Bel continued to speak. With the determination of someone trying to retrieve something dear, she kept trying, hoping her words would reach Citrina's heart.

"I was so glad, Rina. You're the first friend I ever made, and I got to give you a gift I made with my own hands. And you kept it. And even wore it. It made me so happy. I'm *still* happy..." She gently took Citrina's hands in hers. "That's why I decided to hold on as tightly as I can. Because I cherish our friendship. And I won't ever let go."

Citrina's face twitched. For a moment, it looked as if she were about to cry, but her ubiquitous smile won again. She wore it like a shield, keeping both others' and her own feelings at bay.

"Tell me, Bel... Do you understand what I was doing? I was trying to kill you, you get that? Because I'm a Serpent. That's what I do. I kill people. Even my friends. Even your beloved Miss Mia."

Bel, unfazed by this admission, smiled playfully.

"In that case, I'll let you in on a secret. It's a very *secret* secret, but I'll tell you because you're my friend." She lowered her voice to a dramatic whisper. "The truth…is that I've come *this* close to being killed before. Actually, I probably still am this close. Once I wake up from this dream, I'm going to be killed by a bunch of terrifying men I've never met before."

"…What?"

"That's why…I don't really mind all that much. If I have to point a weapon at my friend to survive, then I'd rather let my friend kill me… because I don't want to give up. I'd rather die…still true to the things that matter to me. Besides…"

And that was when her earnest passion gave way to levity.

"This is Grandmother Mia we're talking about. I'm pretty sure she won't die quite so easily. She's the Great Sage of the Empire, after all," she said with immense pride.

Chapter 30: She Who Believes in Citrina's Mushroom Heart

Mia stepped off the boat and promptly shuddered at the gloom surrounding her. A backward glance revealed the distant glow of a torch-lit Saint-Noel, its glimmering form a stark reminder of the world she'd inhabited just a few short hours ago, and the one in which she now stood. The moon alone saved her from absolute darkness. Slowly, her eyes began to adapt to its faint light.

"Well, it looks like I'll manage... Hey, you, tell me something. Where exactly is this Bandoor Village supposed to be?"

"Bandoor Village? That'd be past the grassland to the north. There's an old road that leads there, but the place has been abandoned for years. Nothing but broken buildings and... Oh, but I guess that makes it the perfect place for a secret date, doesn't it?"

The merchant gave her a conspiratorial grin. Clearly, his mind was enjoying a swim through the gutter. Mia, however, found this an enlightening thought. No wonder he hadn't asked any questions about the absence of her attendant. A self-absorbed princess intent on slumming...would certainly shun the company of attendants. It was indeed the perfect cover story for her sneaking off the island alone. In this merchant's eyes, she was undoubtedly the spitting image of young, enamored royalty with more passion than sense. Which was perfectly fine; she couldn't care less what the man thought of her.

"If I just have to follow a road, then that seems doable," she said, looking to the north.

"If you're worried about getting lost, you can use that horse." The man pointed. "I'm told it knows the way there."

Mia followed his finger to find a…somewhat unimpressive steed. It paled considerably next to Kuolan. Which was not exactly a fair assessment. Having seen nothing but a string of moonhares since the fall—credit to Kuolan, Kayou, and Skyred Hare—she'd developed what was probably an overly critical eye with regard to equine quality.

Out with the mushroommeister, in with the mountmeister.

"The thought is appreciated," she said, shaking her head, "but I'll ride my own horse, thank you very much."

Hmph, I mean, it's probably not a bad horse, but Kuolan's definitely faster. I bet they gave me this horse because they knew that even on the off chance I try and escape, it's slow enough for them to catch me without any trouble. Nice try, but I've got you figured out.

"All right, then…"

She gave Kuolan's neck a pat, gripped his saddle, then began pumping her legs rhythmically as she chanted in decidedly grandmotherly fashion, "And a one, and a two, and *upsy-daisy*," before climbing onto its back with an emphatically laborious grunt on the "up." To her credit, warming up one's muscles before exertion was a good idea. The chanting and grunting were perhaps extraneous, but if it prevented her from throwing out her back, then, well…more power to her.

Note that it was definitely not because age was taking its toll after her long years spent out of shape. She was fresh as a daisy and no one may say otherwise!

The merchant watched her antics with disinterest.

"If you say so. Watch yourself out there."

He promptly returned to the boat. Mia wondered if he had more passengers to ferry. Would he pick up some other merchants waiting to depart? Or, emboldened by this experience, would he assist in ferrying other students off the island as well? There was certainly no shortage of couples who'd jump at the opportunity to sneak off the island on a secret date.

He'd be a fool to do so. If Miss Rafina catches him, he'll never hear the end of it. But that's his business. Everyone must reap what they sow, after all…

She had neither the time nor the desire to warn him. He'd made his choices, and whatever befell him afterward would simply be his just deserts.

"Let's go, Kuolan."

Her steed's gruff whinny echoed through the moonlit grassland.

The merchant had spoken true, and Mia soon came upon a road leading north. Guided by the faint lunar light, she followed the road toward the abandoned town.

"This road looks as abandoned as the village."

She'd expected as much. These people were about to commit some seriously evil deeds. They'd obviously choose a secluded place to do so. Unfortunately, foreknowledge of this fact did not make it any less daunting to traverse the grasslands alone.

"Ooooh… I heard it's pretty safe around here, but who knows if that's really true? What if I run into some wild animals? Getting assassinated sounds terrible, but getting eaten sounds even worse! Ugh, I hate this…"

The ominous darkness ahead seemed like perfect cover for ferocious beasts to lie in wait, ready to pounce. As soon as this thought crossed her mind, everything suddenly seemed a lot scarier. Her timid heart sought comfort and found it in the unflappably steady steps of Kuolan, who marched down the path without the slightest sense of concern. Matching the rhythm of his gait—something she'd grown accustomed to after all the practice she'd had—gave her a familiar task to focus on that dampened her rising dread.

"I'm counting on you, Kuolan. The second a scary beast shows up, we're making a run for it, okay?"

"Neeeigh."

Kuolan replied in Horse and turned his head toward her as if to say, "Leave it to me, boss!" Slightly reassured by the gesture, Mia smiled.

"By the way, is it just me or do you seem a lot happier lately? Are things going well with Kayou?"

"Neee-ei-eigh."

"Is that so? Well, good for you. But remember to be nice to your kid, okay? And make sure you never force them to call you 'papa,' or they'll hate you for it."

Alas, the encroaching terror proved too much, and she cracked. In a desperate attempt to distract herself, she'd begun to have a conversation with her horse! Not even Malong of the proud Kingdom of Equestria could manage such a sublime feat of interspecies communication. It was the kind of thing that made one worry if one day, she'd find herself disgusted by the barbarism of humans and gallop away to join her brethren in the land of the horses.

Her potential renunciation of membership in human society aside…

The pleasant chat she was having with Kuolan came to an abrupt end when a shadow leapt into view.

"Eeek!"

Mia all but jumped in place. Kuolan, already breaking into a run, was stopped by the shadow placing itself squarely in their path. The horse let out a low, rumbling grunt. While usually bold to the point of belligerence, he held his ground cautiously and refrained from any sudden movement, for he recognized the creature that stood before them…

"I-Is that a wolf?"

And a huge one at that. It stood tall as Kuolan and had thick muscles enveloping its frame. It was the very image of power. Compared to the horse, it was a different beast—literally. Whereas the former's body was meant for running, the latter's was clearly built to pounce and kill. The wolf fixed Mia with its predator's gaze, sending a chill up…nowhere, actually.

My, how odd. I don't seem to be all that scared. A glare from Dion is far more terrifying.

As it turns out, her frequent encounters with the Empire's Finest Mia-Beheader had caused her to inadvertently develop a tolerance to menacing glares and murderous gazes. On top of that…

Hm, as a matter of fact, this wolf doesn't even look like it means to attack us.

She'd even developed the ability to distinguish between different flavors of menacing glares. A budding connoisseur of murderous intent, she was well on her way to becoming a murdermeister!

…Perhaps murdermeister isn't the best term to use. Anyway.

The wolf shot a glance at her face, then spun around and began walking down the path. It seemed to be acting as a guide.

"Maybe this wolf…is one of our enemy's minions?"

She recalled the passage in the Princess Chronicles describing how she'd been gobbled up by wolves. At a glance, the account suggested that her enemies had simply killed her and disposed of her corpse in the wild. Given the behavior of this wolf, however, it seemed plausible that her furry foes actually had an active paw in both her death and the subsequent concealment of the evidence.

"Regardless, it looks like it's not going to attack us right away. Let's follow the wolf for now, Kuolan."

"Nee-eigh."

As usual, Kuolan responded in Horse.

After trailing the wolf for a time, Mia came upon a creepy, clearly-abandoned village.

"This must be Bandoor Village, then? Which means…"

Beyond the dilapidated ruins of houses, the red flicker of flames emanated from the center of the village.

"That bonfire must be where Bel is being held."

With a heavy sigh, she dismounted and gave Kuolan's neck a pat.

"Stay on your toes, Kuolan. Or whatever the horse version of toes is. I want you to be ready to run at a moment's notice."

She left the final part unsaid.

Not that we're likely to be given the chance.

No matter how she imagined things playing out, successfully rescuing Bel and riding off to safety with the two of them on Kuolan's back just didn't seem like a realistic outcome.

Which is fine, I guess… After all, my main objective here is to figure out who's actually behind all this.

"Ah, Your Highness. You've arrived."

Suddenly a voice that matched the darkness of the night entered her ears. Startled, she spun toward it to find…

"Welcome to our temporary abode. We are most honored to have you. Oh? And what horse might that be?"

…A woman with her head lowered in a curtsy so jarringly formal it left no doubt as to its insincerity.

"You…" said Mia, realizing she recognized the woman. "You're Miss Barbara. Which means…"

Barbara chuckled.

"Indeed. This way please. Oh, the horse can stay. You alone will be more than sufficient."

"…You're not planning to have that wolf eat my horse, are you?"

"There's no need to worry. The wolf is well-trained, and it has been strictly instructed to never eat *horses*."

Mia let go of Kuolan's reins with extreme reluctance.

"Well, I'm off then. Listen, Kuolan. If things go south, you go south too, okay? Don't wait."

With that, she walked to the bonfire.

"Ah—"

Standing there were Bel, hands bound behind her back, and a masked man with a wolf at his side. Mia's eyes, however, were pulled to the figure of the third person.

"Ah... So it was you, Rina..."

Beside Bel was Citrina.

"Greetings, Your Highness," Citrina said with a sweet smile. "I'm honored that you decided to make the long and arduous journey here."

She held her skirt daintily and curtsied.

"You're too modest," Mia replied. "You went to all the trouble of inviting me. The least I could do was show up."

As she engaged in this surreal back-and-forth, the conversation she'd had with Ludwig at the end of last summer echoed in her mind.

She really pulled the wool over my eyes. I was warned that the Yellowmoons were suspicious, and yet... What a terrible failure on my part...

Though mortified by how thoroughly she'd been deceived, she still couldn't bring herself to think badly of Citrina. What if, she wondered, there were extenuating circumstances? Wasn't it possible that for some reason, she'd had no choice but to obey the instructions of bad people?

Thinking back, it was thanks to her that Kayou managed to give birth to her foal. Citrina really saved the day. Things would probably have turned out much worse if she hadn't stepped in. Would someone like that...willingly take part in evil?

Despite the damning context, Mia continued to grasp at straws in a stubborn refusal to believe that Citrina was evil. She grasped, however, not out of desperation but conviction, for you see...

Besides, Citrina likes mushrooms, and nobody who likes mushrooms can be a bad person. Therefore, there must be something forcing her to do this!

...She firmly believed that one of those straws would support the weight of her confirmation bias. As the Mushroom Princess, she deemed it a simple fact of nature that mushroom lovers were all good people. And Citrina, with her vast troves of fungal knowledge, had to be extra good!

Just for the record, Barbara wasn't there for the mushroom hunting trip, so she didn't count. There was no doubt in Mia's mind that the old woman was evil through and through.

But that leaves me with a tough decision... Can I trust Citrina here and now?

Needless to say, extenuation was not absolution. Unwilling or not, the fact remained that Citrina was complicit in Bel's kidnapping. However, her extenuating circumstances would be significant when the time came for her to atone. After all, if she was inherently good, then she might be persuaded to become an ally.

After a brief but intense moment of consideration, Mia made up her mind.

All right. I'm going all in. Whatever happens, I'm going to believe in Rina until the very end.

Her reasoning was, again, very simple.

Because nobody who loves mushrooms can be a bad person! It's a physical impossibility!

She instinctively knew this to be true. It was like a sixth sense. A Mushroom Prinsense, if you will. Emboldened by this infallible logic, she spoke.

"Rina...I know that you have your reasons for doing this. That you've been given no choice."

Her voice was calm and confident, as though it were rooted in an abundance of certainty. Having decided that she'd believe in Citrina until the very end, Mia fixed her with an unwavering gaze.

And if I'm wrong, and she's actually rotten to the core, well... That's fine too, because I'm going to die here either way. It doesn't even matter!

And thus, it was revealed that her belief was predicated on decisional irrelevance. The Mushroom Princess's resolve was as tough as her title! That is, soft, squishy, and a great dish for individuals without teeth!

"...Huh?"

Citrina froze. The dubious derivation of Mia's words did not diminish their impact.

"...Why?" Citrina said after a long pause, the confidence in her mien giving way to distress. "Why you too? How come you're saying the same things to Rina too?"

"Why, you ask? Because I don't think you'd do this willingly, of course. I believe in you, Rina."

No one who likes mushrooms can be a bad person! Driven by her unshakable faith in the character-elucidating power of mushrooms, Mia continued to speak with confidence.

"Talk to me, Rina. Tell me why. You're being forced to do this, right? I know you are. You're Bel's friend. There's no way you'd do this willingly."

"Miss Mia..." Bel brightened slightly at Mia's words. "That's right. I thought it was weird too. Rina wouldn't do this by herself. She's obviously being bullied into it by bad people!"

The young girl then glared at Barbara, who shrugged calmly as the look bounced off her.

"Oh, how blessed are the ignorant. Mmm... I wonder what you'd think if you knew what milady has done..."

"No! Barbara, don't!" begged a visibly distraught Citrina.

Barbara rolled her eyes before turning to Mia.

"Why even ask such questions in the first place, hm, Your Highness? What can you possibly do with the answer? You won't be leaving here alive, after all."

As she finished the last word, the wolf rose slowly to its feet from beside its master, like an executioner waiting for their cue. Mia's heart skipped a beat at the sight. She quickly chanted the magic phrase three times.

It's better than Dion… It's better than Dion… It's better than Dion!

Somehow, she felt a little less scared afterward. Mia's little fear-repelling spell actually seemed to work. It came at the cost of a vision of Dion, eyebrow raised in displeasure at having his image appropriated for her wizardry. She quickly swatted the unnerving picture out of her mind.

Have no fear, me! Sure, this is a dangerous situation, but it's nothing compared to having Dion Alaia come after my head!

She smiled boldly back at Barbara.

"My, that's rather presumptuous of you. Sure, I might die here, but that won't be the end of me. There are plenty of things I can do with the answer afterward."

The look she gave the old woman was a silent declaration of *Like going back to the past and ruining all your evil plans!*

"…Now, now. Nobody likes a sore loser, Your Highness."

"*Am* I being a sore loser, Barbara?"

She technically was. Mostly, at least. There was no guarantee she could make the trip through time again. But Mia was no featherless fledgling. She might be a chicken, but she was a chicken that had *seen some shit.* So, she posed the question with her chest held high and arms akimbo.

"...Perhaps a play for time then. But—"

Just as Barbara frowned in contemplation, she disappeared from view! Rather, *everything* disappeared from view. A sudden eruption of thick white smoke enveloped everything.

"What the—" exclaimed a bewildered Mia.

With her sight hampered, her nose took up the slack, picking out a scent in the white smog. It was faint, but she recognized it— lucioluna grass. Specifically, the bath herbs she'd used. The next instant, something slammed into her.

"Yeeow!"

She fell down with a shriek. Looking up, she discovered that the one who'd crashed into her was...

"Bel?!"

"Miss Mia?!"

...Bel, and her arms were no longer tied behind her.

Chapter 31: A Radiant Princess Mia Lights Up the Dark Night!

The smoke filled the area in an instant, but Bel was watching during that instant, so she saw everything. It all happened in a heartbeat right in front of her eyes.

While Barbara was distracted, Citrina had walked over to the bonfire, where she'd picked up the water she'd boiled for tea...and dropped something in. An explosion of white smoke immediately followed. Soon, no one dared move, for not a thing could be seen. Or so Bel had thought until she felt the rope around her arms give way.

"...Huh?"

Surprised by the sudden freedom, she was about to turn around when a shove to her back sent her lurching forward. Behind her, a faint voice echoed in the smog.

"...Goodbye, Bel. Be well."

"Huh? Rina?! Ri— Ow!"

Stumbling headfirst through the thick smoke, she promptly crashed into someone else.

"Yeeow!"

The victim let out an undignified shriek. It was, of course, none other than the person who was supposed to be coming to her rescue.

"...Huh? Miss Mia!"

"Wha— Bel?! How?"

Mia's astonishment lasted for only a second, for she soon realized something else.

Wait, this is our chance! Time to scram!

Fortunately, mental flexibility was one of her strong points, and she quickly burst into motion.

"Kuolan!"

She urgently called her steed's name, the slim window of opportunity affording her no time for further instruction. Kuolan didn't need any. He charged through the smoke and stopped at her side. Mia deftly flipped onto its back and hoisted Bel up in front of her.

…Well, that was how she envisioned it, anyway.

In actuality, her bestriding process included her usual sequence of preemptive leg pumping and motivational chanting, which was followed by an intensely laborious and decidedly ungraceful effort to heave Bel onto the saddle. Still, the sheer urgency of the situation had triggered a primal amplification of Mia's physical prowess, and she ultimately managed to get both of them seated fairly quickly.

"B-But Rina!" exclaimed Bel, peering desperately into the smoke. "She's still—"

"We can't help her. Not right now. But…" Mia paused to gaze into the smog as well. Then, she continued, "We *will*. One way or another, we'll come back to save her. But for now, we *run*!"

With that, she gave the order.

"Go, Kuolan! Get us out of here!"

Thus began the most dramatic escape of Mia's life, wherein a desperate flight for survival would culminate in an epic race between heroine and villain.

At Mia's command, Kuolan all but exploded into motion, instantly breaking into a full-speed gallop. She wrapped her arms around Bel and pressed their bodies forward to withstand the intense shift in momentum that threatened to fling them off. Smoke surrounded them on all sides, impairing Mia's sense of direction. Which wasn't much of a problem, actually, thanks to a potent technique she'd acquired through her autumn riding practice.

Mia, you see, had mastered the Flotsam—the secret art of reinless riding in which the rider conformed to the horse. In other words, she just let Kuolan do whatever he wanted and tried her best not to get in the way. So long as the horse knew how to get back, they'd be fine. All she had to do was blankly stare off into the distance for a while.

They soon broke through the smoke. A quick glance backward revealed a large cloud of brilliant white had swallowed the entire village. Brilliant, as in *glowing*.

"That…must be the same bath herbs that Chloe gave me."

She recalled when she'd gone to the bathhouse with Tiona, and how Citrina had shown up soon after.

Does that mean she asked Chloe to give her some? If so, that would suggest Rina saw this coming and was intending on helping us from the very beginning…

The thought threatened to pull her into a bout of rumination. She shook it out of her mind.

"There's no point mulling it over right now. The most important thing is that we managed to get away. Once we're back together with everyone, we can figure out a way to rescue her. Oh, but we'll need a boat to get back on the island… That merchant is almost certainly gone by now. I guess that means we'll have to hide somewhere and wait until morning. The moon's out tonight, but it's still pretty dark everywhere. It can't be that hard to find a hiding— Hm?"

It was then that Mia noticed a strange phenomenon. For some reason, her immediate surroundings looked…brighter than they should be. She glanced upward, wondering if the moonlight had grown brighter. It seemed the same as before. She looked back down. And that was when she realized the source of the enhanced illumination…was them!

Specifically, it was her and Bel who were glowing. Kuolan had not turned radiant. The pale light highlighted their forms against the dark backdrop of night, making it look as if they were floating. At a distance, they resembled a pair of fairies darting through the air. If a certain author of supposedly nonfiction content had witnessed the sight, the Princess Chronicles would surely have gained another few passages of spectacular nonsense.

"How— What in the moons is this?"

A moment's confusion, but clarity soon followed. To digress a tad, while Mia's little gray cells generally existed in a state of perpetual inaction, there were a couple of trigger words that could excite them. "Sweets" for one. "Mushrooms" too. But there was another… Any time "bath" was mentioned, her brain would go into overdrive. And what among recent events involved the bath? The bath herbs, of course, and their pleasant aroma. The aroma of lucioluna grass…

"Lucioluna grass… Lucioluna… Wait, *lucio*luna? That sounds like it glows!"

It hadn't occurred to Mia until that moment, but the name's etymology spoke for itself. Lucioluna grass—a grass that gives off light when the moon is out. Naturally, bath herbs made from it would have the same property. This fact had unfortunately eluded her due to its pale light being unnoticeable when it was bright out. Unfortunate, because right now, it was not bright out, and its light was definitely not unnoticeable.

"Okay, this might be useful when I'm walking around at night, but how am I supposed to hide…" she muttered amidst a mounting sense of panic.

Only for that panic to triple when three glowing forms burst out of the shining white smoke behind her. All imbued with the same light, it was impossible to mistake their identities—the masked man atop a horse and two massive wolves!

"Eeeeek! They're coming! They're coming for us, Kuolan!"

Her shriek proved unnecessary, as Kuolan had already sped up at the first sight of their pursuers. She almost bit her tongue as the violent acceleration hit her like an invisible wall. With a grunt, she hunkered down as her steed went from fast gallop to furious gallop. And so, once again, she became the wind.

…But the wind wasn't fast enough!

A quick glance backward was followed by a terrified shriek.

"Eeeeeeek! They're getting closer! Kuolan! They're catching up!"

She could barely believe her eyes, particularly because she knew how fast Kuolan was. Yet the man's horse was undoubtedly gaining on them. Like a spectral knight of death, his glowing silhouette grew closer second by terrifying second.

He was so damn *fast*!

For a moment, Mia considered the possibility that the combined weight of her and Bel was slowing Kuolan down, but she quickly dismissed the notion.

"No, I can't be that heavy… Kuolan should be able to handle the two of us no problem."

She was soon proven right as the pair of wolves began to fall behind. Kuolan wasn't slow. Her foe's horse was just too fast!

"F-F-Faster, Kuolan! Come on, please go faster!"

All she got for her efforts was a curt huff. There was a hint of irritation to it, as if to say, "Ah shaddap, I'm gallopin' here!"

Little did she know, her desperate moonlit flight had only just begun.

Chapter 32: Extending the Thin Thread of Fate

That's…a moonhare. Must be one of the horses that Equestria ceded to Saint-Noel Academy. A fine steed. But…

The wolfmaster coolly regarded the fleeing princess and her horse. For whatever reason—the smoke, perhaps—she was glowing, which granted him a clear view of how she rode.

Not a bad rider, this Princess Mia. She's giving her horse free rein.

Doubly impressive was the sight when accounting for the fact that she maintained good form while supporting a younger girl who wasn't used to riding. Triply, perhaps, given her gender and regal status…

Unfortunately for her…it's not enough to outrun me.

He calmly uttered a command to his horse.

"…Go, Eilai."

His steed, its black-silver hair gleaming, let out an affirmative whinny. It promptly upped its speed, leaving their lupine escort in the dust. Within seconds, the gap all but closed. He drew his sword. Its blade caught the moon and gleamed with menace.

"…I shall have your head."

"Eeeeeeek!"

There were but three horse-lengths between him and his shrieking prey. In response, the fleeing horse increased its speed as well, and the gap grew again. It also kicked a splatter of dirt at him.

A smart horse then. Very good.

The wolfmaster veered left to evade the projectile, briefly distancing himself from Mia. Then, preserving his momentum, he traced a semicircle back toward her to cut her off. As he approached again, however, his eyes caught something in the distance.

Hm? What's that?

In the all-encompassing gloom, there was a small red flicker. It arced through the air…right at his head!

"Hngh!"

He quickly swiped at it with his sword. A brief sensation of impact was followed by a burst of flames nearby.

"A fire arrow?"

Soon after, a girl's voice echoed through the night.

"Your Highness!"

He peered ahead into the darkness from which the fiery missile had come. The light emanating from him, though faint, was nonetheless hampering his own vision. Still, he could make out the outline of a horse with two riders. One held the reins and the other a bow.

Attendants, then. Here to rescue the princess. Very well.

Anne and Tiona had been furiously trying to track down Mia's whereabouts on Saint-Noel Island. Fortunately for them, many of the townspeople were familiar with Mia, and it hadn't taken long for them to discover that she'd left the island by boat. The sight of a Saint-Noel student with a horse had been peculiar enough to leave an impression, and thanks to Anne's tireless efforts to maintain good relations with folks throughout the town, many had willingly come to the flustered maid's aid.

With this new knowledge, the pair of them had decided to follow Mia off the island. With the help of a merchant Anne was well-acquainted with, they'd managed to procure a boat.

"The problem is what we do once we get to the other side..." said Tiona as she narrowed her eyes worryingly at the darkness across the lake.

Their leads had ended with "Mia left the island." After that, the trail might go cold. Was it even possible to find out more by asking around?

"Hey, Anne, you got a second?" asked the merchant, who approached the two anxious girls. "See, normally, I'd take you to the dock on the other side, but people are gonna raise a ruckus if they find out I took students off the island, so I'm gonna have to drop you off some place where people aren't watching."

The merchant's words only darkened their despair. Whoever ferried Mia across the lake would surely have done the same. Searching for witnesses would be futile. Just then, they came upon another boat heading in the opposite direction.

"Huh. Funny. Didn't expect anyone else to come this way."

Hearing the merchant's puzzled tone, the two girls traded a look. "Do you think..."

"...That that's the boat Her Highness was on?"

They ran to the back of the boat and studied the craft making its way toward Saint-Noel. There was no way to stop it and question whoever was aboard. But...

"Excuse me, but could you head toward the place that boat came from and let us off there?" asked Anne.

It was abundantly clear to the two of them that Mia had been caught up in some serious trouble. Once she got off her boat, she wouldn't have sat there twiddling her thumbs. They knew this, and yet, they could only hope against hope that they'd find her there.

"Milady... Please."

Anne's desperate prayer was ultimately in vain. Upon disembarking they found no trace of Mia. With their last ray of hope fading into the all-consuming darkness, they nonetheless mounted a stubborn effort to search the area. Alas, by the time the torch they'd received from the merchant yielded its last flicker, glistening grief was openly flowing down Anne's cheeks.

"Milady… Where…did you go…" she said through short, gasping sobs.

"Anne!" Tiona gasped and pointed. "Look!"

Anne wiped a hand across her tear-blurred eyes and looked in the direction of Tiona's outstretched arm.

"Huh? Is that…"

Tethered loosely to a tree was the unmistakable outline of a horse.

"What is a horse doing out here?"

Tiona regarded it with puzzlement. Anne did too, but only for a second before her expression hardened with resolve.

"Miss Tiona, please get on behind me."

"Huh? What?"

Anne gripped the sides of the saddle. Her fingers tightened as she remembered—again, for how could she ever forget—that day… when they went to the Kingdom of Remno without her. The day she was left behind. She'd wanted nothing more than to be at Mia's side at all times. It was her greatest wish, but it was betrayed. Because she didn't know how to use the thing in her hands right now. Because she couldn't ride.

So, she'd begun practicing, the words *never again* fueling her as she struggled to learn. She already had enough regret to last her the rest of her life. She would not allow the saddle to separate her from Mia a second time.

And now, a horse had appeared before her. Mia was doubtless in serious trouble, and fate had deemed fit to present her with a horse. What she should do next was abundantly clear.

"Whenever milady rides, she always lets the horse have its way. I should do the same…"

Anne's equestrian role model was Mia. She'd watched her mistress closely whenever she rode, and as a result, she now considered the Flotsam to be the ideal way to ride. Which…wasn't entirely correct, but anyway…

Her mind was made up. She was going to follow in the footsteps of her dear mistress, both in method and in spirit.

"Hurry, Miss Tiona!"

"U-Um, right. Okay. I'm coming," said Tiona, who quickly mustered her own resolve and followed Anne up onto the horse, seating herself behind the maid.

Anne took one last glance back to make sure Tiona was seated firmly behind her, then spurred the horse into motion. She knew not where she was headed. She simply let the horse have its way.

Completely unaware, of course, that it was a horse specifically prepared by the Chaos Serpents to deliver Mia to their meeting spot.

"Anne! Over there!"

After a period of bumpy riding while holding Anne for support, Tiona caught a glimmer in the distance. It was a faint light, but there was something enchanting about the way it glided toward them like a moon fairy soaring through the nightscape. And when she fixed her eyes upon it, she realized that the light was emanating from a person astride a horse. A person who happened to be…

"Eeeeeeeek!"

…Screaming her lungs out in a voice that Tiona recognized at once.

"That's…Her Highness!" exclaimed Anne.

They'd found her at last. And right in the nick of time, it seemed.

"Is she in danger?"

There was a sense of desperation to Mia's shrill cry.

I've never heard Her Highness let out an undignified scream like that, thought Tiona. *She must be in serious trouble!*

That alone was enough to convince her that Mia's life was in grave and immediate danger. Of course, Mia was actually a frequent emitter of undignified screams and pathetic squeals, but in Tiona's mind, she was a paragon of poise and coolheaded composure.

"Hold us steady, Anne. I'm going to give her some cover fire."

She drew an arrow from the quiver on her back. It was a standard practice arrow, but its tip had been modified to burn. She held the arrowhead to her newly-acquired torch, and it burst promptly into vigorous flames.

Amazing as always, Liora. It works like a charm.

She spared a moment to give silent thanks. Then, she nocked the arrow.

The revolution in Remno had left more than one person with heart-wrenching regret. Tiona as well recalled that time with bitter frustration.

"I couldn't do anything…"

She'd *been there.* Right beside Mia. But she hadn't done a thing. Useless from beginning to end. Haunted by regret, she'd resolved to pick up archery, hoping it would give her strength. To fight, yes, but far more importantly, to do something—*anything*—to help Mia. To be *useful.*

She focused her gaze. Two shimmering objects wavered in the distance, both imbued with the same pale light. Which was the assailant and which was Mia? It was impossible to tell. Her arms tensed. A drop of sweat descended from her brow. Her aim had to be true; even the slightest risk of hitting Mia was unacceptable. But how could she tell? The bowstring trembled with her hand.

Which one is Her Highness? Is my aim good enough? Can I… Can I really do this?

Just then, one of the glowing figures veered wide. Then it followed a crescent path as it curved back toward the other. That was when she saw the flash. For a single, pivotal moment, a stray moonbeam fell upon the pursuing form. Within its faint radiance, there was a cold, harsh gleam.

"That's…a sword!"

The foe's blade was illuminated by the moon.

Her Highness would never fight with a sword! And there's some distance between them right now! From this angle… Now!

With decisive deftness, Tiona loosed the flaming arrow.

The blazing missile was a culmination of the girls' collective resolve. Pathos crystallized, it arced through the air like a shooting star. Anne alone would not have sufficed; she could have rode to the scene, but she'd be of little use afterward. Tiona could handle both horse and bow, but not both at once. Their presence here was, therefore, the result of their mutual effort. Their combined wills had borne the fruit of their timely arrival on the stage during the climactic scene of Mia's death-defying escape.

The fire arrow shot straight toward their foe.

Astray again. The attempts are growing increasingly laughable.

After the first arrow, subsequent shots all flew well over the wolfmaster's head. Their aim was laughably poor. Poorer yet was the choice to use fire; the flaming points betrayed their trajectory. This critical flaw meant that even if their aim had been true, he'd have little difficulty cutting them down. A concentrated volley to set the field ablaze could, perhaps, prove effective, but these pitiful attempts at marksmanship while illuminating the trails with fire was nothing but utter foolishness.

If not foolishness, then perhaps extreme caution? The arrows are made conspicuous to ensure the princess is not struck by accident...

They might have dissuaded the average bandit from further pursuit. For the wolfmaster, who'd cleaved the arrows of the Empire's Finest out of the air, they were but impotent distractions.

Though... While they pose no threat to me, they're still a nuisance. What is their purpose? With such poor aim, what if a stray shot finds its way toward the princess? Surely, she is no warrior. Visible though these shots are, how can they be sure she will evade them?

He had no trouble parrying arrows, but it seemed a tall order for the girls ahead.

...An idle worry for one whose head I'm about to claim. Last rites, then. Consider yourself prayed for, he thought as he signaled his horse to go faster.

He quickly gained on Mia. His sword raised, he swept it down across her neck. Rather...he was just about to when—

"On my cue!"

The archer ahead raised her voice. Her words stirred up a hint of doubt in his mind.

Cue? For what?

Was she speaking to the girl in front of her holding the reins? If so, what was there for her to do on cue? Was the message meant for the princess then? How was she meant to react? His doubt grew from an inkling to a cloud. Something wasn't adding up.

A split second later, another fire arrow flickered to life ahead. It flew toward him in a shallow curve. Perhaps it was their increased proximity, but this time, its aim was true, forcing him to swing his sword at the arrow instead of the princess. Then, mid-swing, his ears caught the dissonance.

Two sharp whistles. *Two* fletchings splitting the air.

Instantly, he dove forward, flattening himself against his steed. An arrowhead grazed his shoulder, its trajectory perpendicular to the other. His cloud of doubt finally cleared to reveal the answer.

Gah… A fine shot. So they had a second archer…

"Tsk… No bullseye."

Liora Lulu, her small form silhouetted against the dark grassland backdrop, clicked her tongue in annoyance.

"This time…I won't miss," she said, nocking a second arrow.

She'd been instructed by Tiona to go find help when they were still on the island. What was she doing here then, you ask? Well, there were a number of reasons, but they could more or less be summed up as "she was worried about Tiona."

Having astutely perceived the severity of the situation from Anne's perturbation, Liora'd done only the *bare minimum* necessary to technically comply with Tiona's instructions before setting out after her. She arrived at the dock just as a boat was pulling in. It was of course the boat belonging to the merchant who'd ferried Mia across the lake. Emboldened by his success, he'd returned to make some more quick cash.

"No goods to carry, the entry inspections are lax…and I'm paid in gold. All for ferrying one student off the island. Hah, this is great. I should build a business around this."

His buoyant mood did not last long. The karmic scythe came for him quickly, reaping the bitter fruits of his own deeds. Soon after landing, he was caught by the townspeople who'd witnessed Anne's distress. Putting two and two together, they quickly gave him the beating of his life, which Liora arrived just in time to witness.

With ample information in hand, she had a much easier time charting her course across the lake. Ultimately, she managed to catch up with Anne and Tiona in the middle of their mad dash across the grassland.

Suspecting an impending battle based on the merchant's confessions, she crafted some makeshift fire arrows, dulling the points to ensure they'd be less than lethal if one were to strike Mia by accident. They'd still hurt, of course. A *lot*. But Liora operated on the principle of "if there isn't a hole in you that I can see through, you're probably fine."

She's a rough-and-tumble sort of girl. It's part of her charm.

On top of that, she'd given Tiona a role to play as well. Handed a new torch and the improvised fire arrows, Tiona's job was to distract the enemy and keep them busy. In the process, she had to achieve the arguably more important goal of lighting up the surroundings so Liora would have an easier time aiming.

Tiona was certainly no pushover when it came to her bow arm. But with so much on the line, the slightest error could result in a tragically porous princess, so Liora had her mistress provide cover fire. She herself would shoulder the responsibility of shooting to kill.

Granted, it wasn't like Liora had divine providence on her side. There was still a chance of her hitting Mia by accident. It was just lower than Tiona's.

"Your Highness... If I hit you...I'm really sorry."

...Was Mia *really* going to make it out of this alive?

"Eeeeeeek!"

Mia shrieked in horror at the string of flaming missiles flying toward her.

"Gah! That was so close! Eeep! That one too! Dodge them, Kuolan! Dodge the— Eeeek! I think I felt that one! Bel, keep your head down, you hear?"

Objectively speaking, the arrows gave her a wide berth, but they whistled while flying past her, and that was more than enough to convince her inner chicken to put on a squawking concert.

Bel, meanwhile, just sat with her head down the whole time. Unlike Mia, this wasn't her first arrow-laced rodeo, so to speak. The surrounding commotion failed to fluster her. What worried her…

"Rina…"

…Was the friend they'd abandoned. So deeply did she dwell on this thought that nothing—not the flaming arrows overhead, nor the menacing pursuer behind them—could win her attention. She barely even heard her grandmother's rampant squeals inches away from her.

"Eeeeeeek! We're going to die! This is it! We're totally going to die!"

Not even that one.

Thus, Bel's image of her grandmother as a stolid, dignified individual would live to see another day. Rejoice, Mia!

Now, after a while, even a coward like Mia began to clue in to the fact that the fire arrows weren't coming anywhere close to hitting her. This realization brought about a measure of composure, allowing her to venture a glance backward. Her eyes immediately widened, for her assailant's horse had fallen a ways behind them.

"My, what's— Oh, I know! The fire arrows must have scared him into slowing down!"

Needless to say, Liora's sharpshooting went completely unnoticed by her.

"Oho ho, what a wimp, getting scared by shots like these. There's no way they'd ever hit us!" she said, gloating with extremely undeserved smugness, considering her behavior just moments before.

But that was just how her brain worked. It prioritized convenience over truth; inconvenient thoughts, whether true or not, were promptly discarded.

At this rate, I think I might actually have a chance of getting away!

Her spirits had just begun to lift when something heavy slammed into them from the side, knocking them—and herself—right back to the ground.

"Ah—"

"Gaaaaaaaaaah!"

You may figure out for yourselves which utterance came from who. Regardless, Mia and Bel were thrown from their steed and hit the ground rolling. As the world spun repeatedly on its axis, Mia caught a glimpse of the massive shadow that had tackled Kuolan. A shadow that was now bearing down on her menacingly.

O-Oh no… I completely forgot about the wolves.

Like the wolfmaster, Mia had also been distracted by the fire arrows and inadvertently slowed down. Consequently, the wolves managed to catch up, and one had knocked her from her horse. That was all. Just a slight lapse in concentration. And it had cost her dearly.

"Say your prayers."

The wolfmaster, already dismounted, walked up from behind the wolves.

Oh, stupid me, getting my hopes up… So this is it. It ends here, she thought as she gazed up at the blade in his hand. *I-I guess it's okay though. I figured out who the bad guys are, at least. Next time, I'll be able to do better. If…there is a next time…*

He approached her. She watched, counting the distance between them in steps. Five more… Four more…

She shut her eyes tight. With every ounce of will she could muster, she mouthed a silent prayer. What did she pray for, you ask?

Please! Please please please don't let it hurt too much!

What did you *think* she was going to pray for?

The pain…never came. Instead, there was the sharp ring of metal meeting metal.

"…Sorry, but no prayers today. She's important. To me, and to everyone. I won't let you lay a finger on her."

Thus, Liora Lulu's bare minimum had arrived on the scene. Upon returning to the academy, the first person she'd found had been…

"A-Abel!"

Abel Remno winced bashfully at Mia's effusive gasp.

"Oh, merciful moons! Abel! You're here! You came for me! Ooooh, thank the moons, Abel's here to save me!"

Mia's exuberant cries of joy were not matched by Abel. He kept his eyes trained firmly on his foe. Every one of his hairs stood on end. Nervous sweat seeped from his palms. The man in front of him was dangerous. Everything about him, from the poise in his stance to the tilt of his blade, screamed *deadly*. Abel tightened his grip on his sword, knowing he was staring down an opponent rivaling Remno's champion, Bernardo Virgil the Adamantine Spear, or the Empire's Finest, Dion Alaia.

This man…is an expert killer. That much is certain.

Being very careful not to let the man out of his sight, Abel took in his surroundings.

The wolves are a problem. I need to do somethi— Hm?

Kuolan suddenly appeared behind them. He plodded leisurely to Mia's side before glaring at the wolves with a belligerent huff. He was joined by Abel's steed, Kayou, who placed itself in front of Mia as if to protect her.

The thought is certainly appreciated, but horses against wolves? I'm not sure…

He was promptly forced to reconsider when, to his surprise, the wolves glowered at the horses but stopped in their tracks.

"Huh. Son of a swordseller. I see what's going on."

It took him only a moment to decipher the situation. Horses were assets. Valuable ones. A swift warsteed was worth a thousand gold pieces. The enemy's wolves had likely been trained not to attack horses.

"It looks like for the time being, we won't have to worry about the wolves. Stay close to those horses, Mia."

"Got it! I'll be right here next to— Hm? My, Kuolan, are your nostrils twit— Gaaah!"

There was a loud *hack-a-pchoo*, followed by the splatter of slime, then the dull thud of Mia hitting the ground. Abel, however, dared not dwell on this sequence of slapstick. He quickly turned his attention back toward the man in front of him.

"Thanks for training those wolves so well. All I have to do now is take you down."

"Abel... The Second Prince of Remno then..." the masked man murmured pensively.

"Oh? You've heard of me? I'm honored," said Abel. There was no humor in his voice. Or his glare. He raised his sword, adopting an overhead stance.

Strictly speaking, the circumstances had not changed much in his favor. He still faced an assassin whose prowess rivaled the likes of Dion Alaia. Though the man hadn't attacked, his lupine allies seemed ready to pounce on any opening.

Abel could attempt a furious assault. If he paid no heed to his own survival, full-on aggression would theoretically allow him to trade some blows and buy time. Buying time, however, wasn't enough. Their only way out of this lethal predicament was for him to defeat this formidable foe, or at least force him to retreat.

...Can I do that?

A wave of anxiety suddenly bubbled up in him. He let it, feeling it climb up through his chest and into his throat. Then...

"Phew..."

...He expelled it with a long breath. Free from distraction, he refocused his mind.

"Here I come!"

His task was simple. Momentous and critical, but also simple. As such, all that remained was for him to act. He launched himself forward with a long stride, the stomp of his foot threatening to crater the ground beneath. At the same time, he swung. It was a motion he'd etched into every fiber of his muscle through tireless practice. A motion he knew and trusted. From high atop his head, his blade came crashing down in a lethal blur, leaving moonlit afterimages in its split-second wake. It was a mesmerizing strike, the trail such a perfect crescent that it seemed the moon itself had descended to earth. It was also a ferocious strike, so swift and true that even the genius, Sion Sol Sunkland, might not have reacted in time.

Ker-chaaang!

A heavy clang echoed in the night. Under the pale celestial beacon, two fighters stood with their swords locked.

Damn it. He barely even flinched.

Abel clicked his tongue. He'd put everything he had into that one strike, only to have it be blocked with frustrating ease. The masked man peered at him through the crossed blades and spoke in a cold voice.

"A fine strike. But not enough to slay me."

He retaliated with a slash of his own. Abel narrowly avoided being cleft in two, parrying with the flat of his blade. Then came the next slash. And the next. A relentless barrage that kept him firmly on the defensive.

Ugh, this guy's a beast. No surprise there, but damn.

Outmatched by his opponent's strength and speed, he failed to completely repel the furious onslaught. The masked man's blade found flesh time and again, though never managing a lethal wound. Fresh crimson dotted the grassland's moonlit canvas.

"I...won't let you win!" said Abel through gritted teeth.

Though bloodied, he refused to bend, for he knew well the value of that which he was protecting. *She* was behind him. That thought alone kept his sword up and knees firm. He couldn't afford to lose her here. Couldn't afford to give up! His resolve was as steel, unbreakable and true. But—

Ka-chiing!

A shrill ring entered his ears. The sound of something snapping. He hastily backed off a few steps and held up his sword to defend himself, only to grimace. The metal of its blade failed to match the mettle of his mind.

"To battle me with that plaything of a sword... Such folly," the masked man scoffed in a low, rumbling voice.

The weapon Abel had brought...was a training sword. Its edge had been dulled, and its durability was hardly fit for actual combat. Weapons were strictly controlled on Saint-Noel Island, and possession required express approval to be granted beforehand. That kind of approval took time—time that he hadn't had. He couldn't afford the slightest delay.

After being informed by Liora of Mia's irregular behavior, he had immediately dashed off, training sword in hand, to the stable, where he jumped onto Kayou, the only horse who could catch up to Kuolan, and promptly rode off on his emergency rescue mission. It was only through this urgent commitment to speed that he and Liora managed to make it in the nick of time...but in their hurry, they failed to procure the instruments necessary to defeat the wolfmaster.

Despite their best efforts, the heavy doors of destiny refused to open. The scale of fortune remained unmoved. The thread of fate proved an inch too short to reach the future for which they yearned.

Until the dogged will of a certain girl grabbed the thread's flailing end and pulled it taut. The thin thread was stretched very tightly…but it held, finally extending just far enough to touch the conjoining end beyond. Two silvers' worth of loyalty she dropped on the scale of fortune. And with it, the beam tipped, summoning their most formidable ally in Saint-Noel to this decisive field of battle.

This ally's voice reverberated through the night.

"Abel! Catch!"

At the same time, the masked man lashed out with a sideward swipe. Abel leapt into the air, his legs folding toward his chest to clear the strike, and threw his arm upward at the sky. As if drawn by his will, a sword landed squarely in his palm.

"I owe you one, Sion!"

He drew it in midair. It's ebony glint was proof of finely forged steel. This was no toy. It was a weapon made to cut down thousands on the battlefield. Placing both hands on the hilt, he brought the blade of the military-grade longsword crashing down on his opponent. The deafening clang of metal was followed by a quiet but labored grunt as the tremendous force of Abel's blow made the masked man stumble backward.

"My condolences to your arms, sir, which I presume are feeling fairly numb right now," quipped Sion. "That boy swings like a lumberjack. And hits even harder."

He strolled onto the scene with an easy pace and a casual smile.

Sion Sol Sunkland, prodigy of the sword, drew his weapon with a calm, quiet grace. His gaze briefly shifted toward Kuolan, then Mia, who stood in the horse's shadow. She was a mess. Her clothes were drenched, and dark splotches of mud covered her cheeks and hair.

"You've done our friend a great discourtesy. I do hope you're prepared for our reprisal," he said, his cool tone betrayed by the anger burning in his eyes.

...Just for the record, while Mia's dishevelment could, admittedly, be partly attributed to the fact that she was knocked off her horse, it was mostly because said horse then proceeded to sneeze on her, causing her to stumble and fall into a puddle of mud. Of course, these details were unknown to Sion.

Chapter 33: Keithwood the Workcamel and the Extra Heavy Straw

Looks like we really cut it close.

Keithwood, who'd arrived with Sion, took in the surroundings. Mia and Bel were standing close together. A pair of horses flanked them in a protective ring. Two wolves—the enemy's minions, presumably—circled the group, ready to pounce on any opening.

Too close, honestly. Way too close.

He breathed out a sigh of relief, though it was followed by a chill when he considered how they'd averted tragedy—for now, at least—by only the thinnest of whiskers.

Under orders from Sion, he'd been doing his usual rounds of the academy when he discovered the bloody sight of Lynsha near the rear gate. As he ran to her side, preparing to help her to the infirmary, she clutched his arm and forced out just enough breath to mention Bel's kidnapping at the hands of Citrina and Barbara before passing out.

The urgency of the situation dawning on him, he rushed to inform Sion before running off to procure assistance. However, a search for Mia's usual acquaintances proved bewilderingly unfruitful; every relevant individual seemed to have vanished. Furthermore, he'd found the ransom letter abandoned on the floor of Mia's room. Upon returning to Sion, who'd already changed into battle wear with his sword at his hip, they quickly decided to leave the island.

Lynsha's message had impressed upon them the gravity of the situation. As a result, they acted with less hesitation than everyone else. The fact that even so, they arrived with not a moment to spare was something that would likely haunt Keithwood for days to come.

Princess Mia is priceless. Losing her would be an incalculable loss. Thank the sun we made it in time.

Sion's voice pulled him out of his thoughts.

"Keithwood, I'll let you handle the wolves. If possible, get rid of them and open up an escape route for us."

Keithwood grimaced at his master's command.

"Really, milord? Your demands are always unreasonable, but this one is definitely extra unreasonable," he grumbled.

They were, after all, a pair of *wolves.* And very big ones at that. The average person would already be running away in terror, never mind fighting them.

Granted, the two-legged one doesn't look like a pushover either. Guess I'll have to pull my weight here. And then some.

And so, the workcamel picked up the extra heavy straw, and proceeded to fling it onto his long-overloaded back.

Keithwood had carefully watched the masked man defend himself against Abel's crushing blow. He recognized the enormous power behind Abel's swings. Weathering one head-on was usually a recipe for disaster. If the receiving blade didn't snap, the receiving arms might. Heck, reacting fast enough to defend oneself was a minor miracle in itself.

Their foe, meanwhile, had done so with nary an effort. Whoever this man was, he was *good.*

Sion probably also figures that our chances of beating maskface there are slim. Which doesn't leave me with a whole lot of wiggle room, does it? All right. The wolves it is then. I need to get rid of them fast and secure our escape.

Vicious though they were, wolves were still beasts. Surely they had to be easier to defeat than an armed and highly competent man. So he thought, at least, until the mere motion of drawing his sword prompted one of the wolves to attack.

"Whoa!"

It pounced out of nowhere, jaws opening wide. He dodged hastily, only for the wolf to swerve with him, its gaping jaw following the motion of his body as if it had predicted his reaction.

"What the—"

In the fraction of a second he had to think, he decided that further evasion was impossible. Abandoning all semblance of defense, he leaned into the attack, twisting his sword toward the wolf's neck to drive it up through its throat.

Sword through the neck. If I kill the thing right when it bites me, I can minimize the damage I take. An arm for a wolf. Worth it.

This grisly bargain, however, did not come to pass. The wolf met his eyes and suddenly stopped in place before backing off.

"Scorching sun, what?" Keithwood exclaimed in shock.

The wolf bounded backward a few more times. A second later, arrows fell on its paw prints. Another arrow, this one with a brightly burning tip, flew toward the other wolf, who didn't budge. It landed wide of its mark. The wolves showed no fear of fire, dodging only when the arrows' aim was true.

We have an archer on our side, huh. That helps. But...

Undeterred by the long-range threat, the wolves kept their eyes on Keithwood. Seeing this, he understood what had happened.

Not only did it hop away from the arrows with ease, it sensed I was going to let it bite me to go in for the kill, so it backed off. These aren't regular wolves. They're trained for battle.

They stood like warriors in lupine form, and their deft movements suggested a familiarity with the tendencies of swordsmen.

He wasn't, Keithwood realized, fighting a pair of giant wolves. He was up against two trained soldiers who fought with jaws and claws. With the speed and power of wolves, to boot.

Beating them...is going to be backbreaking. Maybe literally. In that case...

Not dropping his guard, he addressed Sion without turning his head.

"Milord, these aren't regular wolves. Defeating them doesn't seem a likely outcome. May I change my approach to stall for time instead?"

"...Fair enough. I suppose there's no need for us to attempt immediate escape if it's not really feasible. We'll take this slow then. Drag it out."

Sion's response elicited a private grin from Keithwood.

Good thing he caught my drift. Now, let's see if maskface takes the bait.

He was interrupted by a growl.

"Ah, right. Sorry to keep you two waiting."

Turning back toward the wolves, he shrugged.

"Still, against these fellows, even stalling for time is plenty risky. Let's hope I make it out of this with all my limbs intact... I swear, I don't get paid enough for this."

Bel, who'd been watching these goings-on from the sidelines, squealed in delight.

"Omigosh omigosh! Look, Miss Mia! It's him! The Libra King! The Libra King is here to save us!"

Her idol, Sion Sol Sunkland, had come to her rescue. It would be unrealistic to expect her *not* to erupt with excitement.

"Oh, and there's Grandfather Abel too, of course!" she added, clearly as a courtesy.

Poor Grandfather Abel. The fanatic affection of Maniabel would never truly be his.

In any case, the arrival of reinforcements had greatly improved her spirits.

"Now that help's here, maybe…"

They could go back to rescue Citrina. That thought was the source of her renewed cheer.

By the way, unlike Mia, while Bel had incurred some degree of muddiness from her tumble off the horse, she remained mostly presentable The reason was that she'd astutely perceived the wriggling of Kuolan's nostrils and deftly stepped out of the way. Never let it be said that Bel hadn't learned from her grandmother. She was adapting the principle of Mia First into Bel First, at least when it came to avoiding horse mucus.

"Yaaaay! Go go Libra King! Come on, Miss Mia, let's cheer together. Yaaaay! Go go Libra King!"

While a wide-eyed Bel pumped her fists in the air cheerleader-style, a grimy Princess Mia lifted hers to shoulder height and said in a half-hearted tone, "Yaaaay…"

Ugh… Why me…

Though hardly a stranger to Kuolan's nasal discharge by now, every time he sneezed on Mia, it still ruined her mood.

W-Well, then again, he did do a lot to help me… I guess I can't complain. Besides, now that I think about it, Abel's here to save me. I have to cheer him on properly.

She glanced at Bel, who was eagerly pumping her little fists in the air.

I…would have preferred to do so in a more presentable fashion though. Ugh, this was supposed to be the big moment. The pivotal scene where the knight in shining armor comes to rescue the princess. If only it wasn't ruined by the fact that the princess is soaking wet and covered in slime…

After briefly wallowing in self-pity, she decided to adopt a more positive outlook.

No, I'm going about this all wrong. Regardless of the situation, I'm still the heroine here, so I need to get my act together!

She gave her cheeks a few invigorating smacks and raised her voice.

"Show them what you've got! I'm rooting for you! Both of you!"

With the self-styled heroine cheering him on, Abel went on the offensive.

"Take this!"

Again, he used his signature technique, adopting an overhead stance. It was the same motion as before. The masked man all but rolled his eyes at the monotonous approach.

"Fool…"

He huffed in disdain and prepared to take a lateral step to avoid the vertical strike. Indeed, power here meant little when intent had been laid bare. Predictability was the bane of a swordsman, especially against an exceptionally skilled opponent.

Abel, of course, was well aware of this. Still, he committed to the overhead swing. Was it stubbornness? Of course not. His reason was simple; he knew his swings were lethal.

"Fool?" Abel grinned at the word. "We'll see who's the fool."

His foe had deemed him a fool, and in doing so, given him an opening.

The next instant, the masked man's eyes sprung to twice their size.

"How—"

Abel's sword became a blur. It fell faster and with far more force than before. The man's sidestep kept him unharmed, but half his mask fluttered away in the wind.

It was an absurdly powerful swing from Abel, incomparable to his last. A technique of pure offense, it allowed for no recourse, no next step in case the opponent dodged. It left him wide open, completely unable to repel a counterattack from his foe. No sane fighter would commit to such unbridled aggression…without good reason. And Abel had a good reason.

"Leaves you sort of open, doesn't it, Abel? Not the most practical move, in my humble opinion."

The fatal opening left by the attack vanished as Sion stepped in to fill it. The masked man, already in motion to strike back, tsked and withdrew.

"No. Not unless you're here, Sion," replied Abel, cracking a quick smile. "Which means I'm going in full power, all the way."

His words could be taken as a sign of faith in his friend. Should he leave himself open, he trusted Sion to step in and cover him. But at the same time, it had a deeper meaning. Should he *fall*, he also trusted Sion to step in and take his place.

Before, Abel's death would have inevitably spelled doom for Mia as well. Not anymore. Sion's arrival meant that Abel could try for more. If the masked man escaped, he could make another attempt on Mia's life. Better to put an end to the threat here, even if he had to risk overextending himself in the process. After all, even if he died…

"No, you won't." Sion cut him off. "If you're thinking of defeating this man at the cost of your own life, Abel, then you can back the hell off."

There was no humor in his voice.

"…My, that's odd," murmured Mia.

The two princes were fighting in concert. Side by side, they battled with their lives on the line to protect her. That was the kind of thing to be relished. Which she did, entertaining such blithe thoughts as *Mmm… It feels pretty good knowing that they're fighting for me*. Abel's face was a mask of concentration. That alone was a sight to behold. But even Sion was making every effort to keep her safe. She felt every bit the heroine of a romantic drama.

The dreaminess of it all gradually took her mind off the fact that her life was still very much in danger. She started to feel comfortable with the situation. A little too comfortable, in fact.

"Something isn't right…"

She frowned, trying to put her finger on the strange feeling. It was almost like she was…out of place. As if she didn't belong. She gazed at the two princes.

"Leaves you sort of open, doesn't it, Abel? Not the most practical move, in my humble opinion."

"No. Not unless you're here, Sion."

In front of her, a dazzling spectacle of friendship was on display. Two handsome princes fighting side by side, while they shared trust and traded banter. She watched, fascinated by the scene…until a thought occurred to her.

Wait. Wasn't I supposed to be the heroine here?

They were fighting for *her*. She was supposed to be center stage. So why did she feel so left out? Until just a moment ago, all signs pointed to the story reaching a climax, with two knights in shining armor riding in to save the princess. Which had happened. Sort of. The knights rode in, but the princess exited stage left! Now all eyes were on the pair's rousing camaraderie, and no one was paying any attention to her.

Wh-Why do I feel like I've been in this situation before? What was it last time? Hmm… Oh, I remember! The sandwiches! It was when we were making the sandwiches!

Memories of her marginalization in the culinary taskforce resurfaced. Hoping to avoid a repeat of that demoralizing experience, she vowed to reclaim her spot as the heroine of the moment. Then, remembering her present appearance, she promptly rescinded her oath and hung her head.

Right… I almost forgot. How can I be the heroine…when I look like this?

She gazed forlornly at all the snot and mud covering her clothes.

"If you're thinking of defeating this man at the cost of your own life, Abel, then you can back the hell off," said Sion as he pressed his sword into his foe's.

Pushing hard, he forced the wolfmaster away from the other prince.

"What do you mean by that?" asked Abel.

He righted his stance, ready to join in the attack at the next opening. Sion, however, gave him no such chance.

"Don't lose sight of the goal. We're not here to defeat this man. Our goal is to get back to Saint-Noel with everyone alive."

"But this man is—"

"Look at her! Do you see the expression on her face?"

It took Abel a moment to parse the meaning before quickly turning toward Mia. Only then did he realize that she'd fallen silent. She'd been cheering for them not long ago. Now, her gaze was downcast, and she looked on the verge of tears.

"Don't you see her sorrow? Why do you think she feels that way?" exclaimed Sion. "Because you're disregarding your own life!"

The words pierced Abel's heart, sharply and more painfully than any sword ever could. Seeking an advantage at the cost of life…was the kind of thing that Mia would never do nor wish for. More than anything else, she hated the squandering of life.

"*Think*, man! Think about how she hopes to see you fight. Then, if you believe yourself capable of doing so… If you can give her joy instead of sorrow, *then*, come and fight by my side."

Sion leapt back from the masked man, as though affording himself a moment's respite, only to dash right back in. His mercurial style, coupled with his swift motions, were effective in disorienting his opponent. But only for a moment. The masked man reacted in time to the feint and strike, countering with a blow of his own. The screech of grating steel filled the night.

I see. I... I almost broke Mia's heart...

Abel looked to Mia, who favored him with the faintest of smiles.

I let myself be consumed by anger...and I lost sight of everything else. Good thing Sion was here. I owe him one.

He drew a long breath, let it out slowly, then raised his voice.

"I am Abel Remno, and I fight to protect those I hold dear!"

...It hardly bears mentioning at this point, but Mia had not suddenly become a martial-artsmeister as well. She definitely couldn't read Abel's mind through the way he was fighting. Frankly, all his sword swings were just blurs to her eyes and therefore looked the same, no matter the motivation behind them.

Sadly, no one was at leisure to point out this glaring flaw in Sion's logic. A missed opportunity, truly.

The princes fought as one, their coordination honed through long hours at the training grounds. In practicing together, they'd gotten to know each other's habits. Working further in their favor was the natural synergy of their sword styles.

Abel's strikes were bold and single-minded. Their power was immense but they lacked versatility. He made no attempt to adapt to his opponents, opting to smash through whatever tactic they employed through overwhelming force alone. His style was simple. Easily predicted by his foes, yes, but also by his allies.

And his ally was the sword prodigy, Sion Sol Sunkland, known for the staggering versatility of his technical mastery. Adapting his style to complement Abel's was an effortless task. Abel could crack the opponent's guard with his crushing strokes, then Sion would capitalize on the opening with his shifting strikes. Their combined assault was immaculate, relentless, and brutally effective.

"Formidable…"

The wolfmaster muttered a grudging acknowledgment. He wasn't losing the fight, per se. Neither prince was truly his equal in skill, and every two or three exchanges, his blade would draw blood. The wounds he inflicted, however, did not dull the duo's attacks. They only added crescent mists of crimson to their every move. Should they keep fighting like this, he'd surely kill them both sooner or later. The problem was that it would take time. Ideally, he'd call his wolves back, but the pair's attention was being forcibly occupied by Sion's attendant.

"…The tides have turned."

He glanced up at the night sky and clicked his tongue. Its starry canvas was tinted ever so slightly with morning's light. Even in the midst of battle, he'd kept his ears open. And he'd heard the brief exchange between Sion and his attendant.

If they're stalling for time…then backup must be on the way.

It was hard to imagine there wouldn't be. This was an assassination attempt on the Princess of Tearmoon. They'd surely respond in force. He was skilled, but it would be nothing but folly to challenge a furious retinue of imperial pursuers in direct combat. He couldn't afford to waste any more time here and risk capture.

"…Time to go."

He shouted a command at his wolves, prompting Abel to slash at him again. He met the blow with a heavy clang. The prince glared at him through their clashing blades.

"Do you think we'll just let you leave?"

The wolfmaster snorted.

"I *am* leaving. You may attempt to stop me, Second Prince of Remno, but know that it will cost you a limb or two."

He kicked at the boy's stomach, using the rebounding force to push himself back and create some distance. Swiveling, he leapt fluidly onto a shadowy form—his trusty steed—that had appeared out of the dawning blue.

None attempted pursuit as he rode away.

None pursued…because none could. Abel and Sion watched as the wolfmaster disappeared into the distance. When the man's form melted into the surrounding shadow, they collapsed onto the ground.

"Scorching sun… He finally left… Ugh, everything hurts."

Sion let out a long breath. Tension drained out of his body. Its vacancy was promptly filled by a flaring wave of pain. He grimaced.

"What a beast… That man could give Sir Dion a run for his money, don't you think?" said Abel with a matching wince. "By the way, are reinforcements actually on the way?"

"None at all."

They traded a knowing look.

"It was a bluff, of course," said Sion with a shrug. "We didn't have time. In fact, we need to head back to Saint-Noel soon so I can put together a pursuing party."

"Are you two okay?!"

Just then, he heard Mia's voice followed by the sound of her rapidly approaching footsteps. Turning, he found her trailed by Bel—now thankfully unabducted—along with Anne and Tiona on a horse. Behind them, a bow-carrying Liora was running toward them as well.

He gazed at the oncoming girls for a moment. Abel did the same. Eventually, they shared a wry laugh.

"Did the pain get to your head, milord, or is there some humor in this situation that I'm missing?" quipped an equally wound-riddled Keithwood.

Fangs and claws had taken their toll on flesh and fabric alike. He was no less a bloody mess than the two princes.

"I assure you my head is quite fine, Keithwood. And so is your sense of humor. I was just wondering how we fared in the eyes of our good princess with regard to the way in which we resolved this incident. I do believe we've earned ourselves at least a passing grade. Right, Abel?"

The two princes shared another laugh. This time it was far removed from the danger and bloodshed of the world.

Chapter 34: Barbara...Sees Through Mia's Little Game (...What Game?)

The sun was peeking over the horizon by the time the wolfmaster returned. Upon dismounting, he delivered a swift and terse report.

"They got away. We have failed."

Barbara sighed deeply.

"Bah, I figured as much, but good grief…"

She walked over to a listless Citrina, who was standing by herself, and struck her across the face.

"Ow—"

The sound was short and sharp. Caught off guard, Citrina teetered and lost her balance, only to be forcibly righted by a violent tug on her arm. Barbara pulled her close.

"Cursed child… Useless…"

She was about to strike her a second time when the wolfmaster interjected.

"We have no time. The enemy has help on the way. They will soon give chase."

"…Help on the way? Do they, now? And who did you hear that from?"

"No one in particular. They spoke of stalling for time."

"Stalling… Considering they said it within earshot of you, it's very likely a ruse. Ack, this is why I hate working with those who have swords for brains. Silly. So silly," Barbara spat before giving Citrina's shoulder a violent shove.

Citrina fell backward, landing painfully on her tailbone, which she nursed with one hand while the other cradled her bruising cheek.

"And you, milady, what a foolish thing you've done. So foolish."

Barbara looked down at her, voice thick with contempt. Citrina made no reply. Instead, she uttered a private whisper.

"So... Bel made it out safely then... That's good..."

"How could you be so utterly foolish," Barbara continued. "You've been *had*, milady. The Great Sage of the Empire tricked you with her cunning words."

"Did she? How so?"

The question came from the wolfmaster. Barbara rolled her eyes at him.

"Isn't it obvious? The princess used moral pressure. She exploited milady's conscience to manipulate her."

"Exploited in what way?"

"Have you forgotten what the princess did? She looked milady in the eye and said 'I believe in you.' Right after being presented with incontrovertible proof that milady had been deceiving her this whole time. Who in their right mind would say that under those circumstances? No one. Unless they had another motive. Don't you see? It's all part of the princess's ploy. By offering unconditional trust, she hoped to weigh down milady's conscience to the point of cracking. And she *succeeded*. Because she recognized how weak the will of this useless child is..."

"That's not true, Barbara... It's not a ploy. She believed in Rina. She honestly bel— Mmm!"

Citrina was cut off by a hand closing around her cheeks. She made no attempt to resist as her face was pulled to within an inch of Barbara's, who glared at her. Ultimately, her resigned expression drew a sigh out of the irritated attendant.

"Ugh, after all the time I spent training you to be a Serpent... I should have drawn the line long ago. A *true* Serpent would naturally have paid no heed to such things. But a failure of a Serpent like you... clearly can't help but fall under her spell. Ah, good grief, you wretched thing... Oh, which reminds me." Barbara paused to smile as a thought occurred to her. "That smoke back there... Tell me, was it the princess who taught you how to do that?"

Citrina's ensuing silence was answer enough. Barbara shook her head.

"Which means...in return for your role in helping her escape, the Great Sage of the Empire chose to absolve you of guilt in this current matter. In doing so, she has done you a greater favor than you have her, and it is through exploiting this debt that she intends to make the House of Yellowmoon hers. After all, like you, the Duke of Yellowmoon is at best mediocre and ineffective. I doubt the princess will have much trouble wheedling him."

The wolfmaster narrowed his eyes.

"What do we do with the girl then? Kill her and feed the body to the wolves? We could also leave the corpse for all to see. It will serve as a warning. In any case, traitors must be put to death."

His hand went to the hilt of his sword, but Barbara stopped him with a slow shake of her head.

"Though the logic may escape people like you, let me assure you that what you are proposing is unwise."

"Why? Kill her to set an example. It will send a powerful message to our opponents."

"Are those ears of yours for show? Recall, if you even can, how the princess said that even if she died here, that wouldn't be the end of her."

He gave her a dubious look.

"I do remember. But surely, that is just the empty threat of cornered prey."

Barbara shook her head again.

"Your judgment leaves much to be desired. Of course it isn't. Or are you honestly suggesting that the Great Sage of the Empire, who nipped the Tearmoon revolution in the bud and doused the Remno revolution soon after...would stoop to the language of a sore loser?" she asked, her certainty of the answer apparent in the sarcasm dripping from her voice.

"Then what did she mean?"

"The wise know how to make use of death. Amongst the leaders of history, there are rare examples of brilliant kings who used even their own ends as a tool to further their sweeping stratagems. I fear our particular sage has done something similar. Knowing that her death was all but certain, she likely planned to utilize it in some fashion. The simplest possibility that comes to mind would be...a banner, for example. Her death could strengthen the bonds between her allies... perhaps even rally them further against us in their anti-Serpent efforts. Regardless, the princess was certain that though her body may perish, her will would not die with it."

After that bout of pontification, Barbara's hand encircled Citrina's slender neck.

"Nngh..."

Her nails dug into the callow flesh, eliciting a grimace.

"And those who would extract value from even their own deaths... would never allow the death of another to go unutilized, would they? The death of milady will only give the princess another tool to use against us. Don't you see? Should we kill milady here, we will surely be playing into her hands. She will use it to inflame the desire for revenge."

Barbara stared into Citrina's eyes.

"The Duke of Yellowmoon is most fond of this daughter of his. Kill her, and he will be out for our blood. And you can be sure the Great Sage of the Empire will not pass up such a golden opportunity to bolster her ranks."

"Then what do we do? Take her with us and train her to be an assassin?" the wolfmaster asked with furrowed brows.

Barbara rolled her eyes.

"That's what got us here in the first place, in case you forgot. We have no need for an assassin who can't even kill a friend. She would only be a liability."

She released Citrina, the motion casual and quick, as if she hadn't been trying to strangle the girl just a moment before.

"But she is not without value. We can still use her...so long as we do so in the correct fashion. We shall make this girl into the knife that severs the bond between Mia Luna Tearmoon and her friends."

With a wicked smile, she regarded Citrina again.

"Traitors must be put to death. That goes without saying. But we must *make good use* of their deaths as well. In any case, let us flee before they send men after us. Time is of the essence, and I'll need plenty of it to make the necessary preparations..."

Unfortunately, Barbara's preparations would be quickly dismantled, because they *did* send men. Far sooner than she'd anticipated. They just didn't send them after her. Rather, they'd been strategically deployed elsewhere.

Together with Citrina and the wolfmaster, Barbara traveled north from Belluga, soon reaching the border with Sunkland, only to find it guarded by ranks of preemptively stationed Sunkland cavalry. So impeccable was the positioning that it was as if someone had exactly anticipated their planned escape route, creating a blockade that left them floundering.

This prudent arrangement was, in fact, not the work of Mia and her friends. There wasn't enough time for them to return to Saint-Noel and issue the necessary instructions. It couldn't even be credited to her reliable right hand, Anne, whose behind-the-scenes diligence often laid the groundwork for future success. No... This was the product of her *other* hand, Ludwig of the left.

Barbara regarded the pinpoint dismantling of their route to safety...and smiled.

"You think you've backed us into a corner with this, Mia Luna Tearmoon?"

Sunkland's patrol troops were no pushovers. Alone, the wolfmaster might yet manage to breach their lines, but the added baggage of her and Citrina would make such an effort impossible. After a swift assessment of the situation, Barbara made a decision.

"Well, now that it's come to this, I suppose I have little choice left... I would give my life to drive a wedge between those who oppose the Serpents."

Thus, the wolfmaster and Barbara went their separate ways, the latter taking Citrina with her as she made her way toward the only place that could still offer them positional advantage and safe harbor—the Yellowmoon domain.

Little did Barbara know, the path to the Yellowmoons had been left unguarded for a reason—an intentional hole in the ever-tightening net of capture.

And little did Mia know, in this particular case, her left hand had been particularly busy in the background.

Unbeknownst to both, dawn was quietly breaking over the long night of conspiracy.

Chapter 35: Princess Mia...Enjoys a Bath of Supreme Bliss(?)

After returning to Saint-Noel, the first thing Mia did was, of course, take a nice long bath. For her sake, it should be noted that she hadn't forgotten about Citrina. The boys took it upon themselves to organize a search party and, seeing her grimy state, the three gentlemen kindly advised her to enjoy a good soak and get some rest. Military deployment and command were far outside of Mia's limited field of expertise, so even if she stayed around, she'd just get in the way. It was better for her to let them handle all the work. Which she was more than glad to do.

Before making a beeline for the bath, she'd actually asked Bel to join her, but the younger girl had been so worried about Citrina that she'd decided to tag along with the boys. By now, they were probably together in a room with Rafina, discussing all sorts of serious things. Which made Mia all the more glad that she was elsewhere. As she walked into the bath chamber, a cloud of vapor enveloped her.

"Aaah... Nothing relaxes a girl like the warmth of a bath— Hm?"

She frowned as a scent entered her nose. It was coming from the bath, and it smelled nice.

"This...smells like princess roses? Mmm, it's very pleasant. But where is it coming from? Did someone put in some bath salt?"

At this point, Mia's brain had already clocked out for the day. After surviving a long night of death-defying encounters, she'd fully entered epilogue mode, leaving her danger sensors entirely unmanned.

Which was too bad for her, because had she left even a skeleton crew on the bridge, they would have reminded her where exactly princess roses were grown in Saint-Noel, and what it would mean for her to meet the caretaker of that secret garden alone right now. She should have realized these things, but alas...her dulled senses pushed her thoughts in a different direction.

"Bath salt... That reminds me, Rina gave me some once, didn't she..."

Memories resurfaced of how the kindhearted girl had, seeing Mia weary after riding practice, offered her a special blend of fatigue-relieving salts. Not long ago, that girl had used the same smoke-producing herbs to get her out of a desperate situation. Citrina had undoubtedly saved her life. She owed her a great deal.

"Which means...Barbara is probably the main villain in this whole thing, and Rina was acting under compulsion. Then, at the last second, she betrayed Barbara to save me. That must be what happened."

Attempting to infer the circumstances that led to this incident, Mia concluded that Citrina, having realized what Barbara was trying to do, must have asked Chloe in advance to give her some smoke-producing bath salt, which she had held on to in case of emergencies.

"This is no small debt. I have to repay her. And to do that, I have to save her first. If not for myself, then for Bel."

Citrina was her dear granddaughter's friend. That was reason enough for Mia to yearn for her rescue.

"This...will not be easy," she murmured as she began her pre-bath cleansing ritual.

Normally, Anne would be standing by, ready to help at a moment's notice. Right now though, she was off procuring a change of clothes from their room, leaving Mia alone in the bath chamber. As she worked up a good lather with the soap and started rubbing it over herself, she suddenly noticed something.

"…My, how strange. My arms seem a little jigglier than they should be."

A quick review of recent events produced snapshots of the enemy rider effortlessly catching up to her and Kuolan, followed by a montage of her *living in the moment* phase and the diet it had entailed.

"…I'm probably just imagining things. Me? Jiggly? Nonsense. I'm not jiggly. I can't be jiggly. I'm physically incapable of becoming jiggly!"

Her excessive fixation on the word distracted her from a more important observation. The way her mind quickly replayed recent memories, starting with those of Citrina, followed by riding Kuolan, then shifting to the decadent glory of her moment-living days… It was ominously similar to how impending death would cause one's life to flash before their eyes. Devoid of this insight, she remained ignorant of the fact that her subconscious was warning her of severe and imminent danger.

Just as she finished rinsing the shampoo out of her hair and was taking a moment to bask in the sensation of cleanliness, the door to the chamber abruptly slid open. Hearing the noise, she glanced over, figuring Anne had come back. In her unguarded state, she was *not* ready for the sight that greeted her. Walking in was not Anne, but…

"Gosh, Mia. Good to see you."

A polite smile rested upon the face of none other than Rafina Orca Belluga!

"Ah, good to see you too, Miss Rafina."

In fact, Mia was so unready that she entirely failed to mount any sort of response, fight-or-flight or otherwise. Even her primal survival instincts had taken leave of her.

She must have been terribly busy with the ceremony and everything. Then, she probably had to deal with Abel and the others asking for a search party to be put together… Phew, it's not easy to be the daughter of Duke Belluga, is it?

As Rafina began washing her hair, Mia stepped into the pool. As she lowered herself into the water the lovely fragrance filled her nose, making the sensation doubly pleasurable.

"Ooof..."

With her trademark old man noise, she sighed as she stretched out her limbs.

Aaaah... It feels so good. So indescribably good. I can feel all the stiffness in my joints melting away... Truly, nothing beats a good bath!

As she savored the moment, Rafina spoke.

"So? How do you like my special bath salt blend?"

"Oh, it's marvelous. Did you make this yourself?"

"I did," Rafina said with a giggle. "It works wonders on fatigue. Just pulls the exhaustion right out of you..."

For some reason, her voice caused a chill to shoot up Mia's spine. It was an eerie experience. She was steeped in bath water. She could feel the heat enveloping her body. Still, she couldn't help but shiver.

What in the moons was that?

Before she could think any further, Rafina continued.

"After all, you seem so exhausted today. So I made this blend specially for you. I thought you'd appreciate it." She turned as she finished washing her hair and looked straight at Mia. "I heard that you...had a very exciting day off the island. Something about a death-defying adventure, I believe?"

A slow, humorless smile crept across her lips, causing Mia to shudder again.

W-Wait... I-Is she...angry?

At long last, the implications of her current situation dawned on her. She was alone in the bathhouse with an inexplicably angry Rafina. In other words, she was in deep doo-doo!

Rafina finished washing her body and rose. With measured steps, she walked toward the pool with the aura of a lion baring its teeth.

Eeeek! She is! She's definitely angry! Very very angry!

That thought was enough to kick her brain out of its stupor. It worked with frenzied urgency, trying to figure out why Rafina sounded downright livid. Soon, it produced an answer.

Th-That's right! The party! Miss Rafina was looking forward to the stew party we'd planned for today!

She remembered how excited Rafina had been when talking about the student council's stew party, which had been planned for tonight. That clearly wasn't happening anymore. The loss of the stew party then, Mia deduced, must be the source of Rafina's fury. Part of her felt like pointing out how it wasn't *her* fault the party got canceled, but Mia was well aware that speaking reason to anger was futile.

Granted, I don't blame her for getting so angry. Losing your cool because a stew party fell through is totally understandable. They're delicious, after all, thought Mia. *Hm, this also suggests that Miss Rafina is probably a closet gastronome like me!*

She snuck a glance at Rafina's middle...and gasped! For Rafina's stomach was perfectly flat!

That makes no sense... If she's as into food as I am, then there's no way she'd be...

Mia gave her own sides a pinch. She shook her head, then heaved a sigh laden with all the injustices of the world.

Never mind that though. She pulled her mind back from its digression. *I've made a terrible mistake. This was no time to be soaking in the bath. I should have gone with everyone to apologize to Miss Rafina before doing anything else!*

It was too late to remedy that lapse in judgment though. Worse yet, she was unlucky enough to have run into Rafina in a place where they'd be alone.

No... Not unlucky. This was planned. She said so herself. The bath salt is hers. In other words, this was her trap, and I walked right into— Yeep!

The sound of a small splash made her jump. Nervously, she looked in its direction to find Rafina lowering herself into the water.

"Phew... You're right. It's a pleasant smell. Very...calming. For the mind."

Rafina sighed quietly and stretched.

D-Doesn't that mean she's so furious that she needs aromatherapy to keep herself in check?

Mia began producing splashing sounds of her own, though hers were from her uncontrollable shudders of fear.

"W-Well then, I think it's time for me to go..."

She promptly attempted to escape. Whatever the consequences, it couldn't be worse than being stuck here alone with an angry Rafina.

"Mia? A little early to be leaving, isn't it? Won't you stay a little longer?"

A slender hand rose from the water and wrapped itself around Mia's wrist. A quiet giggle followed.

"Isn't it fun bathing with a friend? What's the rush? Or am I..."

Rafina abruptly swiveled to face Mia. With widened eyes, she looked up at her and asked, "Or am I not your friend, Mia?"

Her smile had vanished. Her gaze was fixed in what could only be described as an intense glare.

"O-O-Of course you are, Miss Rafina. You're my dear friend."

Mia hastily sat back down in the pool. Sweat entirely unrelated to the heat in the room began rolling down her back.

"Am I? Well, you could have fooled me... I thought for sure you'd rescinded your friendship..." Rafina said with a curious hand-cheek head-tilt gesture.

"A-Absolutely not!" Mia asserted vehemently. "You're my friend, Miss Rafina! A very important friend!"

"Then why… Why did you walk into danger all by yourself… without saying a word to me?"

That was when Mia noticed the unmistakable shimmer of tears in Rafina's eyes.

"Eh? U-Uh… Miss Rafina?"

"You said I shouldn't hold onto everything. You were the one who told me to share my burdens. But when it's your turn, you just… How could you… Do you know how worried I was?"

Rafina's voice trembled with emotion.

Mia's brain trembled with confusion.

When had she ever told Rafina to share her burdens? If Rafina was handling everything and doing a good job of it, then by the moons, Mia would much rather have her keep it up so she could slack off. This, however, was a question she kept to herself. With her danger sensors in working order again, she recognized that voicing it would inevitably lead to a "me and my stupid mouth" situation.

O-Okay, I have no idea what's going on, but I should just go with what she's saying for now. That should be safe. It does seem like she was genuinely worried about me, after all.

She nodded along, adding, "I do feel very sorry about this turn of events. Though I had very little choice in the matter, it's true that I made you worry…"

Silence ensued. She held her breath under Rafina's withering gaze. Eventually, Rafina shook her head.

"I know… Of course I do. It's not your fault. You had no choice but to go alone…to save Miss Bel. Still, I wish you'd said something. Anything. I knew you were deeply troubled lately, but there was nothing I could do to help. I felt so powerless.

It was terrible, and I never want to feel like that again," she said as she breathed out what seemed like a lifetime's worth of frustration.

"Miss Rafina…"

Mia couldn't help but be touched by this candid outpouring of emotion. It gladdened her to know how deeply Rafina cared about her.

"I heard a bit of the story from Bel. I can only imagine how you felt when you learned that people were plotting an attempt on your life. You must have been beside yourself with anxiety."

"Oh, I *was*. It was terrible. I'm not sure how I coped, honestly…"

Finally, someone understood how she'd felt these past few days! So glad was she to have found a sympathetic ear that she started tearing up. However…

"And you couldn't tell anyone about it either, could you? For Miss Citrina's sake. For the chance to bring her back from the brink."

"…Hm?"

…The conversation suddenly took an odd turn.

Bring her back from the brink? *What in the moons is she talking about?*

Undeterred by Mia's look of confusion, Rafina kept going.

"Using those bath salts that produce smoke in this pool was your way of showing Miss Citrina another path she could take. You left a door of opportunity open for her. There was no guarantee whether she could pull it off successfully, but that wasn't the point. What you wanted to do was give her a chance to repent. And that's why you let the assassination plot play out, going so far as to brave the risk of death yourself."

"…*Huh?*"

Mia's confusion deepened. Rafina's expression, meanwhile, grew wistful.

"You're a good person, Mia. The way you approach others with such kindness, and your willingness to risk your life to help them… They're virtues of the highest order. And it makes me all the more proud to be your friend… But it still hurts. It hurts to know that you left without saying a word to me. That I let you do so. I know I probably couldn't have done much even if you had come to me for help, but I still wish you would have…" said Rafina, her voice growing steadily softer. "And that's why…you can forget I ever said any of this. I'm sorry. It's nothing more than the silly grumblings of a silly girl. I'm glad you're back safe, Mia. That's enough for me."

"Miss Rafina…"

Mia regarded this outpouring of candidness from her friend, and let out a long breath. Of relief, that is!

Oh, thank the moons! It looks like she's not actually angry!

"But I won't give up, Mia. I'll keep improving. Until I become the kind of person you'd want to seek advice from. And the kind of person…who's worthy of giving you that advice."

Rafina smiled. It was a tender smile, but for some reason, it filled Mia with a vague sense of dread. She couldn't quite put her finger on it, but it felt like a grave misunderstanding had gone unexamined. The kind of misunderstanding that heaved oodles of raised expectations upon her. Her look of concern prompted Rafina to give her a reassuring nod.

"Just leave the rest to us. All you need to think about today, Mia, is getting plenty of rest. Monica is handling matters right now, so there's no need to worry."

"I-I see. Well, I suppose I'll just go do that then…"

Given the chance to shut her brain off, Mia promptly did so. Whatever the case, she'd survived, and she was now safe and sound.

It's not like losing sleep over it will change much anyway.

And lose sleep she did not, for after climbing out of the pool, she retreated to her quarters and crawled into bed where, aided by the lingering heat of the bath radiating from her body, she slept like a rock for an entire day.

...Which was *way* too much sleep, but anyway.

Chapter 36: Mia Pandemic! –Monica... Realizes the Terrible Truth!–

"Excuse me, Princess Mia…"

The distant sound of knocking and a faraway mention of her name roused Mia from slumber.

"Mmm… Mm?"

She slowly sat up, groggily rubbed the sleep out of her eyes, and looked around. She was treated to the familiar sight of her room, only something felt off.

My, that's strange… Usually, Anne would answer the door.

As she made to get out of bed, she discovered the reason. There, holding herself in the fetal position on the floor beside the bed, was a sleeping Anne.

"My…"

The maid's soft, rhythmic breathing tugged the corners of Mia's lips upward in a fond smile.

She rushed to my rescue last night, after all. She must be exhausted.

It should be noted that Mia was currently harboring a chronological misconception. After sleeping for a whole day straight, it was now morning again. Therefore, the time frame of her daring adventure was in fact from two nights ago to yesterday morning. Mia's perception of time was off from reality by a full cycle of the sun and moon through the sky. During the Lost Day, Anne had been her usual hardworking self, not slacking off in the slightest. However, this detail was lost on the time-bending princess.

"I do wonder though. Why is she sleeping down there?"

Needless to say, Anne normally slept in her bed. What was she doing snoozing away on the ground beside Mia's then? Mia pursed her lips, perplexed, but an idea soon came to her.

"Maybe...it's because she's worried I'll run off on my own again."

Presumably, fearing a repeat disappearance, Anne had curled up right beside her beloved princess, not bothering to even change into nightwear.

"Hm..."

Mia considered her options. In case of emergencies, she'd made it a point to figure out how to handle most things on her own. Tasks such as changing her clothes were, by now, trivial. Normally, if Anne was getting some extra rest to recover from a weary day, she'd let her sleep and change on her own to head out to greet the visitor. Today though...

Maybe I shouldn't go off on my own. Anne might get upset if she wakes up to find me missing.

She gave Anne's shoulder a shake, figuring she'd play the part of the selfish princess today out of consideration.

So, after allowing a drowsy-eyed Anne to help her into her clothes, Mia opened the door. The person who walked in was Rafina's maid, Monica, bearing a message from her mistress.

"Milady would like to invite you to a breakfast party. Would you care to join her?"

"Breakfast, you say..." Mia gave her tummy a probing rub. "Hm... I think I would appreciate some food right now. My stomach feels emptier than usual this morning. I wonder why..."

It promptly growled as if in protest of her extended period of slumber.

The breakfast party was hosted in the academy's Secret Gardens. "Ah, there you are, Mia."

"Good morning, Miss Rafina. Thank you very much for inviting me."

Mia curtsied and took a look at the attendees. They were all people who'd come to rescue her. Abel and Sion were present. Tiona and Bel as well. So were Keithwood and Liora. This particular composition of members set off an alarm in Mia's head.

Getting these people together for breakfast means there's pretty much only one topic of conversation that will come up.

Her vigilance lasted until the food arrived.

Hm, well. Whatever the case, eating comes first. I am very hungry though. Why is that, I wonder...

She immediately reached across the table for the bread. Taking a loaf, she broke it in half with a pleasing crunch. A wisp of hot air rose from the center, carrying with it the luscious aroma of well-baked dough. She gulped hungrily in anticipation before tearing off a bite-size piece and placing it in her mouth. Its crispy exterior gave way to soft insides that melted on her tongue.

Such delicious baking. The workmanship is simply exceptional. Saint-Noel never fails to impress. Who would have thought tasting a single piece of bread at Miss Rafina's breakfast party could be such a profound experience?

Her inadvertent day-long fast made everything taste five times better.

Next, she took a thick glob of the golden honey jam before her and spread it across the bread. The added sweetness was complemented by a bite of fresh, crunchy salad. Then, she enjoyed a sip of rich vegetable-and-smoked-meat soup. Just as she capped it off by placing a sweet slice of fruit in her mouth, Rafina spoke.

"Well then, everyone, shall we get down to business? The reason I gathered you here today is, as I'm sure you've all guessed, to discuss the incident that occurred on the day of the Holy Eve Festival. Monica?"

On cue, Monica walked up to the table and respectfully bowed her head.

"First, I believe an update regarding Lynsha is in order," said the maid. "Fortunately, her injuries were not grave. After receiving treatment, she was able to resume her daily activities the following day."

"Oh, I went to see her this morning. I'm so glad she's okay," said a smiling Bel before she deflated a little and lowered her gaze. "I'm glad that...at least Lynsha is okay..."

"Bel..." Mia whispered, noticing that the young girl's breakfast remained completely untouched.

She picked up the jar of honey beside her and placed it in front of Bel, then said, "It's not time to give up yet. Rina's not a lost cause. We can still save her. So for now, eat up and keep your head up."

"Miss Mia..."

Bel looked up, at which point her eyes took in the dwindling food before Mia and widened with understanding.

"Oh, I'm sorry, but when I went to see Lynsha, I actually snacked on a lot of Perujin fruits that were given to her, and I'm really full now..." She laughed bashfully. "Perujin berries are really tasty."

"...Oh, Bel."

The comment reaffirmed for Mia that the girl before her was indeed of her blood.

Right you are. In the morning, nothing beats sugar.

Like grandmother, like granddaughter. Both shared a morning sweet tooth. And despite initial appearances, both also shared a perfectly functional appetite.

"Getting back to the topic at hand," said Monica, "regarding the whereabouts of the three individuals, Citrina Yellowmoon, her attendant Barbara, and the man who controls wolves, who together plotted an assassination against Princess Mia... We've received word that they attempted to flee toward Sunkland, where they ran into patrolling Sunkland cavalry."

"Ah. So they tried to cross the border to my homeland. But what's this about patrolling cavalry?" said Sion, raising an eyebrow.

Monica smiled.

"As a matter of fact, we were informed in advance of the wolf assassin's involvement by Ludwig."

Ludwig? Mia was reminded of a message she'd received. *Oh, now that she mentions it, I do remember Ludwig saying something about how someone had tried to kill him back in Tearmoon.*

Ludwig's scrupulously tidy handwriting reappeared in her mind. The letter had indeed mentioned an assassin who used wolves. Which was very much old news now, but throughout the fall, Mia's mind had been occupied by her impending assassination on the night of the Holy Eve Festival. She'd hardly possessed the spare mental capacity to consider all the letter's details.

Gah, that was a mistake. If I'd known the enemy would bring wolves, I'd have brought a meaty bone with me...

A vision of herself waving a bone around and making a fool of her enemy's wolves popped into her mind.

"Keep your eyes on the bone, doggies. Now, fetch!"

It was an enjoyable vision, so she indulged it a little longer, stopping only when the content of the discussion caught her attention again.

"Furthermore, on the day before the festival, we received an emergency message from Ludwig, telling us that the assassin with wolves would travel through Belluga and approach the border with Sunkland."

"Oh? I wasn't aware of that," said Mia. "I did ask Ludwig to investigate the connection between the House of Yellowmoon and the Chaos Serpents though. If he discovered something during that process, then I wouldn't have much of a say in how he handled it."

"I see. The urgent nature of the information might indeed have necessitated immediate correspondence. What we received was an extremely terse letter sent by messenger pigeon. It outlined the wolf-man's escape route and suggested locations for posting guards."

The Tearmoon Empire and the Holy Principality of Belluga were in fairly close proximity to each other. Even so, regular mail delivered by horse—the kind Mia often sent—took days to reach the recipient. Messenger pigeons, meanwhile, could do the same in far less time. Monica was, essentially, affording an extenuating reason for her having access to a piece of information that Mia didn't.

In truth though, Mia had given Ludwig free rein over his investigation and wasn't bothered in the least. For someone like her who subscribed to the "yes-man is best man" philosophy, Ludwig was the ideal vassal. She wouldn't dream of faulting his handling! Not when it allowed her to respond to all his reports with either "Yes!" or "Great!"

I must say though, Ludwig is so wonderfully dependable. As usual, as long as I leave it to him, everything just turns out fine.

Mia smiled with satisfaction.

Princess Mia...is quite the character. I'd always known it, but...

As she delivered her report, Monica felt a growing respect for the princess. Normally, the smarter a powerful figure was, the more they tended to micromanage their subjects. At the very least, they'd try to keep tabs on everything. Subordinates who acted arbitrarily without prior consultation usually incurred the displeasure of their superiors.

Mia's reaction, meanwhile, flew in the face of all common sense. She seemed nothing if not pleased. It was, in a way, a subtle but profound display of faith—a display impossible for those not endowed with absolute confidence. Confidence in her subjects, for she trusted them to do the right thing, and at the same time, confidence in her own ability to follow up should they fail. Monica regarded Mia, appreciating her in a new light, before continuing.

"Following Ludwig's report, we contacted Sunkland."

Officially, Sunkland's spy agency, the Wind Crows, had remained inoperative after the Remno incident. They'd undergone an internal purge of White Crows and were in the process of reorganization. Realistically, it went without saying that the Kingdom of Sunkland couldn't afford to shut down their entire intelligence network just like that. A core team of personnel remained active and ready to respond to emergencies.

Monica had delivered her message, hoping it would be picked up by a Wind Crow agent. It had been, and they'd responded swiftly. Without asking for further details, they'd immediately deployed their fastest cavalry.

"In accordance with Ludwig's instructions, they stationed themselves at the suggested spots and lay in wait. The operation was a success. The enemy fell for the ambush."

"Really? Does that mean…"

Bel's eyes lit up with expectation, only for their spark to be doused by a shake of Monica's head.

"Unfortunately, the enemy evaded capture. The wolf-man slipped past our lines and vanished. The carriage bearing the young lady of Yellowmoon and her minion Barbara changed course and made for Belluga. We believe they are headed for the Tearmoon Empire. Specifically, the Yellowmoon domain."

"They went back home? Seriously? That seems...sort of stupid. Are you sure they'd do that?" asked Abel.

Monica grinned.

"They were led to do so. Ludwig advised us to avoid completely encircling the enemy, for a trapped foe is a more dangerous foe. Instead, we followed his instructions and left an opening in the direction of Tearmoon as our forces closed in."

Abel nodded in understanding.

"I see. Makes sense. I wouldn't want to force that man to make a last stand either."

"Indeed. Soldiers with nowhere to go also have nothing to lose, and can at times do a terrible amount of damage before they perish. If that assassin is a skilled fighter, cornering him without ample preparation would be dangerous. Of course, the cavalry we had on patrol didn't even manage to corner him to begin with..."

It was still worthwhile, because it meant that the encirclement was just loose enough for the wolfmaster to escape on his own. That fact proved pivotal, not only dividing the enemy but also bringing Citrina—the one they wished to take back—within their reach again. As she worked through the logic, Monica was suddenly struck by a realization that gave her chills.

It's like...I'm having déjà vu. This is playing out in the exact same fashion as that time in Remno...

Back when she was in the Kingdom of Remno operating under the White Crow, Graham, she'd seen firsthand how the Great Sage of the Empire had systematically dismantled the White Crows' conspiracy piece by piece while simultaneously rebuilding it into a new outcome that favored her. It was like watching a sleight of hand trick being performed on the scale of an entire kingdom. The way things just came together in the end boggled her mind.

For example, had this assassination attempt not occurred, Ludwig's instructions would have fallen flat. Without a successful encirclement, the assassins from Tearmoon would likely have escaped with ease.

That wasn't, however, what had happened. The assassination attempt had occurred, and the blockade had worked. In the end, Mia got the exact outcome she'd wanted. Was this evidence of meticulous calculation? To Monica, it seemed to be nothing but.

Of course, a part of her mind pleaded for rationality. To the best of her knowledge, there was no possible way for someone to exert control over so many factors. That kind of calculation had to be impossible. Yet at the same time, she couldn't deny that the facts laid before her argued otherwise.

Lately, Mia had been visibly uneasy. That clearly suggested she'd somehow learned about the conspiracy against her. Then, the discreet manner in which she'd demonstrated the effect of the smoke-producing bath herbs to Citrina in the communal baths showed she'd already been aware of her compatriot's complicity. Nonetheless, she'd made no attempt to thwart their plot right then and there, undoubtedly for Citrina's sake. It was her way of giving her a chance to repent and in the process, reclaim her loyalty.

And now, regardless of how implausible it all might seem, the reality was that Mia had stopped Citrina from being whisked away to distant lands, instead placing her in a location that was firmly within reach. After, it should be noted, Citrina had made clear through her own actions a desire to atone.

"Everything Miss Mia did, she did to save Rina. I'm sure of it!"

Bel's confident assertion echoed in Monica's mind. She found it difficult to disagree with the girl.

It would take a tad too much willful ignorance to dismiss all of this as simple coincidence...

There was a certain reverence to her expression as she slowly turned her gaze toward Mia.

"...Princess Mia, just how many steps ahead do you think?"

Mia did not answer, responding with little more than a noncommittal smile.

I should ask Rafina what she thinks later... Perhaps she'll have a more objective view on the princess's actions.

Monica did bring the topic up with Rafina afterward, though it only served to further reinforce her awe of Mia's unfathomable mind.

In other words, it was business as usual.

Chapter 37: A World without Punchlines

With the Holy Eve Festival concluded, it was time for the winter holidays at Saint-Noel Academy. In previous years, Mia had always left for Lunatear ten days after the festival, after which she'd attend her birthday festival. This year, she departed early, for there was something she had to get done.

Mia and her entourage made their way not toward the imperial capital, but to the Rudolvon Outcounty. The route took them through the south of Belluga into Tearmoon. It was, as a piece of time-leaping trivia, the same path through which the Sunkland army had invaded when revolution had consumed the empire. From there, they proceeded in secret toward the Yellowmoon domain.

You know, there's something really satisfying about marching down this route. This is what I call poetic justice.

After all, it was through this very route that the Chaos Serpents had—indirectly but still unequivocally—cornered Mia. Now she was using it to corner them back. Every step she took filled her with vindictive glee.

Bypassing the Sealence Forest by following its perimeter, their carriages headed due north, soon arriving at a village near the Yellowmoon capital. There, they rendezvoused with Ludwig and the Princess Guard, who stood in a line at the village entrance to greet her.

"We are overjoyed by the safe return of Your Highness," said Ludwig, taking a knee before Mia as she stepped out of the carriage.

"Yes, it's certainly good to be back."

Despite gesturing for him to rise, Ludwig continued kneeling and kept his head down, prompting a curious frown from Mia.

"Is...there something else you wish to say?"

After a period of silence, Ludwig replied in a grave tone, his gaze still downcast.

"No, Your Highness. I have nothing to say for myself. The blunder I have committed is inexcusable, and I can only apologize."

"Oh? A blunder, you say?"

"Despite anticipating the fact that that assassin's path would lead him through Belluga, I failed to keep Your Highness out of harm's way..." he said, voice heavy with regret.

Mia's eyes widened at the sight.

My! A glum Ludwig? Now that's not something you see everyday! Fascinating!

She couldn't help but stare. After all the lectures and admonishment she'd suffered from him in the previous timeline, the sight of him dejected was downright novel.

With that said, I can't exactly leave him like this. He doesn't look very...productive. There's still going to be a famine to deal with soon, and I'm going to need him at his best...

She nodded to herself in thought. Then she spoke in a gentle voice.

"Arise, please. If not for you, then for me. What you speak of is not your fault, Ludwig. There will always be events that defy our expectations. As you can see, I have returned unharmed. Is that not enough?"

"But..."

He remained kneeling. Seeing this, she placed a hand under his arm and gave it a gentle tug, prompting him to look up.

"Unfortunately, we don't have time to split hairs right now. We need to rescue Citrina as soon as possible. I'd appreciate it if you'd join me in the carriage and brief me on the situation."

Ludwig held her gaze for a moment, then breathed a short sigh.

"I thank you, Your Highness, for granting me this chance to atone for my failings," he said, bowing his head once more.

Mia shook hers.

"Enough with the failings. Less atoning, more rescuing. Come on, hurry up."

Stepping into the carriage, Ludwig took note of the people inside.

There was Prince Sion and his attendant Keithwood, along with Prince Abel. These were familiar faces. The fourth person, however...

"Pleased to make your acquaintance, Ludwig Hewitt. I've heard much about you from Princess Mia."

Dressed in a maid's uniform, Monica Buendia gave him a courteous smile.

"Likewise, Miss Monica. The assistance you have been providing in this matter is greatly appreciated," replied Ludwig, returning her smile.

After exchanging friendly greetings with the other passengers, his expression sobered.

"Now, pardon my brusqueness, but let us get down to business. I have it on good authority that Lady Citrina and her attendant Barbara have already returned to the Duke's residence."

As soon as he said that, tension filled the air.

"By *returned*, do you mean they're still there, Ludwig?" asked Abel. "They're staying at the Yellowmoon manor?"

Ludwig nodded, saying, "They arrived there yesterday."

"A trap, then? It seems to me that they're waiting for us..." Abel said as he crossed his arms. "I thought for sure they'd try to raise an army out of desperation."

In taking Citrina back with her to the Yellowmoon domain, Barbara had already limited her own options. They could either force the empire into civil war or uproot their whole clan to escape abroad and live in hiding.

"Personally, I figured they'd up and vanish," said Sion. "They might be one of the four, but I can't see them achieving anything but their own demise through an open revolt right now. On what grounds would they rise up? Without just cause, how many men could they possibly rally? It would be a waste of soldiers' lives. The way I see it, they'd be better off lying low somewhere and planning their next move…"

At that, Sion fell into silent contemplation. The Serpents were frightening because they lacked a fixed identity. Their shapeless, enigmatic nature meant they could be anywhere, hiding just out of sight. That uncertainty was a source of fear. Equally vexing was the fact that they seemed to operate largely as a loose collection of lone actors and displayed no tendency to gather in one place. Eliminating one or two of their members did little to the whole.

But it would do a lot to those one or two members. Once any single Serpent's identity was revealed, they became only a minor menace. They were, in a way, like a swarm of locusts; eradicating the swarm is challenging, but each individual locust poses little threat on its own.

"Judging by the fact," Sion finally continued, "that they're not coming out of the manor, it might indeed be a trap…"

It was a difficult situation that furrowed the brows of everyone in the carriage, Mia included. For her, there was an added layer of complexity. Normally, in a situation like this, she'd simply tell her father that there was an attempt on her life. He'd doubtlessly mobilize the imperial army in response. Even the most devious of traps couldn't possibly stop an army from razing the whole manor.

However, if she were to take that approach, Barbara, along with Duke Yellowmoon's whole family, would be sentenced to death for their complicity in orchestrating the incident.

I won't be able to save Rina.

She thought of Bel, who sat in the carriage behind theirs. For the sake of her granddaughter, she needed to bring Citrina back safe and sound.

Besides, if we got the army involved, Duke Yellowmoon would probably respond by raising his own troops.

She knew that if it came to war, her side was guaranteed victory, but winning wouldn't lead to a bright future. The death of Duke Yellowmoon would cause widespread chaos throughout his domain. People would die. Fields would burn. And the next war would become that much harder to fight...because the next war would be against the great famine.

This whole affair, in other words, was nothing but a preliminary skirmish in Mia's eyes. What mattered was securing as many advantages as possible for the true battle ahead. To that end, she couldn't afford an extensive military engagement. If a fight was unavoidable, its scope had to be small and victory had to be swift. The only forces she could move freely were the Princess Guard and...Dion.

The Princess Guard and Dion.

She paused to consider the absurdity of that thought.

Well, I mean, Dion's pretty much a one-man army anyway. It makes sense to think of him in the same category.

While she was affirming her belief that Dion was more military unit than man, Ludwig spoke.

"Have no fear. Should obstacles appear, I shall see to it that they are removed." His voice was quiet, but it didn't contain a shred of doubt. "The Princess Guard is already in the process of apprehending members of the Chaos Serpents in the empire."

The statement elicited a round of gasps. Everyone in the carriage—save for one individual—understood how immensely difficult it was to ferret out Serpents hiding among the populace. They all wished to know how it was being done.

Naturally, all eyes shifted toward Mia, who declared, "Are they now? That's certainly reassuring. Good work."

And that was it! She made no attempt to inquire further, offering only a few words of appreciation. Nevertheless, no one protested the absence of details, interpreting her laissez-faire attitude as a sign of absolute faith in Ludwig's ability to get the job done. There was, they assumed, a simple and tacit understanding between them; she spoke her wishes, and he made them come true. She gave him her trust, he lived up to it. Therefore, he did not and need not explain.

Or, some then inferred, perhaps she didn't ask because she already knew, and it was her own meticulous instructions that Ludwig was carrying out.

The truth, though…

My, it sounds like finding Serpents is actually pretty easy. That reminds me, weren't they supposed to reveal themselves if you read them the Central Orthodox Church's Holy Book? Frankly, they sound like pushovers. Maybe I should give reading to them a go next time.

…Was that Mia hadn't the foggiest clue what was going on. The backbreaking efforts of her subjects were entirely lost on her. And her profound ungratefulness was lost on them. Meanwhile, the rest of the carriage had all drawn their own misguided conclusions. Frankly, it was hard to tell if anyone correctly understood anything. The whole conversation was a long joke waiting for its punchline. But alas, it would never be delivered.

Chapter 38: Citrina's Homecoming

Some narrative backtracking is in order.

It was the middle of night when Barbara reached Duke Yellowmoon's manor with Citrina in tow. This caught Lorenz, who'd been pacing aimlessly about in the courtyard in thought, completely off guard, sending him into a hasty scramble to welcome his daughter upon her sudden return.

"Come in, come in," he said. "What's going on— Ah, you have company."

As Barbara and Citrina entered the manor, three other men followed them in. They were fully armed, and each wore a mask with the same striking, snake-like design around the eyes. Lorenz was no stranger to the masks. They marked those enamored of the destruction of order, the Chaos Serpents. Those who would gladly give their lives to further its ends.

Lorenz couldn't resist a scowl. These men were not like the wolfmaster. There was a darkness about them. They reeked of decay and degeneration. The thought of his daughter being near such men was deeply unpleasant.

Citrina stood in silence, visibly upset. The haste with which they'd returned was evident in the dirt on her face and her disheveled uniform. She showed no signs of serious injury, but to Lorenz's eyes she seemed on the verge of falling apart. With her head hung, she made no attempt to look up. His heart ached at the sight of her exhaustion, and he rushed to her side…only to be stopped by a blade that pointed itself at his nose.

"Wh-What is the meaning of this?"

"This girl, in her foolishness, has betrayed us, milord. She betrayed the Serpents," hissed Barbara as she gave Citrina's back a shove.

Citrina crumpled forward onto her knees like a puppet whose strings had been cut.

"Well, milady? Do you not feel that you owe milord an apology? Your stupidity has deeply inconvenienced him. How do you intend to atone?"

Citrina shuddered. She turned her face up to him at last.

"I'm sorry… Th-Thinking about friendship made Rina do something stupid. I put those worthless feelings first…and ended up helping Her Highness escape." Tears fell from the dying embers that were her eyes. "I'm sorry…for being such a useless daughter."

"Rina… Come on, let's get you on your feet first." Lorenz placed his hands on her shoulders. "What happened out there—"

"Thanks to milady's foolish whims, we failed to assassinate Princess Mia," Barbara spat.

"What in the— Assassinate Princess Mia?!"

Lorenz stared at Barbara in shock, but she only sighed.

"Such folly. We've shown our hand. An attempt on the princess's life must not leave any witnesses. It is the simplest of concepts, but milady was so caught up with playing pretend that it seems to have gone right over her head. Had you obeyed the Serpents' orders, you would have enjoyed a nice period of prosperity as a Yellowmoon, but instead…"

Barbara spitefully played with Citrina's hair, twisting it around her fingers.

"W-Well, in any case," said Lorenz, hastily trying to redirect the conversation, "what's failed is failed. Not much to do about that now. Let us hurry up and make plans for escape then."

"Escape? What escape?"

"*Our* escape, of course! You can't possibly be thinking of challenging the empire through open revolt!"

"Of course not," Barbara replied with a wave of her hand. "They will crush us, and that will be it. An entirely futile attempt."

Even the Redmoons with their elite private army couldn't hope to wage war against the imperial army alone. For the Yellowmoons, whose faction more resembled a loose rabble than a front—many who aligned themselves with the Yellowmoons did so with a sigh rather than a cheer—it would be suicide.

"Then why—"

"What, milord, is there to gain from escape? What will you and this pathetic daughter of yours do afterward?"

Barbara grabbed Citrina's hair and violently yanked her face close to her own.

"Ow—"

Citrina swallowed a cry of pain and squeezed her eyes shut.

"What *can* you even do on the run?" spat Barbara. "What use will you be? Are we to train you in the arts of assassination and have you try again with the princess?"

She released Citrina equally violently before shrugging.

"Regrettably, I do believe this girl will never become a Serpent. Not while she entertains her silly fascination with worthless sentiments such as friendship."

"Then... D-Do you propose we confront them here in the manor?"

"Do I? Let us consider your question. Do you believe these men will have a chance against her? After she has already defeated our strongest asset, the wolfmaster? No, their blades will not draw the princess's blood," she said, shaking her head at her followers. "Or do you, milord, know of someone who can best that cursed Dion Alaia in combat?"

"I...don't believe so."

"Then clearly, that is not what I propose."

Barbara gave an unnervingly sweet smile before continuing.

"A small worm does not fight a lion by standing up to it. It will simply be crushed. A worm can only ail a lion from the inside." She slowly turned toward Lorenz and held his gaze. "You Yellowmoons are worms, aren't you? Poisonous ones, at that. As the oldest of the loyal, you should not accept a pointless death under the lion's paw. Instead, you should make like the poisonous worms you are, and have yourselves ripped apart and devoured to spread your toxin through your foes. It is through that toxin you will stain the princess's reputation and further the goal of the Serpents."

Her smile turned gentle.

"Now then... Let us prepare, milord. Milady too. We must make ready to welcome the Great Sage of the Empire, and it would be disrespectful to do so wearing such filthy clothes. We shall greet her in a most peaceful fashion, on our best behavior, and wearing our prettiest things. Anything we can do to torment them further for the choice they must make is— Oh?" She raised an eyebrow. "By the way, milord, where is Bisset?"

"O-Oh... He told me he was going out on an errand."

"Goodness gracious." Barbara chuckled. "Abandoned at last by even your butler. My condolences, milord. But fear not, for I, and all us Serpents, shall remain by your side until the very end."

Chapter 39: The Advent of Empress Magistratus Mia and Her Arbitrary Arbitrations... Does Not Come to Pass

"We have arrived, Your Highness. Do mind your step."

Mia's carriage entered the Yellowmoon capital, Foret-Jaune, rather uneventfully. Though stopped by guards for routine inspection, they encountered no other impediments on their way to the town center where Duke Yellowmoon's manor was located.

"I'd expected *some* resistance. At least an obstacle or two..." said Sion.

"Yeah, it's a little creepy how smooth this trip was. Smells even more like a trap," agreed Abel.

Mia, after hearing the princes' comments, started feeling a little nervous herself.

They have a point... I guess there is a sense of danger in the air. But where's Mr. I-Show-Up-Where-the-Danger-Is?

She glanced around curiously.

"If it's Sir Dion you're looking for," said Ludwig with almost telepathic precision, "he's currently on a different mission."

"Is he now? I see. Hm..."

Frankly, the thought of kicking in Duke Yellowmoon's front door without Dion was making her anxious.

"Ha ha ha, I'm sure you'd rather have Captain Dion with you, Your Highness, but don't you worry. We won't let anyone lay a finger on you. Give us a little credit, yeah?"

Vanos, now captain of the Princess Guard, gave her a reassuring grin.

"…You're right, of course. I'm counting on you to protect me then."

She nodded at him, but soon added, "But not by throwing away your own lives, all right? Even if it's for me. Your lives are valuable, and I want you to treat them as such."

The comment was spurred by the memory of another duke's red-headed daughter.

If this man dies for my sake, Ruby's going to be very upset at me… I'd rather not deal with that.

"We know, Your Highness. There's not a man under your command who'll 'throw his life away,'" replied Vanos with a laugh.

Mia found herself only partially reassured.

Mmm… Vanos seems like exactly the type to jump into harm's way. I can totally see him taking a sword for me. Oh moons, it's times like these when I wish Dion were here. He'd charge into an army, then come back whistling.

She sighed and turned her gaze toward the manor. Just as she did, someone appeared at the front door.

"Wha—"

Eyes widening, she stared at the figure.

"Welcome, Your Highness. Milord and milady await you inside."

Standing there with her head bowed too low to be sincerely respectful was the Yellowmoon maid, Barbara. The two princes immediately gripped their sword hilts.

"You've got some nerve, just strolling out here like that."

Barbara brushed off the open hostility with a smile.

"Prince Sion, if you wish for milady Citrina to be returned unharmed, then I advise prudence in your actions from here on in."

"Is that a demand for us to drop our weapons?"

Sion gave her a sharp look, but she remained unfazed.

"I wouldn't dream of doing such a thing," she said with a shake of her head. "That would be an infringement of royal privilege. Please, enter accompanied by your arms. The sword is the symbol of a ruler. To wear it is his right. It is, after all, the mark of royalty to wield the sword as he pleases and slay those who oppose them, is it not?"

Her remark and ensuing cackle were met by a cool, quiet response.

"A king wields his sword only against evil. Evil such as yourself."

"My oh my, is that how it works? Spoken like a true upholder of justice and righteousness, Prince Sion. Well, in that case, I suppose I should play my part as your villainess." She chuckled and continued in a theatrically malicious voice. "Think twice before drawing that sword of yours then, if you wish to retrieve milady in one piece."

Her gaze slithered its way from Sion to Abel and Keithwood. Then she said, "Now, do come in, though as guests of Duke Yellowmoon, I will remind you to conduct yourselves in an appropriate manner."

Her demeanor remained wholly respectful, save for her mocking grin. With a flourish, she bade them enter and led the way.

Having gained such disconcertingly easy entrance to the manor, Mia and her friends could but step cautiously into their enemy's lair.

Inside, they discovered a modest decor at odds with the pomp and extravagance often associated with powerful nobles. A long hallway stretched before them, its walls adorned by what seemed like endless portraits of unfamiliar faces.

Is it just me, or are there a lot of boring old men in these portraits? There's literally nothing striking about any of them.

Mia's musing was interrupted by Barbara, who noticed her gazing at the portraits.

"Displayed on these walls are the heads of the House of Yellowmoon. Generation after generation, they and their cursed bloodline have done the Tearmoon Empire's dirty work."

"I see. Hm…"

Mia nodded with interest.

Then again, a lot of them do look pretty coldhearted, she thought as she regarded the portraits anew.

Mia, you see, was easily influenced.

The hallway opened into a large courtyard filled with vegetation. Across it was…

"Th-That's…"

Three masked men stood over a kneeling one, their blades pointed at his neck. The man held at swordpoint was dressed richly. Beside him sat a young girl.

"Rina!"

Bel exclaimed at the sight of her friend. Slowly Citrina lifted her head and met Bel's gaze. She smiled a sweet smile, but it didn't last.

"…Bel."

Her pleasant front crumbled, revealing a girl on the verge of tears. With deliberate steps, Barbara walked over to her and turned around to face the guests.

"Now then…let us begin, shall we? The time of judgment is upon us. The House of Yellowmoon must be tried for their sins."

"Judgment? What do you mean?" asked Mia. "What are you going to do to them?"

Barbara looked at her with glee.

"What am *I* going to do? Nothing. Absolutely nothing."

"The nerve of this woman. They weren't lying when they said depravity breeds shamelessness," said Abel.

Barbara shrugged.

"Judge me as you will, but later. Once this is over, Prince Abel, you may dispense upon me whatever justice you please. But right now, it is not me who is on trial." She walked behind Citrina and placed her hands on her shoulders. "Those who must be tried are the members of the cursed house of Yellowmoon."

"The cursed house of Yellowmoon..." Mia echoed, as she recalled the generations of Lord Yellowmoons that adorned the hallway.

"As I'm sure you're aware, those of the Yellowmoon bloodline have throughout the ages operated in the shadows of Tearmoon's history, assassinating countless important individuals and erasing entire families of nobles."

"That's no—"

Lorenz ventured a protest, but cold metal was pressed even harder against his neck, forcing him to stop. His unspoken sentiments, however, did not remain buried. Ludwig, as if reading his mind, picked up where he'd left off.

"That's not an entirely fair depiction. They were simply eliminating threats to the empire. If a nation is to grow, it will surely encounter power struggles that must be resolved. In that sense, what the House of Yellowmoon has done, while not openly laudable, does not qualify them for harsh trial either," he said as he smartly adjusted his glasses.

Huh. That reminds me. I guess Ludwig did mention something in his letter about the Yellowmoons doing shady things...

While Mia reflected on the contents of a letter she clearly hadn't read very carefully, Barbara put on a thoughtful smile.

"I see. So you claim that the needs of a growing empire exonerate their actions. A reasonable argument, perhaps. But does it apply to *this* pair? In case you weren't aware, both father and daughter

331

are Serpents, and in doing the Chaos Serpents' bidding, they've carried out a number of assassinations." She placed a hand on her cheek in mock contemplation. "Let's see... Just to list off a few... There was the head of an outland noble family whose domain contained a great deal of farmland. He was killed by a special poison, the family was scattered, and the House of Yellowmoon took control of the farmland. Then there was a noble who caught on to what we Serpents were doing. That whole family was wiped out. Oh, speaking of which..."

Barbara clapped her hands once as she glanced at Citrina.

"Milady, it didn't go quite as before, but this isn't the first time you've tried *erasing* one of your friends, is it?"

Citrina's pale eyes snapped open.

"N-No, Barbara. Stop."

She tried to stand, but a nearby man pushed her back down. Undeterred, she struggled free of his grasp.

"Don't! Don't...tell Bel..." she pleaded, voice thick with grief.

This only delighted Barbara, who grinned sadistically.

"You use that sweet little smile of yours to befriend them, then charm their families, and finally kill them all with poison... You poisoned a friend's drink with your own hands, didn't you?"

"Ah..."

Citrina's legs gave way. She crumpled to the ground and pressed her hands to her ears, unwilling—unable—to hear more.

Barbara chuckled.

"Did you know, dear guests, that the Yellowmoons are masters of poison? Milord, for example, has such extensive knowledge of banes and venoms that it makes my own expertise seem like *child's play*," she said, turning back toward Mia's group. "So, O royal upholders of all that is fair and righteous, as you look upon the face of sin..."

She gestured toward the Yellowmoons with a flourish. "What will you do? Surely," she orated with increasing eloquence as her gaze homed in on Mia, "as the Great Sage of the Empire, Your Highness will not leave evil untried? Go on then. By all means. Do bring the gavel of justice down upon these wicked souls."

"Well, uh, I—"

"Or does Your Highness intend to pardon this pair of wrongdoers? Let both father and daughter walk free, unreproved in spite of all they've done?" Barbara's grin grew wider. "I suppose that would be a fine decision as well. After all, what is royalty if not the power to have one's way? To stand tall and crush the principled but inconvenient protests of the lower rabble? But you may wish to think twice before doing so, especially in the presence of your regal compatriot. Isn't that so, Prince Sion?"

Her gaze shifted to him.

"Kings must uphold justice. Is that not the doctrine of Sunkland's royal family? Those with power have a duty to wield it ethically and righteously. Can you overlook amnesty granted purely on the basis of fondness for the princess?"

Sion's lips tightened at the remark.

"And what would the sainted Rafina think of such an act?" Barbara continued, ignoring his expression of displeasure. "Would she look fondly upon the guiltless acquittal of a girl who once killed her own friend? And was complicit in the murder of the friend's parents and the ruin of their entire family?"

Venom coursed through every sentence and dripped from every word. That was Barbara's poison. She would have Mia personally pass judgment on Citrina and Lorenz and condemn their crimes. Or, failing that, deliberately make the decision not to convict them of their guilt. In the former scenario, she would indeed be acting justly.

But to have Citrina die by her hand would undoubtedly create a rift between her and Bel, who'd developed a close friendship with the young Yellowmoon. Her fellow members of the student council would likely harbor complicated feelings toward the affair as well. Such an outcome would leave a scar in her heart and fracture her bond with her friends.

What if she chose the latter then? And pardoned the Yellowmoons? Sion, noted advocate of justice, and Rafina, preacher of holy ways, would not take kindly to such a decision. Therefore, refraining from judgment would breed discord between them and Mia as well. The schism that would form might be small. A minor crack at best. But a crack it would create, and the Serpents would then seize upon that tiny opening. Even if Barbara was arrested here, other Chaos Serpents would come to poke and pry at it until they ripped the bond between Mia and her friends apart.

And they did. Rather, they had. It was this very approach that had brought about the mass poisoning during the Holy Eve Festival, which tormented Rafina to no end and transformed her into the entropic force that was the Empress Prelate. She'd then inadvertently spearheaded the Serpents' crusade against order. Such was their method. If they couldn't eliminate someone through assassination, they'd simply strike at the person's heart instead, for a soul disfigured by scars might very well twist itself into a champion of chaos.

The Serpents' venom was a pernicious one. It seeped unnoticed into the brain and poisoned the mind, every bit as lethal as a blight upon the body. Faced with the insidious technique of a seasoned snake, Mia...

Okay, is it just me or has this old crone been really rude to Rina this whole time?

...Was a tad cross. The way Barbara kept picking on Citrina rubbed her the wrong way.

Mia just didn't have the heart to look away from a person in distress. No matter what Barbara said, she just couldn't see Citrina as an assassin who'd committed unspeakable horrors, only a poor little girl hugging her knees. Which led her to think...

There's no way Rina did those things willingly. I mean, just look at her. She was obviously forced, the poor thing.

In spite of everything, the fact remained that she and Citrina had gone through some of life's most profound experiences together. Like witnessing the creation of new life through the birth of a foal. And picking mushrooms. The questionable parity of those two events aside, they'd *connected*.

I'm pretty sure that Rina herself isn't a bad person. I bet Barbara twisted her arm to get her to do those things. In that case, I can probably save Rina without much repercussion. If Miss Rafina asks, chances are I'll get away with it by saying that there was a girl being bullied in front of me, so I stepped in to save her, and that's all that happened.

It was...a flimsy argument at best, but Mia couldn't care less, because right now, she had absolutely no liability. Even if she were to make a few errors in judgment, Barbara was still the clear villain. There was also Duke Yellowmoon, who was a prime target for blame shifting if the need arose. Being a complete bystander in this discussion of generational crimes, she was practically impervious to fault.

She huffed out a confident breath, feeling a rising sense of excitement. With absolutely no skin in the game, she could say whatever she wished and judge people as she pleased. Behold! It was time for Empress Magistratus Mia and Her Arbitrary Arbitrations!

All right, woman, enough yapping. Time for me to give you a piece of my mind!

As the spirit of Empress Magistratus Mia infused itself into her person, its hammer of justice raised and ready to strike down whomever had the misfortune to incur her resentment…

"Wait, Your Highness. I humbly request just a moment of your time."

…Lorenz Etoile Yellowmoon spoke for the first time.

And that was when the tide began to shift.

"Milord, must I remind you to keep your mouth shut?" said Barbara as she brandished a blade at Lorenz's throat. "It is with great effort that we've managed to bring you unharmed before Her Highness for trial. It would be a shame if injury were to occur in the process."

A shame for him *and* Barbara. The whole point of avoiding open conflict and inviting Mia's group inside was to create this very situation. If a fight broke out, one of her subordinates might end up killing Lorenz in the brawl. That would defeat the point. A mortally wounded Lorenz being put out of his misery by Mia wouldn't suffice either. He had to be whole, sound of mind and body, with decades of life left to enjoy, only to have it all cut short by Mia's hand. *That* was the point.

Lorenz showed no sign of backing off.

"Good gracious, getting rather hot-blooded, aren't we, milord? I suppose I have no choice but to cool you down a little. Let us draw some of that heat out of your veins."

She raised her blade and swung it down at him.

"Father!"

Citrina screamed as the deadly weapon came down on his shoulder. But it failed to draw blood.

"What?!"

Barbara's eyes widened, looking from her blade—now frozen in midair—to the aging face of a man who'd suddenly appeared beside her.

His smartly trimmed mustache complemented his spotless black butler's uniform.

"Now, now, Barbara. That is hardly how a maid should behave toward her master."

"You... I thought you'd already fled for dear life, Bisset. What have you been up to?" she said with a scornful smile at the man holding back her arm.

Sion's brows twitched at the name.

"Did she say...Bisset?" he murmured. "Why does that name sound so familiar?"

Meanwhile, the spirit of Empress Magistratus Mia, who'd been ready to deliver a masterpiece of percussive justice, timidly lowered her hammer and phased out of existence. Mia, you see, was a girl who could read a room. And the room had just *changed*.

"Interrupting milord when he is speaking...is insolence of the highest order. If anyone should keep their mouth, Barbara, it is you."

He wrenched the blade out of Barbara's hand, then lowered his head toward Lorenz.

"I apologize for my tardiness, milord. Exterminating the vermin took longer than expected," he said, before fixing each of the Serpents with a look that warned them to keep their hands off his master.

Barbara heaved a sigh at this turn of events.

"Hmph... So be it. There is little to be gained from violence here. Go ahead, milord. I can't imagine you having anything of value to say, but feel free to speak in your own defense."

She took a step back and made a wordless *the stage is yours* gesture.

Lorenz sighed as well, though his expressed relief.

"Ah, mm, very well. In that case, if I may speak my mind, Your Highness…"

He looked to Mia who, expecting the conversation to proceed without her involvement, barely managed to stop herself from jumping at this sudden mention of her name. However, by now, she was used to getting caught off guard and quickly recomposed herself, readying her mind to respond to any possible development.

"Yes, Duke Yellowmoon? Please, speak freely."

Lorenz held her gaze, as though studying her, and dropped a bombshell of a claim.

"Everything Barbara has said is categorically untrue. Neither I nor my daughter Citrina has ever taken the life of another."

"…Huh?"

This revelatory profession left the entire courtyard in stunned silence. Barbara recovered first, shattering the stillness with a mocking cackle.

"And here I thought you'd offer at least a semblance of a credible defense. What is this nonsense, milord? Have you lost your mind? Do you honestly expect anyone to believe such an absurd claim?" Barbara scoffed.

Mia, frankly, shared her opinion.

Okay, come on now. That's definitely a reach…

But just as she was about to voice this sentiment, she noticed something important—her loyal subject Ludwig was staying mum! Ludwig, who in the previous timeline had never passed up an opportunity to point out in exasperating fashion every one of her remarks that was even remotely incorrect…was completely silent. More than that, his expression didn't show the slightest hint of doubt. His arms crossed complacently, he seemed entirely content to let the duke finish.

Now that...is interesting...

Mia gulped her words back down and kept her mouth closed. Mimicking Ludwig's crossed-arms stance, she adopted a similar "wait and see" approach, keeping her eyes and ears alert for any sign of incoming waves of momentum she could ride. Lorenz glanced at her once more, then took a short breath and continued.

"As you all know, we Yellowmoons have since the inception of the Tearmoon Empire committed ourselves to the covert elimination of those who would impede our progress as an imperial nation. We have done so in accordance with our oath to the first emperor. But... these recent decades have proven remarkably stable. In addition, His Imperial Majesty is of gentle disposition. Not once have we received instructions to carry out an assassination."

"Hm..."

Mia nodded along, finding that Lorenz's statement was consistent with her own understanding.

I don't know if I'd call his disposition "gentle," but father definitely has no interest in anything that doesn't have my name on it. All he cares about is getting me to like him. Also, as far as I know, it's true that the empire hasn't experienced any wars lately.

The amount of political infighting among nobles certainly made up for it, but nevertheless, no menace had ever required one of the Four Houses to personally get involved in its elimination.

"Hah, are you even listening to yourself?" asked Barbara derisively. "That's even more incriminating. With all that free time on your hands, you've had ample leisure to do the Chaos Serpents' bidding." She smirked at him with smug triumph. "I know what you've done. In your efforts to undermine the empire and curse this land with unending turmoil, you've killed many wise men and people who opposed the Serpents.

339

Had you carried out those assassinations as the empire's invisible sword, your crimes might have deserved pardon. But you didn't. You acted on behalf of the Serpents—"

"I," Lorenz interjected, "am a coward, Barbara. Unlike Her Highness. I am not endowed with her courage. Assassination? Why, what a dreadful notion. The thought alone terrifies me. I could never bring myself to do such a thing. Which is why...I deceived you."

"Such drivel. Is fantasy and falsehood the extent of your defense? What do you stand to gain by speaking such obvious lies?" Barbara said, shaking her head like a disappointed parent. "You are indeed a coward, milord. That I will not deny. And that is precisely why you would never dare betray the Serpents. Perhaps in a situation similar to this, when you are in the presence of those who oppose the Serpents, you may yet manage to defy our will. But the present state of affairs is entirely the work of the great sage. You couldn't possibly have let your victims live expecting the princess to create this exact situation far, far down the road. That defies all logic."

"A rare lapse in reasoning coming from you, Barbara. The logic is quite simple. You need only think about it for a moment. The people the Serpents ordered me to kill are inevitably those who pose a threat to them," Lorenz replied in a firm voice. "That is to say, they are people who would be useful allies in fighting against the Serpents. Should I ever rise in rebellion against the Serpents, they are likely to come to my aid. I think that is more than sufficient reason to let them live."

Barbara sneered at his argument.

"An amusing theory, but a mere theory nonetheless. The subjects who serve you are all under our influence. The Wind Crows too. Specifically, the White Crows, who've been working closely with the Yellowmoons. They were under the control of Jem.

Nothing you did could possibly escape our notice. How do you propose to have pulled off this epic feat of deception then? On your own? With so many eyes on you? You somehow faked your victims' deaths, and then simply *whisked them away* to some safe place? You, with all your craven incompetence?"

Barbara's increasingly caustic ridicule elicited only a weak shrug.

"You speak the truth," said Lorenz. "It pains me to admit that I am weak and ineffectual. I possess neither the power to oppose your people, nor even the strength to shield my own daughter from sorrow. It tears at my heart every day…"

He drew a breath. His expression grew placid as he looked at Barbara.

"But he…is not," he said, gesturing at Bisset. "And he is the crucial piece you overlooked."

That was exactly when Ludwig chose to wade into the conversation, speaking as if he'd recalled an interesting tidbit.

"On that note… Prince Sion, I've completely forgotten to relay to you the answer to the question you posed."

"Hm? What question was this again?"

"It was, in fact, Her Highness who brought your question to my attention. Jason, Lucas, Max, Thanasis…and Bisset."

Sion's eyes grew in size as Ludwig rattled off the list of names.

"No way… You mean…"

Monica, not sharing his surprise, nodded in confirmation.

"Yes. The gentleman there who currently goes by Bisset is a former Wind Crow. The legendary architect of Sunkland's intelligence network in Tearmoon."

Bisset shook his head with mild disapproval at her description.

"Now, now. Exaggeration serves none of our interests. It's all ancient history now."

A man without name or face, shapeless and nondescript… That was the aging butler, currently known as Bisset. Meeting him drastically altered the course of Lorenz's life and the fate of the entire house of Yellowmoon. From then on, fortunes also continued to smile on them. Time and again, Lorenz managed to deftly thread the needle, heeding demands for assassinations from the Serpents but never actually carrying them out.

He knew the Serpents. Knew how they slithered into hearts, exploited weaknesses, and pricked at wounds. They were masters of manipulation. His father and grandfather had stained their hands with blood. As a result, they became pawns of the Serpents, who used that fact against them until the end. Unlike other crimes, murder cannot be undone. To take another's life—even once—was to invite their suffocating presence for life. Even a single murder was too much.

Lorenz had no desire to be controlled by their constricting tactics. Also, he just didn't want to kill people. As a man whose heart mewed rather than roared, he hated pain and suffering with equal passion. Having already made the crucial observation that partaking even once in their deadly schemes meant there would be no going back, he lied and deceived himself out of every request.

But in the end, he was given a mission he could no longer evade—a direct order to kill Bisset. At the time, the Chaos Serpents had successfully snuck one of their men into Sunkland's intelligence agency. That man was, of course, Jem. In his attempt to take over the Wind Crows, Bisset proved to be a major obstacle due to his experience and reputation. So, Jem sought to eliminate him. A betrayal by a friend ultimately forced Bisset into dire straits. It was then that Lorenz lent a helping hand and faked Bisset's death to save him. Ever since then, Bisset had served Lorenz as his butler.

Though Barbara was a cunning Serpent, her know-how when it came to espionage was ultimately amateur. For Bisset, a former intelligence elite, fooling her was a simple task. Thus, Lorenz gained the critical components he needed—a route through which important figures could secretly escape abroad, and an ally who could help them do so.

"In the world of intelligence, local collaborators are worth their weight in gold. Therefore, information about them must be withheld even from one's colleagues. This is something I learned from Master Bisset, and true to his own teachings, he never revealed to anyone the identity of his collaborator in Tearmoon," added one of the two maids behind Mia.

So that's the former Wind Crow, Miss Monica...

Lorenz mentally matched the description from reports to the person standing before him, then nodded.

"Indeed. I could have done none of this alone. Covertly transporting assassination targets to safer places abroad... Dropping their carriages off cliffs to make it look like they died... Such acts far exceeded my capabilities. It was all him."

"Nonsense... Complete nonsense. That's not possible," said Barbara, head swaying from side to side in reflexive denial even as the irrefutable truth began to dawn.

With no dead bodies, there was no way to know if their victims were dead or alive. They could have sent detainment requests with personal descriptions to neighboring nations, but no one was likely to have bothered...because there didn't seem to be any need to do so. None of them ever suspected that they, the deceivers, would become the deceived. But then, Barbara remembered something, and she regained her composure.

"Hah... You speak lies, milord. I know you've killed before. Killed him personally, in fact, with those special poisons of yours. I saw the body myself. I even confirmed it was dead."

"My special poisons, you say… Ah, yes, I suppose that's true. I have indeed used poisons before. After all, I have such extensive knowledge of them that…" He looked her in the face. "…it makes your own expertise seem like *child's play.*"

Barbara's mouth opened, but no words came. Understanding flashed across her widening eyes. It wasn't a particularly difficult conclusion to reach. Had she ever stopped to think about it, it would surely have come to her already.

Duke Yellowmoon knew a lot about plants. And medicines. And poisons. That was common knowledge. But *why* did he know so much? How much of his encyclopedic expertise would be necessary if his only goal had been to kill? Did an assassin need to be familiar with every poison under the sun?

No. If death was the objective, a mere handful would suffice. The salamandrake, for example, was potent enough to kill with a single dose. Familiarity with a couple of poisons like that should be more than enough for an assassin. So why did the duke keep going then? With such lethal choices already available, why did he dig deeper, meticulously studying the kaleidoscopic effects of a variety of weaker poisons?

To *not* kill, of course.

He studied them to know what antidotes could be given to counter their effect. And, perhaps, how long he could wait to give them, after the victims have ostensibly drawn their last breaths.

"Do you know why I obsess over poisons, Barbara? It is so I can use ones you don't know and feign the deaths of my victims. Unlike other methods of killing, poison is convenient, because it allows me to deceive your people," he said with a smile of cathartic satisfaction.

It had, of course, all been a gamble. His efforts might have never borne fruit. Like Barbara said, the Yellowmoon faction was not capable of defending themselves against the rest of the empire in the case of war.

The Serpents with their cunning ways could have whispered into the emperor's ear, encouraging him to mobilize the army. They could also have secretly assassinated him and his allies. Had any of those highly possible scenarios occurred, this ace he kept up his sleeve would have been doomed to futility. But they didn't occur, and he managed to slap his trump card down on the table.

Because she's here...

Lorenz glanced at Mia. Ever since her arrival, he'd been carefully studying her, trying to discern if she was truly the trustworthy person the rumors claimed her to be. His answer came in the form of her expression when, faced with Barbara's abuse of Citrina, she glared at the older woman with genuine anger. Willing or not, Citrina had been complicit in an attempt on her life. How many people would be upset by the mistreatment of someone who'd *tried to kill them*? A vindictive "serves you right" seemed the more likely response. Not Mia though. Mia was upset at how Citrina was being treated.

Apparently, Her Highness said she believes in Citrina. Perhaps...that alone should have been enough to deserve my full and unqualified trust.

That was the thought that had finally convinced him to throw in with her and show his long-concealed hand. With his cards revealed, he turned to Mia and said, "That is all, Your Highness. I have spoken all I wish to say and now humbly await your judgment."

Faced with this relentless outpouring of new information, Mia responded in her usual manner.

"...Eh?"

With a slack-jawed stare of profound bewilderment.

Chapter 40: The Advent of Princess Praetor Mia and Her Golden Masterstroke... Does Come to Pass

"Huh? Uhhh… Hmm. Hm hm hm. I, uh, see…"

Mia made an effort not to look too clueless, but on the inside, she was in full panic mode.

Yeep! What is even happening?

The shift in the conversation was so sudden it'd given her whiplash. She'd astutely recognized that Lorenz's revelations had fundamentally changed the nature of the proceedings. This was no longer a trial of Lorenz and Citrina to determine their personal guilt. There *was* no guilt to speak of. They hadn't directly killed anyone. Instead, they'd been protecting important figures from the Serpents. If they deserved anything, it was praise, not penalty.

But this *was* still a trial. And there *was* still guilt to be examined. A guilt so great in scope it made her head spin. The issue Lorenz now placed under examination…was whether children should shoulder blame for their parents' crimes. The guilt he questioned was that of his parents, and their parents, and the generations of ancestors in the Yellowmoon bloodline. Should the punishment for the past actions of his cursed clan be suffered by its modern descendants—him and Citrina.

And he'd posed this question to *her*. She, who would be in a *very awkward* position if ancestral guilt could be inherited. After all, it was old Tearmoon the First who had placed this cursed burden on the Yellowmoons to begin with, forcing all successive generations into the sinful service of the Chaos Serpents. If the Yellowmoons were crooks, then the first emperor was the granddaddy of all criminals. If Lorenz and Citrina bore the guilt of being descendants of conspirators, then Mia... Well, she belonged to the lineage of the principal freaking offender!

No longer was she a casual bystander, content to watch from the gallery with juice and snacks. She was sitting smack dab in the middle of the courtroom! This was no time to be entertaining fantasies about Empress Magistratuses and hammer-wielding.

I-I thought I was supposed to be a spectator. How did I end up in the defendant's seat? Hnnnngh, stupid ancestors and their stupid ideas!

After going on a mental tirade against the first emperor, she forced herself to think, for her next move now demanded considerable caution. Even if she did want to see them get a good flogging, a severe sentence was now out of the question, because whatever punishment she handed out would come right back to her. That kind of careless decision-making would be pretty much asking for a Serpent intervention. They'd doubtlessly start stirring up discourse about how Mia deserved the same penalty as the Yellowmoons.

So, no flogging then. Not that she wanted to do so in the first place. The better—and trickier—question was how far should she go in the other direction? Letting them off scot-free wasn't exactly an option either. Her personal opinion was that inheritable ancestral sin could go choke on a rock fungus. She couldn't care less what nonsense her forebears had been up to, and she wanted to say so to Citrina and her father, but the situation didn't allow it. Her own potential implication in the matter meant that if she gave them a quick and easy pardoning, it might be interpreted as a desire to save her own skin. Again, careless decision-making, Serpent intervention, et cetera.

Ugh, stupid Serpents! I just know they'll make a big deal out of this! The sadistic smile she'd seen on Barbara's face moments before was proof enough.

She also felt the excruciatingly intense gazes of Sion, Keithwood, and Monica on her back, all waiting eagerly to hear her ruling. A half-baked verdict would surely provoke a flurry of complaints.

There was no room for error. She needed a perfect answer, one that would at least be tolerated if not welcomed by all parties. And she needed it now. The only problem was…

Hnnnngh… This is a tough one… This is a very tough one!

…Her brain wasn't playing ball. Still, she kept thinking. To save Citrina…and more importantly, to make sure she herself didn't end up collateral damage. She thought and thought, and just when she thought she was about to pass out from all the thinking she was doing, the spirit of Empress Magistratus Mia descended once again! Imbued with her judicious wisdom, she spoke.

"You have made your case, Duke Lorenz Etoile Yellowmoon, and I have heard it."

The spirit-infused Mia raised in one hand her proverbial hammer of justice…

"So…basically…what you're saying is, neither you nor Rina have ever done the deed yourself. Hm, hm. I see. Very interesting. In that case…"

…And with the other hand, gingerly placed the chisel of justice against the issue. Then, with the most timid of clinks, she began chipping away at it, hoping to sculpt a compromise that everyone could stomach. Strike by nervous strike, she probed its texture with the touch of a sculptor being forced to perform surgery.

"Please, Your Highness," said a disgusted Barbara. "You aren't seriously going to believe the rubbish they're spewing?"

Mia paid her no heed and continued to prod the conversation along with the utmost caution. Lorenz, she figured, had little reason to lie. Even if he managed to temporarily deceive her, he'd only be delaying his inevitable ruin. It'd also spoil everyone's opinion of him, possibly placing him in an even worse situation down the road. Therefore...

"Ludwig, just to make sure, I'd like you to ask Bisset for information regarding the people he sent abroad and to try and make contact with them."

"Already done, Your Highness. The envoys are on their way."

"They are? Good. Your foresight is impressive as always."

Proof was forthcoming, so for now, she decided to reserve judgment on the veracity of Lorenz's claims.

"If Rina and Lorenz have not dirtied their hands..." she said probingly, "then it seems to me that neither of them are guilty."

That was the easy part. If they didn't do it, they weren't guilty. The hard part came next.

"But I believe it is difficult to argue that the House of Yellowmoon... and therefore, Lord Yellowmoon...is completely free of guilt."

Families and lives had, in very real and tragic ways, been ruined by what the House had done. If harm had been done, then the Yellowmoons couldn't be handed a verdict of complete innocence. Therefore...

"Lorenz, you are the Duke of Yellowmoon. As its head, I believe you have a duty to take responsibility for the actions of your House. That is why..."

She paused. In the ensuing silence, she closed her eyes and, with the air of a sculptor appraising the quality of a work nearing completion, considered her next words. Then, raising her hammer and chisel of justice once more, she began chipping away at it again, with all the grace and confidence of a nervous chipmunk, hoping to finally mold it into a shape that would make everyone happy.

"It is my belief," she said in an outwardly dignified manner, "that in order to atone for the harm the House of Yellowmoon has done to its victims, you should make every effort and do everything in your power to save and protect those who have been harmed by the Chaos Serpents."

Which *sounded* like a very noble and principled thing to say but, examined more closely, all she really demanded of Lorenz was a goal. Note the "make every effort" and "do everything in your power," which was language more befitting a New Year's resolution than a courtroom verdict. In other words, she'd left him the "things didn't work out but I tried my best" excuse.

The value in this arrangement was, of course, its reciprocity— whatever she dictated to Lorenz would apply to herself. This way, if anyone tried to fault her for the first emperor's antics, she could just throw her hands up and say, "I tried my hardest to fix things, honest! But this is all I could manage!"

"Also, make absolutely sure to conclude your atonement in your lifetime. Under no circumstances should you leave any residual guilt to be shouldered by your daughter. I repeat, *under no circumstances* should Rina ever be burdened!"

It was important, maybe the most important, so she said it twice. Even if the first emperor's guilt could make its way down the family tree, it should stop at the current emperor's generation. By no means should his poor daughter be forced to deal with that nonsense.

And so, after much meticulous chiseling, the self-serving compromise of a verdict she'd crafted stood tall like a golden Mia statue, radiating its egocentric glory to all who laid eyes on it. Behold! In the statue's right hand, the scale of justice! And in its left, a bunch of sweets! Which signified wisdom! Probably!

Then came her masterstroke—the finishing touch that would breathe bright, light beam-emitting life into its eyes.

"The first emperor—rather, my ancestors have, throughout the long history of our empire, burdened you with a great deal of tribulation. But the days of being beholden to ancient pacts are past." She proceeded to emphatically announce, "The cursed oath of old between my lineage and yours, Duke Yellowmoon, is as of this moment, officially annulled! I, Mia Luna Tearmoon, declare it so!"

Her bold voice carried through the courtyard. As it faded, she let out the kind of satisfied sigh heaved by those who felt they'd done a very good job. Now, if the Yellowmoons did anything crazy in the future, she wouldn't be tied to it. They could assassinate all the people they wanted, and she wouldn't lose a wink of sleep.

Phew... Finally, I can have some peace of mind...

Her breath of relief was met by one of poignant emotion, as Lorenz beheld her with eyes welling with tears of gratitude.

Chapter 41: Thus Shatters the Oath of Old

"No… No! Impossible! This is madness! How can it end like this? It *can't* end like this…"

Her face twisted with hatred, Barbara snarled in a voice so bitter it made Mia's hair stand on end. The furious woman glared at her, then at Lorenz and Citrina.

"Accursed princess… Ha ha… Ha ha ha… I see. So this is the Great Sage of the Empire. Well played. Your entourage of princes seem satisfied as well. But…" A malicious smile crept across her lips. "Things won't all go your way, princess. Oh no, they won't. Because I'm going to slit the throat of these wretched Yellowmoon traitors. Then we'll see how your plan fares."

The three men behind her reacted immediately, surrounding their victims in a last-ditch attempt to mar their opponent's victory. From their position, it was impossible for Mia and her friends to reach the Yellowmoons in time. The only one close enough to act was the butler, Bisset.

The smell of impending violence filled the air. But Mia wasn't worried. Why? Because the fight was, for all intents and purposes, already over.

And…there he is. I swear, it's like he can smell violence or something. And I hate to admit it, but I do feel safer when he's around.

Mia's gaze soared over Barbara's head to land on the figure sneaking up behind her. Dion Alaia wore the wide grin of a boy pulling off a hilarious prank. A prank that involved smashing in the faces of three men without their leader noticing. Then, standing behind a yet-oblivious Barbara, he rested his blade on her shoulder.

Ugh, the way he does that scares the living daylights out of you, thought Mia as she watched. *Gives you visions of your head rolling off your neck.*

A reluctant veteran of decapitation—which had included Dion's trademark sword-on-shoulder stunt—Mia couldn't help but feel sympathy for Barbara, but not enough for her to step in and stop him. She was content with sending thoughts and prayers.

"…Huh?"

The sudden developments proved too bewildering for Barbara to process. She stared at the sword, then at Dion, who beamed at her.

"For a group who went out of their way to avoid fighting me, you made a pretty bad call at the end. Got too greedy for your own good. Had you stuck to your avoidance strategy, you'd have saved these three fellows a lot of pain." He tsked and shook his head. "Gotta learn when to let go."

Barbara frantically looked around. Seeing the unconscious forms of her henchmen on the ground, she bared her teeth.

"Fools… Such fools! Curse you, Alaia. You imperial dog."

"Dog, eh? Guess they'll have to change my title to Empire's Goodest Boy then." He smirked. "I hope you won't mind getting your throat slit by a mutt."

At that, Mia hastily signaled for him to stop.

"Apprehend her alive, please. We might be able to pull some useful information out of her, so I'd like to hand her over to Miss Rafina."

"As you wish," he said before shrugging and binding Barbara's arms. "Honestly, you're too soft on these people. But then again, you're the brains here. I just woof."

A figure dashed past Mia toward the now-freed Yellowmoons.

"Rina!"

Seeing that the situation was fully resolved, Bel made a beeline for Citrina, catching her in a running embrace.

"Rina! Oh, Rina!"

As Bel's arms closed around the slender body and squeezed with all their strength, Citrina's eyes remained vacant. She stared blankly forward, face devoid of expression, as though she couldn't process the series of events that had just occurred. But then, ever so softly...

"...Bel?"

...She spoke her friend's name. Her gray eyes clouded with tears, which soon gave way to a glistening river of emotion that flowed down her delicate cheeks.

"Bel..."

Her lips quivered. Her mouth opened, then closed. An ocean of feelings pushed against her chest, seeking release, but she seemed to have lost all her words. In the end, the only one her trembling voice managed to produce was the name of her dear friend.

"Bel..."

And then, even that was gone, leaving her with only the raw, fitful release of unchecked emotion. She wept. Openly and with all her heart.

"It's okay, Rina... I'm here. And I always will be."

With the most tender of touches, Bel patted her friend's back.

"Does… Does this mean it's over?"

Lorenz watched his daughter's tearful outpouring in a daze. His limbs seemed to have lost the ability to function. His life was no longer at the mercy of enemy blades. The hands holding him down were gone. Nevertheless, he remained on the ground, the thought of compelling his legs to stand too monumental a task for his frayed psyche.

In truth, the only person who could void the oath with the first emperor was the current reigning one. Lorenz was fully aware of that fact, and he could only assume Mia was as well. But she'd said it anyway. And there was a significance to that.

Those words of hers are a shield. With them, I can deflect any future demands to carry out assassinations. On top of that, His Imperial Majesty is deeply fond of Her Highness. Should she request it, he may indeed choose to endorse them.

Despite that knowledge, true relief escaped him. The chains around his soul had been there too long, and their weight, magnified by the empire's long history, was too heavy to remove so easily. His was an ancient curse, cast upon him in the womb. And that burden, with all its crushing gravity and consequence, was no more? Just like that? Without the shedding of a single drop of blood? It didn't seem real. He could but stare with disbelief at the dreamlike sequence playing out before him.

"Cursed Yellowmoons… The Serpents will come for you. One day, we shall sink our fangs into your necks."

Barbara's contemptuous voice drifted into his ears. Curiously, it was the bitterness of her words that drove the intangible specters of fear from his mind, allowing the solid substance of reality to take their place. It dawned on him then. At last. At *long last.*

"Ah, Barbara, she who embodies the Serpents' will… Listen well, for it is now that I can, with the profundity of life lived and fear known, finally speak my mind."

His next words, he spoke to Barbara, but their essence—the deep poignancy contained within them—was surely not meant for her ears alone. There were many who likely deserved them. The Chaos Serpents who'd tormented his house for generations, for example. Or maybe the first emperor, who'd condemned them to this fate. For whomever the words were meant, he spoke them with *verve*.

"Eat shit, Chaos Serpents!" he bellowed with the expression of a man experiencing cathartic vindication. "Eat shit, you steaming turd of a first emperor!"

It was the triumphant cry from the soul of generations of Yellowmoons.

Thus shattered the oath of old, its ancient chains severed by the hands of a young princess in whom flowed the first emperor's blood.

The Yellowmoon manor was quickly occupied by the Princess Guard. Inside, they found only a handful of Serpents, all of whom had already been knocked out by Dion. Presumably, Barbara had preemptively evacuated the majority of her accomplices, with the intent of making a last stand here on her own.

"Huh. The Serpents might be mad, but I suppose there's a method to their madness," said a surprised Mia, who'd expected to see every last underling used as sacrificial pawns in a ruthless attempt to escape.

After the commotion had subsided, Lorenz asked to speak with Mia in his quarters.

"While I'd prefer to know as much about the Serpents as possible, it sounds like this is going to involve a lot of internal Tearmoon affairs, so we'll excuse ourselves from the conversation for now," said Sion.

Abel nodded.

"Agreed. Someone should probably stay with Miss Bel and Miss Citrina too. We'll head over to them."

So, Mia bade a temporary farewell to Sion and Abel, who were followed by Keithwood and Monica.

"Hm… In that case, I guess it'll be Anne, Ludwig, and Dion who come with me."

Being accompanied by Ludwig was fine, since he was the brains of the operation, but the thought of Dion looming behind her was still anxiety-inducing. Not having a reliable bodyguard was even more anxiety-inducing though, so she reluctantly chose to endure his presence, figuring she'd rely on Anne for some psychological solace. Anne, catching her glance, beamed.

"Oh, you can count on me, milady! I've got your back!"

She gave her chest a confident thump, clearly thrilled to be brought along. Maybe a little too thrilled. Mia gave her a resigned smile.

"Well, my back is clearly in good hands then. Ludwig and Dion, I'm also counting on the two of you. Specifically, I'm counting on you to keep an eye on Anne so she doesn't get too excited and put herself in danger."

"Wha— Oh, that's such a mean thing to say!"

The two girls traded giggling quips all the way to Lorenz's room, whereupon Mia was greeted by a pleasant aroma upon opening the door.

"My…"

She sniffed a few times. It smelled of something sweet…and fresh out of the oven.

Black tea and…some sort of pastry, I believe. Ah, there they are on the table. If my eyes don't deceive me, that's a tart made with Perujin apples.

After quietly studying Lorenz for a moment, she privately murmured, "Hm… This man…knows what he's doing!"

In an impressive display of perception, it'd taken her all of a second to detect her opponent's power level. With regard to sweets. Which was just about the most useless type of perception one could display, but anyway…

"I apologize for troubling you during this hectic time, Your Highness, but there are some things that I must bring to your attention." Lorenz got to his feet and bowed at the waist. "By your leave, I would speak upon these matters."

Mia gestured at him to be at ease.

"Please, there is no need for such formality. I also wished to ask about a few things, so this is in fact perfect timing," she said, eyes still laser focused on the steaming tart.

Those taste best when they're fresh. Ah, I wish I could take a bite right now!

She gulped before quickly taking a seat. Then, with the intent tone of someone who wished to sort things out as quickly as possible, she said, "Oh, in case you were wondering, I've decided to overlook the whole business of Rina luring me into a trap. The last thing I want is for father to find out and raise a fuss, so I'd appreciate it if you kept a tight lip. Am I understood?"

It was all too easy to imagine the hysteria that would follow if the doting emperor heard that his beloved daughter came *this* close to losing her life. She'd just experienced a brush with death and survived. She didn't want to then die of a headache in the ensuing fallout. To that end, she made it a point to remind everyone that what happened in Bandoor Village stayed in Bandoor Village.

And let's not forget, there was a tart waiting to be eaten, so the quicker they wrapped this up, the better.

As of this moment, she was no longer just the Mushroom Princess. She was Sweets-Princess-cum-Reconciler Mia! That's Sweet-Pri-Cu-Re Mia for short!

The casual manner with which she pardoned the offense against her was in sharp contrast to Lorenz, who was moved to tears.

"Words cannot express my gratitude, Your Highness…" he said in a trembling voice.

With the weightier topics out of the way, Lorenz finally sat back down across from Mia as Bisset placed the tart on the table and began to cut it. His knife bit into the crust with a pleasing crunch, releasing a waft of buttery steam that was followed by the tantalizing scent of apples. Mia swallowed a mouthful of drool as the aroma drifted up her nose. Her eyes were glued to the tart. She stared at it as if the force of her will alone could speed the process along. Her muscles tensed with anticipation, and her hands began to shake. Noticing this exaggerated reaction of her own body, a wry smile crept across Mia's lips.

That reminds me, ever since we rushed back from Belluga, I haven't had anything sweet to eat...

Already starved for sugar, her brain then suffered through an intense workout. By now, it was running on the wispy fumes of burnt caramel. Immediate refueling was necessary!

She gulped yet again as the plate with her tart slice was finally placed before her. The second Bisset retracted his hand, she devoured it whole. Chewing it chipmunk-style, she savored the crunchiness of the crust breaking apart between her teeth. Its sugary filling flowed across her tongue, enveloping it in sweetness so saturated it bordered on sickly. The rush of tangy apple afterward, however, diluted it just enough to hit the—no pun intended—sweet spot.

Pure bliss permeated her mouth.

"Mmm! I've said it before, and I'll say it again. Nothing beats Perujin fruits!" she exclaimed, beaming through a mouthful of tart.

Bisset stared at her in shock.

"...Your Highness, are you certain that was entirely appropriate? To simply...eat the tart? It has yet to be tested for poison. Though it gives me no joy to dredge up the matter, I must nonetheless respectfully remind you that you are seated in what was, until mere hours ago, still enemy territory."

The curious tilt of Mia's head suggested she couldn't fathom his concern.

"Hm? What an odd thing to say. Poison? And ruin such a delicious tart? Why would anyone do that? I fail to see the point," she said, asserting that no one in their right mind would do something so wasteful to a good tart.

Which made perfect sense in her head, because she wasn't in her right mind either. The long drought of sweets had robbed her brain of all reason and composure. In her current state, she'd gladly sell her palace for a cake. She was nearing the "a cake is worth a thousand forts" stage of sugar deficiency. That is, the terminal stage.

"I must say though, I was quite astonished to discover that you're a former Wind Crow. The way you fooled those Serpents earlier was simply marvelous. A brilliant display of skill and wit."

Having enjoyed a tasty tart, Mia's mood experienced a significant upswing, and she showered Bisset with praise.

"I'm most flattered, Your Highness," said Bisset with a calm and respectful smile.

At that point, Ludwig interrupted the conversation.

"My deepest apologies, Your Highness. I should have notified you as soon as Duke Yellowmoon spoke to me. It is—"

"No, the good gentleman did nothing wrong, Your Highness." Lorenz held out a hand to appease Ludwig. "It is I who requested him to keep this entire affair a secret…in order to ascertain your character. For us Yellowmoons, the true nature of your person was very literally a matter of life and death. We needed to be absolutely sure. Nevertheless, it is a deep affront to have tested you in this way. Please accept my sincerest apologies."

He lowered his head to within an inch of the table. Ludwig followed suit, adding, "Lord Yellowmoon asked to witness your natural disposition. To see whether you would take their side without any foreknowledge of their plans. In order to gain Lord Yellowmoon's trust,

I decided against notifying Your Highness of our correspondence. Though I regret the necessity of such secrecy, I did so in the knowledge that your brilliance would surely prevail. Your Highness is, after all, the kind of person who, when given a single piece of information, will infer ten facts and see a hundred futures."

"Am I now? Well… In that case, I suppose it was a necessary evil. You did the right thing."

Mia nodded, her ego swelling. She was the kind of person who welcomed praise. She was *also* the kind of person who, when given a single piece of information, would infer maybe half a fact from it, then see visions of a hundred sweets from the sheer effort it took. Frankly, even if Ludwig had spilled the beans, it probably wouldn't have changed much.

"In any case, now that there's no longer any need for secrecy," said Mia, "I believe it's time you told us the full story, Duke Lorenz Etoile Yellowmoon."

There were countless things she wanted to know about the Serpents, the House of Yellowmoon, and all the untold stories that had occurred behind the curtains of the empire's history.

"Very well. Where shall I begin…" Lorenz took a moment to consider, took a long breath, then nodded. "Perhaps…the beginning would be best. At the oath between the House of Yellowmoon and the first emperor…"

Lorenz was thoroughly astonished by Mia's actions.

The possibility of it being poisoned…wasn't even a consideration…

She'd eaten the tart without the slightest hesitation and beamed as she declared it delicious. Admittedly, the likelihood of them trying to harm Mia at this point was close to nil. As things now stood, opposing the princess would be an act of suicide for the House of Yellowmoon, likely dooming not only Lorenz but also Citrina. This was a self-evident fact, easily revealed by a rational analysis of the situation. Therefore, she'd harbored no doubts when reaching for the tart...

No, that's not true...

Lorenz knew better, for he'd seen evidence to the contrary. His wary eyes had not missed the slight trembling of Mia's hands. Nor the way *her* eyes had tracked Bisset's fingers with an intense, unblinking focus.

But of course... A wise person wouldn't ignore the possibility of poison. It's unlikely, yes, but the suspicion remains. There's no way to dismiss it entirely. Only the blithest of fools could be completely ignorant of the risk.

It wasn't a lack of hesitation. She'd felt, wrestled with, and defeated her hesitation, all so she could take the first bite of a tart that might kill her. Mia hadn't been ignorant of a potential poisoning; she'd done so in spite of that possibility, out of necessity—the necessity to demonstrate her unequivocal trust in Lorenz.

It wasn't foolhardiness. She'd weighed the risk of being poisoned against winning the trust of us Yellowmoons...and chosen the latter. And that was after *she'd declared that Citrina's grievous treachery was all water under the bridge. The lengths she's going to, it's... I can't even...*

He closed his eyes, taking a moment to delve into past memories. The face of his teacher, to whom his teenage self owed so much, materialized in his mind.

"If you wish to accomplish something, then arm yourself with knowledge. Even if you don't currently know what to strive for, don't stop accruing knowledge. Keep learning, keep studying, tirelessly, in preparation for the day when you do *know. All that remains after is to wait for your opportunity to arise."*

He opened his eyes, the vision giving way to reality. Before him stood the young princess, her visage so reminiscent of the one in his memory. A surge of emotions welled up in his chest, and he exhaled them through a long breath. Then...

"Perhaps...the beginning would be best. At the oath between the House of Yellowmoon and the first emperor..."

...He proceeded to tell the story.

The story of the curse that had bound the House of Yellowmoon for a long, long time.

"As I understand it, the first emperor and our Yellowmoon ancestor were kin. The two had both despaired of the world and resolved to destroy it."

The establishment of anti-agriculturalism and the founding of the Tearmoon Empire were all but means to accomplish one initial goal. It was a revenge plot of epic proportions, devised to drag the entire world into mayhem.

"The Yellowmoons were given two roles to play. The first, which Your Highness likely already knows, was to secretly eliminate threats to the empire and the Serpents. The second...was to become the next imperial family."

"The...next imperial family?" asked a baffled Mia. "What does that mean?"

Lorenz shrugged.

"Exactly what it sounds like. Specifically, when the current imperial family is toppled by famine and revolution, our family is supposed to claim the throne, continuing the dynasty not in name but in essence. And we're meant to be constantly maneuvering behind the scenes to ready ourselves for this eventuality. Then, when someone from our lineage becomes the next ruler, they shall continue the effort to disseminate anti-agriculturalist beliefs throughout the land. We are to reign until revolution claims us again. That is both our role and our reward."

The system known as the Tearmoon Empire was designed to fail. Catastrophic collapse was not a fault but a feature. Anti-agriculturalist beliefs would spoil vast amounts of farmland. The ensuing famine would then give rise to revolution, leading to a messy, protracted civil war in which widespread slaughter would taint the land. And like an undying curse, it would occur again and again, drenching this fertile crescent with endless tears of suffering. The Tearmoon Empire was a self-repeating mechanism, meant to unleash recurring cycles of tragedy upon its victims.

That was why the ensuing dynasty must not be led by a wise ruler. The revolution had to be championed by agents of pure chaos who wished to destroy order, and nothing more. Those who sought the destruction of an old order to instill a new one would not do.

"After the fall of the Tearmoon line, the Yellowmoons would reign. And when the Yellowmoons fell…another destroyer of order would take the throne. That way, dynasty after dynasty, blood and death would continue to stain the land. Such is the creation of the first emperor."

"Hmm… But why would you continue to participate in such an awful scheme?" Mia asked with a puzzled frown. "It'd make some sense if the imperial family is still following in the first emperor's footsteps, but I'd never heard of any such plot. I'm pretty sure fa—His Majesty doesn't have the foggiest clue any of this ever happened."

"Indeed. The imperial family has, as of a number of generations ago, forgotten about the first emperor's ancient will. We Yellowmoons, however, have not. That original oath has become our dream. Our hope. The irresistible light at the end of a long, dark tunnel. Lured by it, we've continued to maneuver in secret throughout the ages."

And that was the curse placed on the Yellowmoons by the first emperor.

The one to inherit the crumbled throne had to be the weakest and most ridiculed of the Four Houses. Those who benefited from the established structures would never start a revolution to destroy it. Thus, the Yellowmoons were made to suffer the denigrating disdain of their peers, year after year, generation after generation. Over time, the malice and humiliation they endured gave rise to a deep desire for a future in which they ruled.

"Our circumstances are but a stepping stone! We endure our current weakness and indignity so that we may prosper in the future. The day this empire falls will be the day our era arrives!"

The more they clung to this hope, the firmer their alliance with the Serpents became.

"Our mothers and fathers, grandparents and ancestors...they all suffered. And they all endured. So that our descendants can thrive. So that one of them becomes the next emperor. Our forebears bore their humiliation for us. We must not let their resolve go to waste."

Part of the curse was their own inability to cut their losses. The heads of Yellowmoon were all faced with the same question. Knowing their clan had endured so much to get to the current point, could they abandon the goal, quashing with their own hands the culmination of lifetimes of effort? How could they allow a wish—a vital hope—harbored by and inherited from their parents to end unrealized with their generation?

"Even so, there have been other heads of Yellowmoon like me, who resented the deeds of death and destruction. But...none of them could escape the Serpents' hold. Once was enough. Stain your hands with blood once, and the Serpents would forever use it for blackmail. A single assassination became a lifelong shackle, and these good people were worn down by their futile struggle against the snakes' demands.

They grew tired…and embraced the promise of future glory, however fleeting it might prove to be, in exchange for peace of mind as they ceded control of their lives to the Serpents."

That was why Lorenz wanted no part in any assassination.

"I see. So that's how it was…" said a pensive Ludwig. "All the more impressive, then, that you've managed to avoid taking a life all this time. Had it been me, I suspect I would have folded long ago."

His sober tone elicited a calm smile from Lorenz.

"I managed, Ludwig, because of the encouragement I received from a certain individual. This person told me that if I wanted to accomplish something, then I should acquire knowledge. I should seek it out, tirelessly and ravenously. Then, I should wait for my opportunity to arise."

True to the advice, he devoted himself to his studies.

"My, what a fascinating individual," said Mia with a sense of wonder.

Lorenz's smile deepened.

"Yes, Your Highness, your grandmother was indeed a fascinating individual. Her Majesty was undoubtedly one of a kind."

"My…grandmother? I see. I never knew her, but…"

"I can see traces of her in you, Your Highness. She…was also a wise woman."

"Wise like me, you say?" Mia pursed her lips and nodded thoughtfully. "Hm, I wish I could have met her then…"

Note that she made no attempt to deny the "wise" part. Not even out of modesty. Mia took her wins where she could get them.

"Ah, but I digress. Let us return to the issues at hand. I believe you still have plenty of questions for me?"

"True. Back on topic then." Lorenz's comment prompted Mia to straighten herself and refocus. "First, the Chaos Serpents. I'd like you to tell us everything you know about them. What kind of an organization are they?"

"An organization? Hm…" he murmured before sinking into silent contemplation.

"Oh? Did I say something strange?"

"…No. But I'm not entirely sure if the Chaos Serpents can be accurately described as an 'organization.'"

"Then…they're not an organization?" asked Mia, frowning.

Lorenz frowned as well.

"I suppose it depends on the definition…but at the very least, they're nothing like the heretical cults that we're familiar with. I'm sure you're aware of this, but unlike cults, the Serpents don't operate as an orderly whole. Each Serpent has their own goals and acts according to their own plans. They might cooperate with other Serpents at times, but not through any hierarchy or power structure. They all move independently, by their own guiding compass, which all happen to point in the same direction."

Lorenz paused for a breath, then concluded, "Which is why…my personal understanding of the Chaos Serpents is that they are not so much an organization as a trend."

"A trend?"

"Yes. Not the reed in the river, but the current that pushes it. A current flowing within the larger course of history…which seeks to destroy order."

Mia visualized the metaphor, imagining herself trying to push back a river. No matter how hard she fought it, how much water she scooped out, she could not stop its flow. If Barbara and Jem were just drops of water in that mighty stream, then foiling them might ultimately be in vain. The stream would keep flowing.

"Pardon. I'm beginning to speak in the abstract. Let me give some specific examples. The people who make up the Chaos Serpents can largely be divided into four categories," said Lorenz as he took a nearby cookie and placed it on the large plate in front of him. The cookie was round, and a small fruit sat at its center.

My, where did that come from? I was so focused on the tart I must have missed it. Mmm, it looks good...

All this serious talk had depleted the sugar she'd consumed from the tart, and she was running on caramel fumes agai— Ah, just kidding. Her sugar mileage wasn't *that* bad. Anyway.

"First, there are those like me. Reluctant collaborators, who had their arms twisted into helping. Next, willing collaborators. Those who are using the Chaos Serpents in an attempt to further their own ends. The first emperor, for example, would in my opinion belong to this category. As far as I can tell, he didn't seem to resonate with the philosophy of the Serpents. He was either using their philosophy for his own purposes, or found that their goals aligned with his, so it made sense to cooperate. In any case, there exist people who assist the Serpents of their own volition," he said, placing a second cookie on the plate.

"Hmm..."

Her arms crossed, Mia nodded along. Her eyes were glued to the new cookie. It was also round, but bore a crosshatched pattern. *What fine handiwork. Was it made here? If so, the Yellowmoons must have a pretty good pastry chef in their service.*

If her thoughts seem a little *distracted*, know that her brain was to blame. It was craving sweets, but it wasn't getting them! An inadequately fueled brain was going to lose focus. That's just how brains worked.

"Then, there are those who resonate with the Serpents' beliefs and work proactively to further their ends. These, we call adherents. The three men Barbara brought were likely adherents."

Lorenz added a third cookie. This one was covered with white powder, almost as if it were adorned with snow. It was something Mia had never seen before, and it caught her attention immediately.

Fascinat— Whoops. Okay, focus. I need to focus on the conversation... Where were we again? Right, Serpent adherents!

"Finally…"

Lorenz took a fourth cookie but paused before placing it down. It was large and leaf-shaped.

My… That cookie…it looks exquisite. Delights both the eyes and the tongue. A work of art, doubtlessly made by a true artisan… That reminds me. I wonder if they can make a horse-shaped cookie. Or maybe a mushroom-shaped cookie. Oh! What if the bottom part of the mushroom is a plain cookie, but the cap is covered with some sort of chocolate or jam? I think I'm onto something here…

There was a surprising prescience to this idea of hers—albeit of the far, far future—but she shook her head and dismissed it.

Ack, come on, focus! We're talking about the Serpents right now! Focus… Focus… Okay. So, Serpent cookies. What's the deal with them again?

Oblivious to the intense battle between a brain and the allure of sweets being fought in front of him, Lorenz continued his explanation.

"There are those who preach the ideology of the Serpents. They go from place to place, spreading the teachings of *The Book of Those Who Crawl the Earth.* These, we refer to as Serpent shamans."

Lorenz added the leaf-shaped cookie to the plate. Then, as Mia eyed the mouth-watering quartet, he snatched them all up in one fell swoop and stuffed them into his mouth. As he munched on them, cheeks even more bloated than Mia's had been, pure delight radiated from his expression.

"Mmmm… The one thing I've always believed about cookies is that nibbling does them a disservice," he said after a satisfied gulp. "Nothing beats the bliss of biting down on a great mouthful of doughy goodness."

Spoken like a true gourmand. Lorenz was clearly a veteran of the F.A.T. lifestyle.

"I... I see..."

Mia managed only a perfunctory response before hanging her head in silence, crushed by the sad reality that those cookies would never be hers.

They looked so good too... Aaah, I wish I could have tried them...

"Serpent shamans... Would it be appropriate to consider these individuals the main body of the Chaos Serpents? Their true essence, so to speak?" asked Ludwig who, noticing that Mia had retreated into quiet contemplation, picked up the conversational slack.

"Not exactly. This is only my personal opinion, but I believe the true essence of the Serpents is something that flows in the deep underbelly of people's hearts. It joins them to one another."

"By which you mean..."

"By which I mean...the Serpents' bible, *The Book of Those Who Crawl the Earth.*"

A soft clink entered Mia's ears, pulling her from her misery. She blinked to find a plate had been set on the table before her.

"Ah—"

On the plate was a heaping myriad of cookies! With bountiful representation of each type of the Lost Quartet to boot! Apparently, Bisset had removed her empty tart plate and replaced it with a cookie platter.

What exemplary butlering! This man clearly knows what he's doing!

She had every intention of reaching for them immediately, but the sudden awareness of a number of intent gazes on her stilled her hand. Both Ludwig and Lorenz were eyeing her expectantly. Even Dion was regarding her with interest. And a smile that somehow conveyed less humor than a glare would have.

U-Uh oh. Something tells me this is no time to be fooling around.

She sighed. With great reluctance, she pulled her eyes away from the cookies.

It's okay. The cookies won't run away. I can always eat them later. It's just a matter of waiting for the right moment. For now, I need to be patient...

She forced the idle clockwork of her brain back into motion. It did so with a crunch, recalling the details of their ongoing conversation.

"...*The Book of Those Who Crawl the Earth*."

The title rang a bell.

"I remember Miss Rafina talking about that. That Jem fellow had a copy with him, didn't he?"

Though she hadn't flipped through it herself, she remembered feeling uncomfortable around it. There was something about the book that, even when recalled through memory, gave her the creeps. There was a crunch as she shuddered.

"Yes," answered Lorenz. "Like you said, it wasn't the original, but he did indeed have a copy."

"What kind of book is it?"

He shook his head.

"Unfortunately, I've never seen the book myself. Only the transcription of 'Kingdombane' that Jem used to have," he said, before letting out a weary chuckle. "Barbara didn't quite trust me enough to divulge any more information. Which was probably justified, considering this long-planned betrayal I've just sprung on her."

"I see... That's a shame. But the way you describe it, with how it joins people and controls them, makes it sound like magic. Is *The Book of Those Who Crawl the Earth* actually some sort of magical tome?" asked Mia, remembering that such things had appeared in Elise's drafts. There was a crunch as she pursed her lips in thought.

"Magic, you say?"

Lorenz frowned, taken aback by the suggestion. However, he soon chuckled.

"Oh? Did something come to mind?"

"No, no. I was simply surprised to hear from Your Highness's mouth the word 'magic.'"

His expression then sobered.

"But…perhaps you are right. Wise, even, to call the book magical. In a way, it's the perfect description. It does, after all, affect the mind in a most mystical manner, transmuting normal people into destroyers of order. The way it drastically changes the lives of people it touches… It might indeed be fitting to consider such power sorcery." Then, noticing Ludwig's expression, he held up his hands and added, "Oh, do not misunderstand me, Ludwig. I'm not suggesting the existence of warlocks and wizardry. Especially when it's perfectly possible to manipulate the hearts of man with techniques far more earthly."

"My, is it? How would one go about doing so?" asked Mia.

Lorenz chuckled at her dubious look.

"How indeed. Let's see… Does Your Highness read at all?"

"Read? Well…I certainly do read. More than most, I'd say."

There was a crunch as she counted with her fingers the books she'd recently read.

"Lately, I've been enjoying a number of romance novels I borrowed from a friend," she said, growing more talkative as the topic shifted to a field of her expertise. "In particular, this one about a knight and a princess in love is just— Hnnngh! There's this scene at a lake, and it's so good!"

"Ha ha ha, I see. Then let me ask again. While you were reading that book, did you ever wish you could experience such love yourself?"

"Experience such love for myself? Hmm… I guess that *would* be very nice."

Mia imagined herself walking along a lake at night with Abel while gazing up at the moon and stars, the air thick with romance as they indulged in saccharine banter…

Yes! Yes! Sweet moons, that sounds amazing!

She was promptly and profoundly influenced by the book.

"Then suppose there was a book that made everyone who read it wish for love. Could you therefore say that this book was a magical tome that had the power to exert influence over the minds of its readers?"

"Huh. Well…"

She found herself seriously considering the question. Framed in that fashion, it did make sense. If the condition for being magical was the ability to exert influence over minds, then regular novels certainly fit the bill. There was a crunch as Mia leaned back and withdrew into her memories.

It wasn't just romance novels. She knew better than anyone how the simplest of tales could have a lasting effect on one's heart. During her hopeless time in the dungeon, Elise's story had been a small but radiant beacon in the darkness. The influence it had exerted on her mind was unquestionable, taking what had and would have continued to be endless days of despair, and changing them, just a little, for the better.

"But surely, it doesn't have the power to change objective reality. To refer to it as 'magic' seems a touch like hyperbole," said Ludwig.

Lorenz smiled at this critique and shook his head.

"I suspect, Ludwig, that you are under a slight misconception. You wouldn't be the first either. Many smart thinkers succumb to the same error. Our minds and the objective reality around us are far more interconnected than you may think." He closed his eyes. "Consider the world. What comprises it? People. People build towns.

Erect kingdoms. Create cultures. Amass knowledge. What guides people then? What determines how they act? It is their minds. Or, you could say, their philosophies, values, and faiths."

"So you mean to say that the Serpents' bible, this *Book of Those Who Crawl the Earth*…is a text that embeds the *desire to destroy order* in the minds of those who read it?" Ludwig frowned at his own comment. "But wait… If memory serves, the copy held by that man Jem was, if anything, a dissertation of methodology on how to topple a kingdom."

The version of the biblical text obtained by Rafina was more of a practical guide, detailing ways to bring a kingdom to its knees. It didn't contain anything that read like an attempt to brainwash the reader.

Lorenz readily affirmed this apparent contradiction.

"You're absolutely right. What was written in that copy were the actual steps one should take to destroy the form of order we know as a kingdom. As you mentioned, it's a how-to, not a manifesto. But consider this, Ludwig. Between handing you a sword and tempting you to kill someone you hate, and giving you nothing and simply telling you to do so, which method do you think would be more likely to entice you to action?"

It was a question of effectiveness. Writing a vaguely-worded call-to-action that amounted to "go out there and wreck yourself some kingdoms" was one thing, but providing a detailed instruction manual for getting it done was another thing entirely. The latter was clearly superior.

"I see," said a contemplative Mia. "Who would have thought something like that exists… And where might these copies be?"

"The Serpent shamans I mentioned earlier are said to always keep a copy on their person. To use when preaching their beliefs, presumably.

Those contain only a portion of the actual book though. I've also heard that higher-ranking shamans have memorized the book's contents and can recite it by heart. As for the exact location of the book itself... it remains a mystery to this day."

Though discouraged by this answer, Mia perked up when Lorenz continued in a lower but more compelling tone.

"However... Just as the Central Orthodox Church has Saint Rafina, I've heard that the Serpents also have their own icon who rallies the shamans. She is known as the high priestess."

"The high priestess...of the Chaos Serpents?"

"Yes, and it is my personal suspicion that this person is holding the original manuscript of *The Book of Those Who Crawl the Earth*."

Mia gulped at this ominous revelation as her hand slid across the table toward the plate. On second thought, maybe she gulped for other reasons. Regardless, she made her move, pointedly not looking down to avoid drawing attention to her action. It wasn't, for the record, because she'd identified the most opportune moment. She just couldn't resist anymore. Figuring she'd waited long enough to have earned at least one bite, she reached for the plate...and felt nothing but empty air.

Huh? M-My... That's odd. Where did all those delicious-looking cookies go?

Surprised, she glanced at the plate, only to find it...

"Milady... You've had far too much to eat," said a frowning Anne. "A tart and five whole cookies... You've been eating through this whole conversation."

"...Huh?"

Mia lifted a questioning eyebrow. Eating? When? It sounded absurd. At least until she touched the corner of her mouth, where she discovered what felt very much like a large crumb. She pushed it into her mouth and bit down. There was an audible crunch.

Wha— But, how? When did I— Huh?

"You're going to start putting on weight if you eat any more."

"But… But…"

Due to having unconsciously eaten the cookies, their taste was entirely lost on her. Just as her expression began to cloud with sorrow, a single cookie was held out to her.

"Oh, milady…" said Anne in a kind but mildly admonishing voice. "Last one, okay?"

She smiled. Mia beamed.

"Oh, you really are the best, Anne! My absolute trustiest subject!"

…Same old Mia, same old exchange. Some things never change.

But some things do.

And so it went. After abolishing the ancient oath, Mia took leave of the Yellowmoon manor. Unfettered from the bonds of old, she was now free to drift with the current of the times. Where it would take her…was still anyone's guess.

Part 3: A New Oath between the Moon and Stars II Fin

Part 3 will continue for a tiny bit longer.

Short Story

Seeds Sprouting in Lands Unknown

The age of the great famine was a hellish time, when the conscience of man lay in rotting corpses, and trust in others was a fatal flaw. Cruelty and selfishness ruled the land.

This next story is a tragedy, but not a special one. It is simply one of the many that made up the Tearmoon Empire during that time.

"Damn it…"

Every ragged breath brought with it the taste of iron. What remained of the leather armor, now more crimson than brown, bore morbid witness to the speed with which the wearer's life was draining away.

The young soldier Ernst stood his ground, shielding the horse-drawn cart behind him. Only privately did he lament his circumstances. How had it come to this, he wondered. Where had he gone wrong?

"You're a stubborn one, I'll give you that. Look, just let go of your blind loyalty to the empire. It ain't even worth the dung on your boots."

The comment came from a man who, until mere minutes ago, had been guarding the cart with him.

"Think about it," continued the man. "That cart's loaded with enough food to feed all of us, or we could sell it all for a fortune and live the rest of our lives like kings. Now, doesn't that sound like a much better idea than guarding it like a damn dog?"

Ernst glared at the man, who scoffed.

"Some skulls are just too thick, I guess."

"Shut up... You're a dirty coward and you know it," said Ernst.

He meant for his tone to be scathing, full of rage, but his heart wasn't in it. Deep down, he agreed with the man. What was the point of devoting oneself to a sinking ship? There was little to gain from risking his life here. Even less from giving it.

But...

Ernst wiped his hands on his trousers, leaving streaks of blood. Then, he lifted his spear again and pointed it at the faces of the traitors before him. The meaning was clear: so long as his spear did not break, neither would his will. He was going to fight to the bitter end.

Inwardly, he sighed again. What was he to do? This was how he'd always been, loyal to a fault.

This cart had a destination. There were hungry people waiting for it. That knowledge alone was enough to dissuade him from any thoughts of banditry. Moreover, it was his job to guard this cart, and he just wouldn't feel right not doing so.

He knew himself to be a boring man. He didn't drink. He didn't gamble. He'd never visited a brothel even once. Was it for fear of betraying his family? No, because he had no family. No wife, no children, no parents. One could hardly ask for a life more free of responsibility. There was almost no reason *not* to plunder this cart and sell the food to fund an ensuing life of decadence. Heck, it was probably the smart thing to do, given the circumstances.

Why, then, was he standing here like a blockhead, apparently determined to give his life in service to duty? He could give no answer except for *this is who I am*. He was a boring, serious person.

But what, he inwardly protested, was wrong with that? So what if there was a famine? So what if it was Hell on earth? Virtues were virtues, the times be damned! They could laugh all they wanted. They could call him brainless. But if he was given a mission, then by God, he was going to do it. Was it ego? Pride? Honor? He didn't care. All he knew was that it mattered.

And with that knowledge held firmly in his heart, he brandished his spear.

"The food on this horse cart is meant for villages suffering from famine. There are starving children, for goodness sake. I'm not going to let it fall into the hands of bandi—"

Sadly, it was too cruel an age to afford his honest diligence the reward it deserved. All he received for his loyalty was the brutality of his ex-comrades. Searing pain accompanied each of their strikes, steadily sapping his arms of their strength. Finally, he fell. Amidst a throng of foes, he perished; the only blood spilt was his own.

However, the stubborn last stand he made was not entirely in vain. His steely resolve gave the merchants on the cart enough time to escape. Though he lost his life, he saved many others. Through the mouths of those merchants, word of his name and actions eventually reached the ears of the empire's princess.

"The transport convoy was…wiped out?"

For a few seconds, Mia said nothing else, utterly dumbstruck by the news. Then she shambled unsteadily over to her bed and toppled onto it.

"Wh-What were the guards doing?"

"Most of them defected to the bandits. Which, while not exactly commendable, is not particularly surprising either. Our ability to pay their wages has been…diminished."

Ludwig looked like he'd just swallowed a mouthful of bile. The grimness of his expression was understandable, considering the supply they'd sent with that convoy had been the precious fruit of a desperate series of negotiations with neighboring kingdoms. They'd just barely managed to scrape together enough food to keep a number of starving villages fed for the near future. Every grain had been worth its weight in gold.

"Gah! I can't believe these people would so easily betray the empire... Unforgivable! Was there nobody who stayed true in their duties to Tearmoon? Not a single loyal soldier?"

"Reports say that there was a young soldier by the name of Ernst who took a stand and tried to carry out the mission alone..."

Mia brightened a little at the news.

"My! How admirable! He must be rewarded. Right away, in fact! Surely, he deserves a medal or two. A promotion as well..."

She trailed off, excitement fading as she realized that Ludwig's dour look remained unchanged.

"Unfortunately," he said, shaking his head, "he perished in battle."

Mia wilted. A hint of sorrow could be seen in her downcast eyes.

"I see... His family then. At least give *them* something..."

"Unfortunately, he has none. No wife or children, no parents."

"I...see..."

Mia bit her lip.

In an age when tragedy abounded, such a story was commonplace. Trite, even. The young soldier Ernst was simply another of the many whose loyalty Mia would never have the chance to repay.

Now, let us skip through the stream of time...

"My, it's been a while since I've dreamt of back then…" murmured Mia as she slowly opened her eyes.

Through the blurry haze of lingering sleep, she looked around. On the desk beside her bed was a half-written letter. It was addressed to Vanos, who now oversaw the Princess Guard, notifying him of her intent to make Ruby their newest member.

"That letter must be why…"

During the age of the great famine, food transports were frequently raided. Sometimes, it was by bandits. Other times, by mobs of rioting villagers. Every so often, it was by the very guards they'd sent to protect the transport. After swallowing countless of these bitter pills, Mia became painfully aware of the need for a unit of troops she could absolutely trust.

"In terms of reliability, nothing beats the Princess Guard, but at the time, they already had their hands full defending the capital."

Now, circumstances were different. She had the Princess Guard, a reliable and mobile force at her beck and call. As for how trustworthy they were… That was probably also a nonissue. So long as Dion Alaia, the Empire's Scariest, was on her side, his former squadmates would never turn against her.

"But the headcount still leaves something to be desired… I wonder if I can pull a couple soldiers over from the Redmoons…"

These thoughts had occupied her mind as she penned the letter, but halfway through, she began to feel drowsy and retired to bed for a nap. The unfinished letter was likely the root of her dream.

"To that end, I need to speak to Ruby and figure out this soldier-sharing thing. We'll have to draw some detailed operation plans…and there'll need to be plenty of training…" she mused before shaking her head. "Ah, but that dream… How uncharacteristic of me to have forgotten about the existence of that loyal soldier…"

Having never met him, she had no face to attribute to the name. That likely contributed to the lapse. Her memory of the man had, until this moment, been buried deep within the recesses of her mind.

"He didn't betray me even at such times as those. I couldn't ask for better proof of a man's character. Whoever this fellow is, he's definitely trustworthy. I need to track him down... Wait, what was his name again? Uh... Loyal soldier... Loyal soldier... Mmmm..."

A series of frustrated mumblings ensued.

"Uh... Hrm, that's odd... Um... Did it start with an A? B? No... C? D? E? Wait, I'm feeling something with E. E... E... Augh, what was it? Ea? Eb? Ec?"

Down the alphabet she went, trying to fish the name out of her mind. The extensive brainwork this led to, along with the nap she'd just had, would doom her to a long, sleepless night plagued by an overactive mind stuck on the task of endlessly piecing letters together.

Moving now to the domain of the Redmoons...

Ruby stood opposite her father.

"You're joining the Princess Guard?!"

"That's right, father. I thought you'd be happy for me."

She arched an eyebrow at her father's grimace. The imperial guard were an elite force. The Princess Guard, even more so. Admittedly, it wasn't quite as glorious as being one of the emperor's personal guard, but this was certainly the next best thing. There was no shortage of prestige and status to be gained from being under the direct command of the princess.

"Well, I'm not *not* happy, but I mean... It's the Princess Guard. According to my sources, they apparently just incorporated a hundred-man squad from the front lines. The front lines! These are fighting men we're talking about. Vulgar and loud and prone to violence. It's a den of brutes there."

"That's just about the last thing I expected to hear from you, father. To the untrained eye, dauntlessness can often be mistaken for crassness. Not to mention, this is the *Princess* Guard. They're literally charged with ensuring Her Highness's safety. Do you really think she'd surround herself with barbarians? Even if it turns out that she selected for competence instead of class, that'd just mean they're a very capable bunch. I'd take that over the reverse any day."

Duke Redmoon regarded the confident manner in which his daughter placed a hand on her hip. He conceded a wry smile.

"Fair points, fair points all. We Redmoons do pride ourselves on our headhunting of quality soldiers. Fussing over class and courtesy runs counter to our philosophy. Very well then. I shall send for an elite troop to be composed of our best soldiers. Take them with you. You may present them to Her Highness as a gift. They shall bear our banner and do us proud."

Soon, at the behest of Duke Redmoon, a retinue of twenty female soldiers were selected to accompany Ruby. They were all the cream of the crop, each and every one sufficiently talented to shoulder the reputation of the Redmoons single-handedly.

Female soldiers were rare in Tearmoon. A small handful of specialists, like the Lulus, did exist, but most of the army consisted of brawny men. The fact that the Redmoons were able to swiftly assemble a crack troop of servicewomen was a testament to their military might.

The person put in charge of this retinue was an old acquaintance of Ruby's—a knight by the name of Celes. Standing as tall as most of her male peers, her strong, lean frame exuded the fierce aura of a seasoned warrior. Having served as Ruby's combat instructor, she was a force to be reckoned with, both in the ring and on the battlefield.

"I must admit, I never expected you to join the imperial guard, Lady Ruby."

Ruby laughed.

"Neither did I, Celes. Life's funny that way. Who would have thought the daughter of Duke Redmoon would subordinate herself to someone else?"

Ruby's shrug prompted a frown from Celes.

"Are you not entirely inclined to proceed with this arrangement in joining the Guard? If so, I will speak to Her Highness personally and do everything in my power to persuade her—"

"No! You should definitely not do that. I swear, every joke just goes right over your head, Celes. You need to learn to ease up."

Ruby shook her head admonishingly. Celes's frown deepened as she groaned in displeasure.

"Your 'jokes,' Lady Ruby, are a mystery to me."

"I'm pretty sure it's not *my* jokes that are the problem. I think it's your sense of humor. Which *is* a problem. How are you going to romance any men like that? Are you seeing anyone right now?"

Celes gave her a flat look, then sighed.

"No. It appears that few men are interested in talking to an uptight woman such as myself. I'm sure my experience with romance pales in comparison to yours."

In Celes's mind, Ruby practically lived in a romance novel at Saint-Noel.

"...Well, I mean, maybe? But uh... More isn't necessarily better when it comes to romance, you know?"

Ruby stammered a little, losing some of her initial verve. After all, "pales in comparison" was not entirely accurate. In fact, for Ruby, who was still carefully nurturing that first tiny flame of love that had flickered to life in her childhood, her romantic experience was, for all intents and purposes, non-existent!

"It's all about going out and meeting people, I think," Ruby continued. "There are plenty of fine fellows in the Princess Guard. I'm sure *someone* there will catch your eye. And when it's time to strike up a conversation, you'll have an easier time if you can crack a joke or two."

Such was the nature of their conversation as they arrived at the headquarters of the Princess Guard in Lunatear. As the building came into view, Ruby suddenly stopped.

"Hm? That's…"

Celes followed her gaze to find a mammoth of a man walking into the building. His clothes bulged the way they did when worn over armor, except in his case, it was sheer muscle. That alone was impressive, but what made Celes's hair stand on end and her sword arm tense was the way he carried himself.

That man…is a fighter.

Even from this distance, she could tell. He radiated an aura unique to those who'd paid their dues on the battlefield and then some. He was *strong*. In every sense of the word. Celes caught herself growling.

I heard that a seasoned hundred-man squad had joined the Princess Guard. That soldier must be one of them. I doubt I'd last three seconds against him…

Surely, she figured, that was also why Ruby had stopped.

"Oh, Vanos…"

Which was why she almost did a double take when she heard Ruby's whisper. Her voice was tense, but it wasn't the kind of nervous tension that arose when daunted by an opponent's strength. Ruby's… was less focused, devoid of her usual boldness. It was clearly the voice of a girl who'd just caught a glance of her crush. Celes eyed the young Redmoon with mild astonishment.

Now that's not a side of Ruby I see very often...

"All right then. I'll wait out here," Celes said with a sympathetic smile.

"Huh? But..."

"I doubt any danger will befall you in the Princess Guard headquarters. Go ahead. I'll stay here and wait for the others to arrive."

"R-Really? Okay then..."

Ruby frowned for a moment, but soon consented. She combed her fingers through her hair a few times.

"Uh, quick question. How do I look? Good?"

She was crushing on him *hard*!

"'Good'? Well..."

Celes thought herself to be the least qualified person imaginable to answer such a question, but she looked her over anyway. Then she answered in an uncertain voice, "You look fine to me."

"Do I? Hm... All right, thanks. I'll see you later then."

Ruby all but ran off, eager steps quickly taking her into the building the giant man had entered. Celes watched her disappear through the door, then shook her head.

"Who'd have thought... Ruby of all people... And apparently, that's the kind of man she's into? Then again...I guess she was always fond of large men."

Her musing was interrupted by an unfamiliar voice.

"Uh, excuse me, but would you happen to be a member of the Princess Guard?"

The question came from behind her, but it didn't catch her by surprise. She'd already heard the footsteps approaching.

"I will be soon. And yourself?"

She turned to find a man of average build. He looked to be about her age or maybe a few years younger. Unlike the object of Ruby's affection, this man did not look like a seasoned veteran.

A new recruit, maybe? Doesn't look very strong... she thought, sizing him up.

He, unaware of his rather unimpressive evaluation, spoke up.

"Ah, my apologies. I should introduce myself. My name is Ernst. I've been assigned to the Princess Guard starting today... I have no idea why, to be honest, but..."

The famed Princess Guard, whose exploits would be told and retold by many future generations, was a rarity in the imperial army. Under the direct command of the Great Sage of the Empire, it was a mixed gender unit. There was a longstanding rumor in the Guard which said that any love which bloomed between its members would go happily. The source of this rumor was unclear, but a number of theories have been posited. One of these claimed that it was based on the epic tale of romance involving the Guard's mountainous captain. Another insisted that its origin lay in the story of a serious-minded soldier and his love.

This is a story unknown to Mia. She was neither protagonist nor narrator. But it *was* her story, because she was the one who'd scattered the seeds. Carried by the wind, it fell far from her view, where it would eventually grow into an endearing tale that bore the fruit of love.

Mia's Diary of Gluttony

The Twelfth Day of the Eleventh Month

I had clam chowder for lunch today. Ever since coming back from the summer cruise, I've been obsessed with seafood. Clams in particular are wonderful. Noelige Lake has a sandy bottom, which apparently makes it so the clams there don't have a muddy taste to them.

The second these clams touched my tongue, they just melted, releasing a mouthful of rich, creamy goodness. Saint-Noel's chefs really know what they're doing. I even wiped the plate clean of cream using my bread. I ate *everything*.

Absolutely delicious!

Highly recommended ☆x5

The Fifteenth Day of the Eleventh Month

I had some mushroom au gratin today. The gratin was rich and cheesy, but very unique. There were little pieces of Belluga mushroom in it, which added this toothsome, chewy texture. The aroma was excellent. It was a triple whammy of fresh mushroom, molten cheese, and the nice toasty crust of a gratin fresh out of the oven.

This was exquisite. I dare say I tasted the heart and soul of Belluga cuisine through the dish.

Recommended ☆x3

This would have been a perfect score if the pieces of mushroom in the cheese were just a little bigger. So close!

It seems like every time I go back to read some previous entries, I realize my diary has turned into a food review. Honestly, I'm getting used to it by now, but this *has* to be some sort of weird curse or something…

Not that I care. There's a good chance I'm going to die on the day of the Holy Eve Festival. So what if I'm doing nothing but writing about food?

In fact, I should be spending every waking moment I've got left eating good food! From now on, this book is officially my food diary! Every page shall be filled with my reviews!

It's time to indulge in fleeting pleasures! Before my time is up, I'm going to taste every last dish available on Saint-Noel Island! I don't even have to eat it all! I'll just take one bite of everything! Who cares if it's wasteful? It won't matter if I'm dead! Oh, delicious delicious decadence, here I come!

The Seventeenth Day of the Eleventh Month

I went to one of my favorite patisseries in town today. The chef there came up with this brilliant idea for a pastry. It's called a crepe, and it's the best thing ever. I always get one when I go there.

Today, there was a new item on the menu. It was called Remno pumpkin pudding. I've always considered pumpkins to be vegetables, so that threw me for a loop. Maybe the head chef's sweet vegetable pastries have become a fad and it's reached here.

I tried a spoonful, and it had this rich sweetness that melts on the tongue. A great item all around.

Recommended ☆x4

It tastes too good, which makes it impossible to eat only one bite. Minus one star.

The Twenty-Second Day of the Eleventh Month

Today, I was browsing the menu for chef's recommendations and found something called a five-mushroom mix. I was supposed to get something else, but this discovery changed my mind, so I ordered it. I tried to eat only half and order the other thing afterward, but that turned out to be a futile plan.

The mushroom mix was brilliant. Each type of mushroom had a different texture, and they all complemented each other. Once I started digging in, there was no way to stop myself. I did manage to leave about half a mouthful in the end, but I couldn't order anything else at that point.

The kitchen staff also gave me a complimentary slice of cake after. It was delicious too.

Highly Recommended ☆x5

A dish mushroom lovers won't want to miss. Wonderful!

The Twenty-Fifth Day of the Eleventh Month

Today, I got Bel and Rina to join me for a bread party.

Anne's baking skills seem to be improving. Also, Lynsha can actually cook. I had no idea...

We ate so much bread. It felt like a bit of a waste to fill my stomach with nothing but bread, but it was a lot of fun, so whatever. Time well spent. We brought the leftover bread to the kitchen and had them make it into soup. They added cheese and eggs to the soup too. It tasted amazing.

It took the whole day though, so I didn't make any progress toward my goal. I'm a little worried about whether I can actually sample every dish in Saint-Noel in time.

The Holy Eve Festival just keeps getting closer.

I'm really looking forward to the mushroom stew party with the student council, but I do wonder how it'll go...

Afterword

Hello, I'm Mochitsuki, and I hope the new year is treating you well.

Thank you for picking up the sixth volume of Tearmoon Empire. Also, sorry about the previous volume's obi strip. It loftily declared that "Part 3 is ending in volume 6!" but, well... Clearly, it didn't! (cries)

The story does have a natural stopping point, but Mia spent so much time mushroom hustling that we didn't manage to get there! Therefore, part 3 will actually end in the next volume! I hope you'll stay with us and keep reading!

I sincerely apologize for Mia's behavior.

Mia: "...Is it just me, or are you acting like the solution to everything is to just shift all the blame to me?"

Mochitsuki: That's not true at all. I have no idea why you'd think that. More importantly, volume seven is next, and surprisingly, it's shaping up to be food-centric, isn't it?

Mia: "Could you be any more obvious about changing the topic? But what do you mean, the next volume will be food-centric?"

Mochitsuki: Well, the story in this volume revolved around mushroom stew, didn't it? That suggests... Actually, did you know that a portion of readers are convinced this story should have the "makes you hungry when reading it" tag?

Mia: "My, is that so? Wait, is that because I keep getting fed all sorts of delicious food?"

Mochitsuki: …Of course not. I have no idea why you'd think that. Moving on, then. The next volume should cover the festivals, both the winter one and the one before summer, so it'll probably be a feast for the tongue…

Mia: "Oh, that's right. There was a part where I'm eating a massive snow sculpture made out of ice candy, wasn't there? And one where I eat through a castle in the woods made out of cake… Just thinking about it is making me excited. I'm looking forward to reliving those delightful memories!"

So, I hope you'll look forward to the seventh volume, wherein Mia will eat, eat, dance, and eat in a vicious cycle of F.A.T.

Note: This preview of the next volume is ninety-nine percent fiction. But there *is* a tiny little bit of truth.

Now, some words of appreciation.

As always, I'd like to thank the illustrator, Gilse, for their beautiful artwork. The pair of youngsters on the cover are absolutely adorable!

Thank you to my editor, F, who is always a great help.

Thank you to my family for their ongoing support.

Finally, thank you to all the readers who continue to accompany Mia on her journey.

I hope we'll meet again in volume seven.

MIA MUSHROOM

MMM HMHM.

THERE ARE SO MANY DIFFERENT SPECIES OF MUSHROOMS!

THAT'S RIGHT. THEY CAN BE DANGEROUS FOR AMATEURS TO HANDLE, SO MAKE SURE YOU'RE CAREFUL WITH THEM, BEL.

MIA MUSH-ROOM...!

WHICH IS WHAT I'LL NAME IT ONCE I FIND THE THING.

JUST SO YOU KNOW, THERE'S SUPPOSED TO BE A LEGENDARY MUSHROOM THAT NO ONE HAS SEEN YET...

KNOWN AS THE MIA MUSH-ROOM.

GASP!

MUSHROOMS THAT LOOK LIKE GRANDMOTHER MIA...

MIA MUSHROOM... I BET IT'S SO TASTY IT'LL MELT YOUR BRAIN WITH A SINGLE BITE.

POOF!

?

THAT'S THE SPIRIT, BEL.

NOW LET'S GO FIND US SOME MIA MUSH-ROOMS!

I'D LOVE TO GET A LOOK AT THESE MIA MUSH-ROOMS!

Squeal

Giggle

Tearmoon Empire Vol.6

THANK YOU FOR PURCHASING OUR BOOK!

Morino

VII

Tearmoon Empire

Nozomu Mochitsuki
Illustrator: Gilse

Author: Kureha
Illustrator: Yamigo

VOLUME 4
ON SALE NOW!

The
White Cat's
Revenge
as Plotted from the
Dragon King's Lap

4

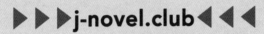

J-Novel Club Lineup

Latest Ebook Releases Series List

...and more!
* Novel and Manga Editions
** Manga Only
Keep an eye out at j-novel.club for further new title announcements!